Voices of America

Voices of America

Veterans and Military Families
Tell Their Own Stories

Editors

Maj. April E. Brown, USMCR (ret.)
and **Ethan Casey**

Associate Editor

Kit Snyder

Fort Worth, Texas

Library of Congress Cataloging-in-Publication Data

Names: Brown, April (Student affairs administrator), editor. | Casey,
   Ethan, 1965- editor. | Snyder, Kit, editor.
Title: Voices of America : Veterans and Military Families Tell Their Own
   Stories / Maj. April Brown, USMCR (ret.) and Ethan Casey, editors ; Kit
   Snyder, associate editor.
Description: Fort Worth : TCU Press, [2020] | Summary: "Voices of America:
   Veterans and Military Families Tell Their Own Stories collects dozens of
   personal accounts of military life from World War II to the present day.
   These narratives from Texas Christian University students, faculty,
   staff, alumni, and family range from deadly combat to downtime, from
   family dynamics to life after military service. Although the
   contributors share a connection with TCU and each experience is unique,
   they share a common bond with all Americans who have served their
   country across far-flung zones of conflict and decades of history, and
   speak with urgent relevance to American society today"-- Provided by
   publisher.
Identifiers: LCCN 2020025977 | ISBN 9780875656731 (paperback) | ISBN
   9780875657097 (ebook)
Subjects: LCSH: Texas Christian University--Alumni and alumnae--Biography.
   | Veterans--United States--Biography. | Families of military
   personnel--United States--Biography. | United States--Armed
   Forces--Biography. | United States--Armed Forces--Military life. |
   LCGFT: Personal narratives. | Autobiographies.
Classification: LCC U52 .V548 2020 | DDC 355.0092/273--dc23
LC record available at https://lccn.loc.gov/2020025977

Design by Elizabeth Cruce Alvarez, Southlake, Texas.

TCU Box 298300
Fort Worth, Texas 76129
817.257.7822
www.prs.tcu.edu
To order books: 1.800.826.8911

Assistant Editors

Sarah Amend

Caleb Ashbrook

Johnny Barfield

Hanna Beyer

Brianna Bickham

Blair Bokelman

Nicholas Bomm

Kaylee Bowers

Kate Bowman

Caroline Brown

Nicole Burns

Canon Charanza

Mary Cordell

Ashlynn Deaton

Erin Dianis

Dean Dillenberg

Olivia Ernst

Cami Fannin

Courtney Franz

Demi Fritz

Jordyn Hampe

Brendan Hartman

Morgan Jacob

Will Jennings

Elyssa Johnson

Samantha Jorgens

Claire Kiser

Addy Kryger

Connor Lundsford

Amanda McFeeley

Mikaela Miller

Rachel Monsees

Meg Moran

Alexis Olivas

Emily Orr

Justin Pollard

Madison Rich

Rebecca Ruch

Lea Shackelford

Autumn Simpson

Alex Smith

Allyson Smith

Rebecca Somers

Hannah Stevens

Courtney Sullivan

Hannah Tenney

Abby Till

Rachel Ziomeck

Contents

Preface

Speaking for Themselves

A huge amount of work over six years, by the two of us and quite a few others, went into the making of this book of personal accounts and statements by some eighty-three American veterans and military family members. The story of that work, and of why this book was thought necessary and how it came about, should be told, but here is not the place to tell that story.

The point of this book is to provide a place where veterans and military family members can speak for themselves, so it's appropriate for the editors to say as little as possible. Beginnings and endings of all stories are arbitrary, and so are many of the inclusion and sequencing choices made about the pieces in this book. A few of them were written by veterans themselves, but most are excerpted from oral history interviews done either by us or by undergraduates enrolled in a series of four seminar classes in TCU's Honors College, taught by Professor Dan Williams, who is also the director of TCU Press. Dr. Williams's students are all credited as assistant editors of this book. We struggled long and hard with decisions on which portions to select from those interviews and how to edit them until, relatively late in the process, the book's natural arrangement declared itself to us: three sections, dealing sequentially with life before, during, and after military service. We're grateful for the almost preternaturally excellent judgment and tact that Kit Snyder, a recent TCU graduate working at TCU Press and personally committed to seeing this project through with us, brought to bear on many of the book's sequencing and titling decisions.

The arrangement is not chronological in historical terms, but it covers a long period, from World War II to near the present day. We were able to interview Alcee Chriss Sr., a member of the legendary Montford Point Marines, in November 2016 (he passed away on August 16, 2018, at the age of ninety-eight), and there are several accounts from Korea, Vietnam, the first Gulf War, and periods of peacetime. (We also have chosen to include three longer written accounts of service during World War II, titled Leading the Way, following each of the book's three sections.) Military service is about combat but also about many other kinds of experience, and so are the pieces in this book. Most are by recent or current TCU students, faculty, staff, and administrators. The governing criterion for inclusion—affiliation with TCU as defined by us, the editors—turned out to be this book's "special sauce," because its arbitrariness renders the range of stories otherwise remarkably representative, first of all locally for TCU and Fort Worth and more widely for Texas, but also nationally. There are lessons and truths in that, for all of us as Americans. One of those is that any American university could—and perhaps should—compile and publish a similar book.

There is a lot more to each veteran's story than could be included here. There are also stories that were left out because they proved too emotionally difficult for the veterans themselves to tell fully or publicly.

One final, important point: War is inherently political, and all of our country's wars have been politically driven or influenced and have taken place within historical and global contexts. Everyone involved with this book, from the editors to the contributors to you, the reader, possesses, and is free to express, political views. That is both a right and a duty of all of us as citizens, civilians, and military members alike. But service members bear an additional obligation to be circumspect about their political feelings, in deference to their obligation to serve the nation by obeying their commander-in-chief, who is the country's elected civilian president, whoever that man or woman might be at any political moment. We have chosen both to honor and to emulate that important custom, by keeping the book's focus on personal experience and earned perspectives. As you read you will surely discern hints and mentions here and there of where particular veterans are coming from politically, but gratuitous overt expressions of partisan feeling have been deliberately kept out of the accounts published here.

April Brown and Ethan Casey
July 2020

Foreword

Stories Have the Power to Unite and Educate

Col. William O. Dwiggins, USMC (ret.)

After serving in the United States Marine Corps for over thirty years, rising from private and retiring as a full colonel, I am currently employed by the Texas Veterans Commission as a District Education Coordinator for higher education. My primary duties are to engage the district's institutions of higher learning and education and to meet with officials and decision makers to persuade them with facts about the uniqueness of veterans and the military-connected student body who desire an education or on-the-job-training certification in an academic environment that is welcoming, safe, and nurturing for them. These individuals struggle under a mask of bravery as they work to reintegrate into their families, community, and normal life after time serving in the military or uniform service.

April Brown is the current director of Veterans Services and Veterans Services Task Force Chair at Texas Christian University. The Task Force is a devoted team of mission-oriented volunteers who assist, guide, and advise student veterans and their military-connected families as they transition and assimilate into Texas Christian University's culture.

Ethan Casey is an American journalist who has written or edited multiple books. Ethan challenges himself by never placing boundaries on experiencing life, people, places, and adventures in this world. After he and I were introduced, Ethan explained that he wanted to learn and research the stories untold by veterans: how their military experiences had shaped their lives. He suggested gathering the stories of our veterans and giving TCU's veteran students a platform to tell their stories of being in the military, as well as the stories of their supporting family members, and compiling them into a book as a living history of military men and women.

The stories in this book will open your eyes to the commitment made by those who serve their country in the military. Veterans see the world around them through the eyes of much older contemporaries, due to their military service. You will find that every story is unique, fascinating, and perhaps a bit of déjà vu. Furthermore, this book will provide you with an opportunity to learn and appreciate the gifts and freedoms many in our country take for granted. And it will allow the community to bear witness to these stories, feel the emotions, and help carry the burdens that these warriors are using their words to share with us. Additionally, you will learn what it truly means when "Taps" is played, and you will understand the words, "All give some, and some give all." Those who read this book will come closer to understanding the sense of military service and the life of a veteran, not only in combat but throughout the whole experience of being in the military.

The Horned Frog Sniper

Eric Freedman

Benjamin Whetstone Schmidt attended TCU as an undergraduate for three semesters, before dropping out to join the United States Marine Corps in May 2008. He served three and a half years in the Marines, including two tours of duty as a sniper in Afghanistan. He was awarded the Navy and Marine Corps Achievement Medal with Combat Valor, the Global War on Terrorism Expeditionary Medal, and the Purple Heart. He was killed in a friendly fire incident during a combat mission in Afghanistan's Helmand province on October 6, 2011. He was twenty-four years old.

Before his second deployment, Lance Corporal Schmidt took care to revise his will, specifying that, should he die in action, his life insurance benefit should be divided equally between his mother, Becky Whetstone, and the Department of History at TCU, to endow an annual scholarship for graduate students. Recipients of the Benjamin W. Schmidt Memorial Scholarship must have a grade point average of at least 3.0 and be involved in community service.

Schmidt's father, David Schmidt, matched his son's contribution and has raised additional funds to enhance the endowment. He and Benjamin's stepmother, Teresa Schmidt, have also established an endowed faculty position and a history symposium held annually at TCU in Benjamin's honor. "The symposium is becoming well known among military historians and is *doing a lot to spread the word about the need for all of us to think about the costs of war," says Kara Vuic, the current Lance Corporal Benjamin Whetstone Schmidt Endowed Professor in History at TCU.*

What follows is a personal tribute to Lance Corporal Benjamin Schmidt written by Eric Freedman, who served with him. This book also includes excerpts from an interview with David and Teresa Schmidt.

Lance Corporal Benjamin Schmidt, or Schmitty, was a leader, a motivator, one who always paid attention to detail. He was my fire team leader and a HOG in our 2nd Battalion, 4th Marines sniper platoon. There

are two types of snipers: HOGs, or Hunters of Gunmen, and PIGs, or Professionally Instructed Gunmen. Lance Corporal Schmidt was a HOG, which means he completed one of the most grueling schools the Marine Corps has to offer. I was a PIG, desperately wanting to earn the title of HOG and prove to myself that I could complete sniper school. Unfortunately for me, I sustained a career-ending injury and was kept around in the platoon in a support role. But this isn't my story.

Marine veteran Benjamin Schmidt.
Courtesy of Kara Vuic.

LCpl Schmidt was someone everyone in the platoon looked up to. He was the life of the party, had a great sense of humor, was a natural leader, and was incredibly smart and talented, especially behind his scope. Most importantly, he was a great instructor. He led classes and taught sniper knowledge incredibly well. I remember after every morning PT (physical training) slay session watching the snipers being dead exhausted after a run, swim, hike, whole body circuit, obstacle course, ruck run, breaking for morning chow, trying to regain life in our beat-down bodies, only to be brought back to the sniper hut to learn! Knowledge is key for a sniper. Most people think all snipers do is pull the trigger on high-value targets and vanish into thin air after that impossible shot. In fact, it all begins with knowledge and practice and repetition, over and over again, until it becomes second nature. And there was no one better at knowledge and passing it down than LCpl Schmidt.

I remember sitting in the sniper hut, learning and writing notes until my hand hurt. The amount of information we had to understand and remember was insane. Not only would we have to be in the best physical shape of our lives, we also had to be mentally sharp and prepared. While I sat and learned with all the other PIGs in the platoon, it was not uncommon for a HOG to walk in and see a PIG yawn or start nodding off, and the HOG would order another slay session. During these incredibly common slay sessions to make sure the PIGs were in the best shape of their lives, I was left back in the sniper hut and would get to pick the brains of the remaining HOGs. This also allowed me to get to know the HOGs better, to learn more about the challenges at sniper school, and actually to be treated like a human, even though I was still a PIG. Not yet knowing the extent of my injury, I still had high hopes of healing and earning my spot in sniper school.

During this extra time with HOGs, I developed a close friendship with almost everyone in the platoon, and I can proudly say that these were some of the best men the Marine Corps had to offer. These were the men that wanted it more. They wanted to be the best, and they wanted to prove they were the best. I like to say that the sniper platoon is the most elite alphas of the Marines. And LCpl Schmidt was one of the best in the sniper platoons. Despite being a seasoned combat Marine, he was incredibly humble and had a big heart for his Marines. One time when the snipers were on a weeklong training mission, I found myself being safety driver, moving snipers from different rally points, being the support for the HOGs and PIGs. After a long day I would volunteer to do the first few hours of fire watch every night, so the snipers could sleep longer. After a few nights of doing this, I was exhausted and in excruciating pain. One night when I was unable to sleep, LCpl Schmidt kept me company, telling me stories about overseas and secrets to getting through sniper school. We swapped inappropriate bar stories, talked about our ladies back home, and connected in a way that only two brothers who are both going through the suck can. Schmitty and I talked for hours about our goals and our dreams, about our plans after the Corps, and of course we swapped boot camp horror stories that now don't seem so bad.

Every sniper needs to be able to shoot, and LCpl Schmidt helped me off my crutches to get in the prone position, to get some glass time on range days. He volunteered to be my spotter and guided me perfectly on target, watching my breathing and trigger control and correcting my body position. We had to put our heels all the way on the ground, which was nearly impossible for me due to my injuries, and HOGs would walk up and down the fire line and stomp on heels that they found in the upright position. I would get so nervous that one of them would forget about my injuries and stomp on my heels. But LCpl Schmidt reminded the other HOGs to leave me alone, and that he had me shooting in the best position I could get into. I remember being on the range and doing support shooting. We found anything we could to rest our rifles on and shoot: from the Humvee, from body parts such as shoulders and back, even the unassisted taint shot. LCpl Schmidt demanded one of my crutches, and we took turns shooting off my crutches. Range days were incredibly fun and challenging at the same time.

During stalking phases, LCpl Schmidt would let me sit up on the Humvee, and he would use his binos to spot for PIGs while they moved, learning how to stalk. He would say to me, "Since you can't be down there, you might as well learn how to not be spotted." He would teach me ways to look for the snipers as they moved, camouflaged from head to toe, building a sniper hide without being seen. This was awesome training for me, since I could see and remember the mistakes being made. I remember Schmitty telling me to stop sweeping left to right as if I were reading, but instead to sweep my eyes opposite, right to left. "You will pick up more movement and mistakes. Keep your hands tucked in between the binos and your eyes to prevent shadows. Tell me what you're seeing." And he showed me ways to pick up on even the slightest movements.

Outside the sniper platoon, LCpl Schmidt found us and a few other snipers out in San Diego partying and enjoying our freedoms. After nearly every long week of training, released for the weekend, we would get dressed up in our polo shirts and hit the town. We had a saying that we were going to get "Schmidt-faced"—and boy, would we drink. After the weeks we had in training, on weekends we would get completely wrecked. This is where the brotherhood started forming; late nights and drunk conversations were an every-weekend occurrence. This is truly an aspect of life in the Marines that most civilians would never understand: going out with your boys, who are more like brothers. The PIGs and HOGs had a clear line of separation during the work week, but on weekends we put all that behind us and no one messed with us: you mess with one of us, you mess with all of us. Getting Schmidt-faced was a rite of passage, and when you thought you were done for the night, LCpl Schmidt would make sure you had just one more.

The Monday morning after, we would put on a fake mean face during the PT slay session, but most of the time nearly everyone ended up puking. The PIGs and I had lots and lots of homework. The HOGs would ask us knowledge questions and, through the drunken haze from the weekend prior, I would remember LCpl Schmidt spitting out knowledge that we had to know the next week while we munched on overpriced pizza at three o'clock in the morning. Remembering enough from the weekend homework assignments to avoid the extra slay sessions, I was thankful for the weekends out with LCpl Schmidt, and for his willingness to make sure we were always prepared for the week to come.

Six years later, my heart was devastated by the news that LCpl Schmidt had been killed in action. LCpl Schmidt is missed daily by friends and family. Every year his mom, Becky, throws a massive party in Arkansas and invites all the Marines who served with him. It is healing and therapy for all who knew him.

One hot summer day in 2017, I found myself here at TCU. My cousin Molly had just graduated, and she invited me for lunch and a tour of the campus. Not knowing anything about TCU, I agreed, and later that afternoon I found myself in front of the veterans' counselor. We discussed options of perhaps becoming a Horned Frog, but I said to myself, "There is no chance that a kid from a divorced family, who barely graduated high school, would get into TCU."

With the conversation wrapping up, the counselor, Ricardo, asked me what I had done in the Marines. I told him how I was attached to security detail for both President Bush and President Obama—a very proud honor for me—and how I was attached to 2/4 after that. "What did you do with 2/4, Devil?" he asked. When I told him I had been attached to the sniper platoon, his joyful demeanor turned serious and he told me to get up and come with him. Thinking about the tragic UT shooting, I wondered if maybe snipers were not welcome here. As we walked in silence, Ricardo brought me to the Reed building and pointed to a plaque on the wall. Goosebumps came out all over my body. The inscription read, "Lance Corporal Benjamin Schmidt Conference Room." We walked in, and on the wall was a framed picture of Ben, his medals, his story, and names of men I had served with. As tears rolled down my face, I asked what the plaque was doing here. Ricardo replied, "He is an honorary Horned Frog," and told me the story of LCpl Schmidt—a story I already knew too well.

Benjamin Schmidt was not just my friend, he was my brother, someone I looked up to and learned from. At that exact moment, I felt as if God was telling me that TCU was exactly where I needed to be. A few hours later, I applied to TCU. Rest easy, Brother, your watch has ended.

I ended up getting into TCU. I am now a graduating senior on track to graduate *cum laude,* and I just applied to join the Criminology master's program. During my time at TCU, I have done everything I possibly could to honor LCpl Schmidt and to inform all those I meet about him. Every time I pass his name in the veterans' plaza, I say a prayer for him and his family. It is incredible to walk in the same halls where he once walked, and to carry his legacy with me for the rest of my life. This May I will walk across the stage at TCU with my head held high, knowing that I have accomplished such a meaningful goal, and that I will be carrying something of Ben's, so he and I can accomplish this achievement together. Thank you, Ben, for your commitment to and sacrifice for this country. You are loved and will never be forgotten.

Fort Worth
February 2020

The Journey Begins

"I thought it was the best thing since sliced bread."

George Wahl

I was born in Chicago. My father was in the Department of Agriculture, so we moved all over the Midwest, eventually settling in Washington, DC. I had all intentions of going to either West Point or the Air Force Academy, but that fell through at the last moment and I was scrambling around. It was June of 1957, and I was waiting for a place to go to college. I found out that Virginia Tech had an ROTC cadet corps program where you wore a cadet uniform seven days a week. That sounded great, so I applied and was accepted. Toward the end of my senior year I was honored as a Distinguished Military Graduate, DMG, which gives you an active Army commission. I said, "Wow, that's great." When you're young, you don't realize what combat is like until you go to it.

I entered the Army Medical Service Corps in October of 1961. I liked it because they sent me to jump school, where I wanted to go, and my first assignment was in the 101st Airborne Division, 327th Airborne Infantry Battle Group. I thought that was the best thing since sliced bread. The Army's really not as bad as I thought. Toward the end of the assignment, I met my wife-to-be, Barbara Steltenkamp, at Hopkinsville, Kentucky. And as it turned out, I got orders for Germany, went to another paratrooper unit, flew back to the United States about six months later, and we got married. One of the keys about staying on active duty is that, if you're married, the spouse and family need to like it. As it turned out, I did not get out of the Army after my six-year requirement. The Army kept on promoting me. Barbara Ann and our family loved it. We loved moving, which is something I cannot say now.

"I discovered that I really liked it."

Michelle Johnson

Goodness! I just always loved it! It was literally my first day as a freshman in high school, registration day. They gave you a manila folder with your name on it and a registration card, and you'd go into the gym where they have all the registration stations, and you'd pick something from each station to fit your class credits for that year. I had picked all the mandatory classes, like government and math and English and social science, but I still had to have an elective. The only couple that were left were ROTC and something sportsmanlike that I knew was not going to be a good situation. So my friend and I walked up to this tall white man wearing Class A's and he said, "Whaddya wanna do? Be in ROTC?" And I said, " . . . Okay?" You know, I was thirteen. I didn't know what I wanted to do.

But I discovered that I really liked it. And looking back on it, I liked feeling like I belonged to something. I liked the structure and having something to do every day, getting to dress up in a uniform once a week, learning the rules about something that I had no idea about before joining ROTC. I had uncles who had served in the Army, an older cousin who was an officer in the Air Force, and my father was an Army man, but aside from that, I didn't know anything about it. That's kind of how I just fell in love with it.

Our ROTC instructor's name was Staff Sergeant William L. Moody. I wonder if he's still alive. He told me, "I see that you've been doing really well, you have excellent grades, you're a good leader, you're a really good cadet. As soon as you graduate, you can go in as a private first class instead of a private. You would be thirty-five when you get out." I said, "Thirty-five?! That's old!" So I didn't do it, because I thought I would be old when I got out of the Army. Plus, my mama had watched Walter Cronkite's exposé on women in the military! She didn't want her baby to go in the Army. After I graduated from high school I went straight into college, even took Military Science at TCU. Things happened. Life happened. I had a daughter, went to college off and on, and worked while raising her. Then I got to a place in my life where I noticed that I still had a strong love for the military. I tried to join the military a couple of times but got scared every time. I made it all the way to Dallas MEPS at least twice. One time I failed this test. The recruiter said it was because I talked too much. Now I know you don't have to tell everything, because the Army will find a way to disqualify you. You don't need to tell everything. Just stick to the question asked.

I enlisted into the Navy Reserve on the eighteenth of February 2005, in the Office Depot break room *[laughs]*. The recruiter was serious about making a point about rushing me to sign those papers and get in. He and his commander showed up on my job at Office Depot in full uniform, marching down that big main aisle. They scared the manager. He thought they were the cops looking for me, because they were dressed in winter blues. He was like, "What were you thinking! Never do that again." I was like, "No problem, you only do it once." So I got enlisted into the Navy Reserve as a non-designated seaman. They told me, "Just enlist now, and you can change it after you get in." Retrospectively, they rushed me like that because they knew I didn't know anything about the military at all, aside from ROTC. They also rushed me because they were trying to "make numbers," make quota. My ignorance—I didn't have to enlist that day. They made like there was never gonna be another opportunity.

"I was actually kinda against war."

Michael Blackert

Nine-eleven was an awakening for me. I come from a long line of military. My grandfather is retired Army, my stepdad is retired Army. Before 9/11, I wasn't really for the war. I was actually kinda against war. I've always been a believer that there were other ways to resolve issues besides war. But living through an experience where they attacked our country made me want to continue that tradition with my family and serve. So I enlisted in 2004, right after we invaded Iraq.

"I refused them."

Jon Lippens

I was thirteen years old when the Germans invaded my country. I'm a Belgian guy, and we fought the same bunch in 1918. I didn't finish high school, because I wouldn't join the Hitler Youth. They wanted me in that black uniform with the swastika on my arm and black boots, and I refused them. Every German said, "Why aren't you in uniform?" and I said, "Because I'm not a member of the Hitler Youth club." And they said, "It's your job to be a Hitler Youth." And I said, "Oh, I didn't know I had a job. How much does it pay?" I really made fun of them. They really meant business, so they gave me a beating for it.

"It made sense to me to go the military route."

Leo Munson

I come from an era where we had ROTC in high school. I was required to take Army ROTC during my four years of high school, and when I went into college it just made sense to continue in ROTC. So I went into the Air Force ROTC program at Colorado State University in 1966 and graduated a second lieutenant in 1970. In the spring of the year I graduated, campuses were being shut down and the events occurred at Kent State.

Colorado State University actually had a building burn down. We were shut down for about a week during the protests. Truthfully, it was very confusing to me. I wasn't a great student. I had a pretty good

Air Force veteran Leo Munson.
Courtesy of Leo Munson.

time, I was a pretty fair skier actually. And I hung around all kinds of different people. I wasn't in a fraternity, but we hung around with fraternity guys. For the most part everyone got along with everybody, and part of the group that I'm going to say were friends of mine were the quote hippies. And they were the ones for the most part that were protesting. So it became very confusing to me to have friendships on one side, and people that were literally trying to shut down an institution on the other side. Which was the intent—not to cause harm to people, but to cause harm to institutions in some cases. I disagreed with the protest, but my friends were not disagreeable when they were around me, nor was I. We had a good time. We had too good of a time.

I viewed joining the military more as a backup plan than anything. I wasn't persuaded or dissuaded from going into the military. The activities in high school were positive activities. So when I went to college it made sense to me to go the military route, in case four years later I didn't have any idea of what I wanted to do, which in effect pretty much happened. I graduated in sociology and psychology, had opportunities to go into graduate school right then, but wisely chose not to, because I was not mature enough to go to graduate school.

I chose to defer for the summer I graduated, then entered active duty in September of 1970 and was stationed in Austin, Texas. From Austin I went to Washington, DC, for ten weeks of training from January through mid-March 1971.

"I'm in the same boat."

Bob Doran

I was born in Winthrop, a town of about eight hundred people in northeast Iowa. I graduated from high school in 1955 and wasn't sure what I wanted to do. I decided to go to Cornell College in Mount Vernon, Iowa, a small liberal arts school. I was really unsettled about attending, and only stayed one year. My classmate and best friend, Clark Dye, also went to Cornell. At the end of the year Clark said, "I'm going to go into the Army." I said, "Really?" And he said, "Yeah. I don't know what I'm gonna do with my life; at least this will give me a couple of years to think about it." And I thought about it and said, "You know, I'm in the same boat. I think I'll join the Army too."

However, I only wanted to serve two years, not the mandatory three years required by enlisting. I found a way around this issue: First join the Army Reserve, and then ask for two years of active duty. This was perfectly legal, and that's what I did. Clark did the exact same thing. We assumed we'd probably serve together, but it didn't turn out that way. Clark ended up at Fort Leonard Wood, Missouri, and I was sent to Fort Hood, Texas, one of the world's largest military bases.

"My family couldn't afford education."

Israel Sanchez

California is a different kind of society from Texas. I'm from central California—Fresno, Bakersfield. Devin Nunes is my congressman. I know what it's like living in a Republican county, but people there are a little bit more accepting. There's still that religious aspect, because it's the Bible Belt of California, but there's still a lot of liberal political views and ideologies.

My family couldn't afford education. I was living in a Pentecostal household, and I was running away from being gay, and little did I know that good old seventeen-year-old me was actually going to end up finding it, and I did. I found myself, I found my identity, I found out who I knew I needed to be, because I was not happy. And that's where I met a Marine who was my brother's recruiter, who ended up becoming my boyfriend at the time. He's the reason I'm doing a lot of this stuff: the outreach, the advocacy for the LGBT community.

"At the beginning it was a financial thing."

Aaron Tombleson

I started in the military right out of high school. I had a scholarship set up, but then I hurt myself in athletics, so I decided to go into the military so I could help out the family and get out of the house. I went into the Marine Corps at 03 level, basic infantry rifleman. I went in in May of 2002 and got out in May of 2009. I got out of boot camp, then was stationed in Washington, DC, after SOI, School of Infantry training. I was stationed in DC for about a year and a half, and I was just a ceremonial marcher. I did funerals, Dover team, taking the fallen comrades off the plane when they reach American soil. I did some parades and stuff at the Iwo Jima memorial in DC. From there I was transferred to Twentynine Palms, California. I was stationed there for the rest of my four years in the military.

At the beginning it was kind of a financial thing. I knew my only option to get into college at that time, right out of high school, was to get it paid for. If I got a scholarship it was gonna be great, but I ended up kind of botching that when I hurt myself. So I decided to use the military, and I went into the Marine Corps because my grandpa was a Marine. He was at Iwo Jima in World War II. I never got to hear anything, and he died before I had a chance to even ask. And I had been hounded by the Marines all through high school. I just denied denied denied, and then I made the decision myself.

When you go in while you're still young, it's a much easier transition. You get used to getting barked orders at or doing things early in the morning. Your body adjusts. Your mental aspect and drive adjust, because the instructors break you down and build you back up. So the adjustment from civilian life to the military was actually pretty easy. Three months you're in boot camp, and you do exactly what they have scheduled for you. So it's actually really easy going in, but it's very hard coming out.

"It was a meal and a small paycheck."

Marty Leewright

I went in when I was seventeen. I was a high school dropout. I lost my biological parents when I was seven. And my adopted mother, who was a nurse, signed for me to go into the military when I was seventeen. I was too young; they didn't knowingly send soldiers to Vietnam when they were seventeen. But they sent me to Germany, and I was in an engineer unit for a year in Karlsruhe and did training and maneuvers in the Black Forest in the middle of winter. As soon as I turned eighteen I got orders for Vietnam. Had a leave at home, then I was shipped over there in December of '69. Spent all of 1970 and the first part of 1971 there.

I didn't have many options as a high school dropout, and I think a lot of the young soldiers that went to Vietnam were guys like me. I was basically living on the streets. I didn't have a high school education, didn't have a whole lot of options, couldn't afford to go to college. It was three meals, it was a roof over my head. I remember going through the supply lines when I was in basic training and advanced individual training and getting all these new clothes. They were Army green, but they were brand new boots, brand new clothes. The food was good. I heard people complain about the food. I loved the food, 'cause there had been times when I'd gone hungry.

So as a seventeen-year-old my attitude when I went in was, I'm gonna stay in the middle of this crowd. I'm not a big, strapping twenty-five- or twenty-six-year-old college graduate that played football, and I don't want to stand out. I was warned about drill sergeants, and I just want to get through this. I actually did pretty well in basic training. I also did very well in the advanced individual training, but I didn't see the big picture at all at that age. I was going in because it was some security, it was a meal, it was a small paycheck, it was the promise of the GI Bill when I got out. And it was an open door for me. It was a dangerous open door, but it was an open door.

I think I was [patriotic]. My adopted mother was a disabled veteran. She had served in World War II as a nurse, and I never did quite understand what her disabilities were, but she could never have children and had several major operations, she had pernicious anemia, but she was proud of her service. And my adopted dad, who left our family about the time that I dropped out of high school, was in the Navy in World War II. My biological father was in the Air Force, actually here in Fort Worth, and he was from Iowa, and that's where I grew up. I left Fort Worth when I was five and grew up in a farming area in Iowa and ran heavy farm equipment, tractors and stuff. I think that's why they put me into that field, because I didn't have much else for skills.

"I needed to actually start working."

Michael Washington Sr.

I grew up in several parts of south Dallas. These places were not your typical suburbs or neighborhood, and crime was present every day. Some would call it the "hood," but I call it life. It was the only way I knew growing up. I graduated from Wilmer-Hutchins High in 2003, and immediately started working for the Texas Department of Transportation (TxDOT). The work was good, but I was under pressure from my mom to pursue a college degree. My mom was a high school dropout and always wanted her children to have a college degree, even if it wasn't possible for her. So after a year of work, I decided to attend Paul Quinn College in Dallas. When I got to school, I started struggling with classes and my finances, so I decided to drop out and continue my job with Tx-DOT. The job was something I could do, and I enjoyed doing, because I wasn't sitting in front of a desk all day. I worked there for several years and I felt that this was the start of my career. But in 2009, the recession started to affect everyone on the job. Layoffs were constant, and cross training to other jobs within the company was the only way to try to dodge being laid off. Unfortunately, I was one of several workers that were let go in early March 2009.

Around my birthday, my cousin came to town and asked, "What are you going to do for work?" I responded: "Maybe find another construction job or work at Game Stop." She said, "I have an idea. Why don't you just join the Army? It would be great for you!" I was very hesitant to join the Army because of the Iraq war. I responded "Nah, I'm not joining. If anything, I would put my application to be in the Navy." So, after our talk, I went into a Navy recruiting office to start my application to join the service. I took the Pre-ASVAB test, height and weight, and fitness test with the Navy recruiters, but the Army recruiters were taking me to MEPS in Dallas and guiding me to the military lifestyle. The Army recruiter stated that it was going to take a little bit over a year to join the Navy, and I didn't have that kind of time. I needed to actually start working. After several months of not being able to reach my Navy recruiter, I switched to join the Army. On February 2, 2010, I swore in, with my family standing beside me. They were nervous for me, and so was I of the unknown.

In the years leading up to me joining the Army, it was tough for me. In late November of 2007, I had lost my brother in downtown Dallas the day after Thanksgiving. He was a security guard working late night, and he didn't allow some group of people to come in. They exchanged words, and he directed them to leave the premise. Later that night, the guys came back and waited on someone else to enter the building, then they rushed in and shot him. This was a difficult time for me and my family. One of the reasons I decided to join the military was because of him. He was a big part of my life, and I looked up to him. So when it was time to pick a military occupational specialty or MOS, I chose Healthcare Specialist/Combat Medic to help others that needed medical care. A few months later, in 2008, I had my first son, and I was so blessed to have him. But I was still learning how to raise a son and dealing with my brother's death. It was very difficult for me.

"So there I was, for twenty-three years."

Shirley Beck

I did the four-year nursing program at TCU and graduated in 1968. I took the course, and when we got our grades and everybody was leaving, the professor said, "Shirley, why did you take this course?" I said, "Well, I want to get into nursing, but I have to have prerequisites." He said, "So where are you going to go?" I said, "John Peter Smith." Which at that time was a charity hospital. He said, "No. I don't think you should do that."

I thought, What does he know that I don't know?

He said, "I'm going to write a letter to the dean of the College of Nursing and tell her that she needs to find some money for you to go to school."

I said, "I can't do that. We don't have the income that I could . . . "

"Don't worry. If she thinks you should be there, she'll find the money."

Four years later I graduated *summa cum laude.* I was the senior scholar in nursing, and ever since then TCU is right here. I'm so thankful for the opportunities and the joyful things I've experienced throughout my career. Every morning you wake up, and you think, "Gosh, is this really happening?" So I really have a soft spot in my heart for TCU.

My husband was made master sergeant. Then I went on and got my master's in psychiatric nursing, and I had grants from the National Institute of Mental Health. And one day I was in my dentist's office and he said, "How are you doing with your nursing program?"

I said, "Well, I'm on the faculty for a couple of years. I finished my master's in psych nursing."

He said, "Oh, our reserve unit needs a head nurse for our psychiatric unit on the manning table, and it has to be a master's-prepared person. Why don't you come and visit us and see if you want to join?"

So there I was, for twenty-three years.

The position was a hospital unit in 94th General Hospital, and their headquarters were in Mesquite, and it was a reserve unit. My dentist was the dental officer in that unit. I went to Desert Storm in '91. Well, we got called up a little earlier, but the war started in January, on my birthday.

I lived at that time north of Dallas. I drove to drill and then we had two weeks of annual training, and our little psych unit went to Terrell

State Hospital to relieve the staff there. Terrell State Hospital is a huge psychiatric treatment center. The troops got training in real psychiatric situations, because they had a vast array of levels of diagnosis up there.

"Our mother insisted that we get educated."

Rodney Baker

I'm number eight of nine kids from a single-family home in Batesville, Mississippi. My mother, Charlene, worked hard to do better by us and for us. The phrase "I'm going to tell Momma" scared the heck out of all of us, because she would beat you. Nowadays they call it child abuse. There was no money to go to college. Batesville is in north Mississippi, about thirty-five miles south of Memphis. Fifteen minutes from Oxford, right off of Highway 6. I still have my eldest sisters there. I have two brothers that are there and their families, and then I have a sister in Memphis, another sister that's a nurse in Hattiesburg, a sister in Washington State and her family; she's also a nurse. And I have a sister that's in DC, and she's a schoolteacher getting ready to retire. Her husband is a former postal rates commissioner. My sister Joyce was a math whiz, and she got a full ride to Ole Miss as a math student, and she's a math teacher now. My sister Belinda actually served in the Army and then used her GI Bill to go to school to be a nurse. So that's how that worked out. My oldest brother who's deceased, Albert, served in the Air Force for a while, then used his GI Bill to go to school also. Again, we didn't have a lot, but our mother insisted that we get educated and use the benefits given to us. That's what we did.

Matter of fact, I didn't find out until after I joined the Navy and had left that there was a scholarship for me to go to college, but I'd already made my commitment to the Navy. That was back in the '80s, when rural areas in Mississippi would take promising students and pay for them to go to school to be dentists or doctors, and then they would come back to those communities and serve. I qualified for one of those and didn't even know it. One of my teachers had put me in for it, and I didn't even know it, just a lack of communication. It's like most rural school systems. Information doesn't get out. The information came, I think, two weeks after I was in boot camp.

"I really didn't have a plan."

Stephen Rivera

I entered the military in 2007. My mom was actually the one who came up with the idea for me to go talk to a recruiter, but when I walked in I was like, "I'm not signing any papers." My mom was like, "Let's just go talk to them; please do it for me." So I was like, "I'm going there, I'm not signing anything, they're not going to talk me into anything." I went in, and he made some great points. So I joined the Navy at age nineteen, just to get some money for college. I really didn't have a plan at all, just kind of needed some guidance as far as what I wanted to do with my life.

I chose a job as a hospital corpsman, which basically is the medical team for the Navy and the Marines. I went to boot camp in Great Lakes, so I joined the Navy in Chicago, so it was literally like my backyard. I passed Great Lakes all the time in high school. I went during the spring so it wasn't snowing, which was nice. My A School, which is the school you go to right afterwards, was also in Chicago, so I literally took a bus from one side of the base to the other. Basically in corps school they teach you everything you know. Like being a medical assistant, how to give shots, how to give IVs. It's obviously a little more strenuous than taking a regular medical school class. If we gave IVs we had to make sure they were secure. They would grab the bag and throw it across the room and the IV had to stay in the patient, because obviously if you're in the field and you're on a Humvee and a bag drops off, you don't want it to rip right out of a patient's arm. So it's a little more intense.

"He realized he needed some discipline."

David and Teresa Schmidt

David Schmidt: [Our son Benjamin] realized that he had been at TCU for three semesters, and he enjoyed TCU a lot. In fact, he probably enjoyed TCU too much. So he came home and told us he was joining the Marine Corps, and we were a little stunned. He had already set it all up. He said he realized he needed some discipline, some structure in his life. So that is what he chose to do, and he did it.

Teresa Schmidt: He said, "I need some focus, and I need some direction." He wanted to continue, but he knew at that point that there were too many distractions. He needed something else to help him channel, get him back in line again.

David Schmidt: We were taken aback. But he had made the arrangements. He basically just told us, "You can come down to my signing-in ceremony in the next two weeks or ten days," or something like that. And so we did it.

"I want to do three years of adventure."

Tim Cole

I entered military service in 1982. My statement is: I did it all wrong, and God blessed it. I was almost twenty-five years old, I had a bachelor's degree in business, I had credits against my MBA, I actually held a nuclear

security clearance. Many of my friends at that age, back in that day, were getting married and buying homes and having families, and I was simply nowhere near that.

I went down to a Marine recruiting station and walked in and said, "I want to go to the Marines." And they tried to explain to me that because of my education I could go to officer school, but I didn't hear that correctly. What I heard was that they were trying to move me into a career. And I said, "No, no, I'm really not interested in a

Marine veteran Tim Cole.
Courtesy of Tim Cole.

career. I just want to go do this three years of adventure." And they said okay, and they signed me up.

I show up at boot camp at twenty-five years old. I was the old man, as old as my drill instructors. So, again, I did it all wrong. These Marine Corps drill instructors were pretty intimidating. No physical abuse, but they were screaming at us all the time. And one day, about a week into it, we were marching along, and this uniformed young man came from the other direction, and I didn't see any marks on his sleeves. He wasn't a corporal or a sergeant. I didn't know then that his rank was on his collar. Well, these mean old drill instructors went all quiet, and saluted him, and said, "Good morning, sir." And he responded, "Good morning." And I thought to myself, "I think we just passed an officer." And I realized at that point that if I had the opportunity to become an officer, I was going to take advantage of it.

"They will have a GI Bill."

Jim Lee

I had dropped out of college for financial reasons, and I was working at a drugstore in Birmingham, when the Korean War broke out in June of 1950. I thought, "I need to get in that, because they will have a GI

Bill," which they did for World War II. They didn't have one at the time, but I knew they would, so I joined the Navy. That's the reason. It wasn't because I wanted to shoot people.

The first part of the transition was going from being a civilian to being in a room full of naked men in San Diego. You had to cut off your hair. You stood in this room with all these naked sailors who were getting checked to see if they were fit to serve. Then we went right into boot camp for twelve weeks.

Navy veteran Jim Lee.
Courtesy of Jim Lee.

For the first month, you didn't really see anything of San Diego. You were on the base, marching all the time. Marching *all* the time, like you were going to be a soldier. It was just awful. You become an automaton. You march everywhere, all the time. You go from one school sort of thing to another. One day you'll go to physical training. The next day you go somewhere to learn about military justice. Then you march to something else. You have to wash all your clothes, and you have to have inspection all the time, every day. Your bunk has to be perfect, your shoes have to be shined, your clothes have to be rolled a certain way and laid out on your sea bag a certain way. If anything is wrong, you don't get to go to shore when your time comes up.

One time I was supposed to go on liberty, but my shoes weren't shined enough to suit them, so I didn't get to go. It breaks some people. We had some people that couldn't do it, and they got some sort of less than honorable discharge. The point of it is to break your spirit, and that's sort of necessary, because you have to do what they tell you to do or you might get killed.

"I wanted to be somebody my family was proud of."

Jake Melton

I went to Korea for my first tour of duty. I was kind of hoping I'd go to Afghanistan, but they sent me to Korea. I was kind of disappointed, but it was a pretty good tour, a lot of fun. I'd never really been outside the country except for Mexico, and it was a whole nother world. It was crowded, and the whole country smelled like *kimchi,* and they really love their professional baseball there. They super celebrate balls and strikes, and it's just insane. I got there soon after the Korean team won [a major baseball championship], and the whole country was still in a state of party, and it was kinda nuts. But it was a good time. They say the easiest way to leave Korea as an E-4 is to go in as an E-5. There's a whole lot of partying going on, lots of drinking.

My whole goal for entering the Army was to go and make a difference. I wanted to be able to come home and be somebody that my family was proud of instead of who I'd kind of become, just nothing to be proud of, nothing remarkable. I was in Korea for eleven months. It was supposed to be a year, but I wrote down the wrong date when I got there. I shortchanged it a month, and I guess the date went through the paperwork and they sent me home a month early. And I went straight to Fort Hood, which is good. I'm from Irving, right here next to Dallas, so I went to Fort Hood. I was pretty excited. They told me, "You've gotten ninety days stabilization." They can't send you anywhere for that period of time. But it was less than a month later that I got my orders to go to Iraq.

"I absolutely hated my job."

Jason Mendoza

I served for seven years in the United States Army. I was a Military Police officer for the first three and a half years. I was stationed in Fort Leonard Wood, Missouri, and there I did garrison work for about a year. The other two, two and a half years I was working with the anti-terrorism unit, stateside. That was very interesting because it was the one time in my military career where we worked with all the branches of the military. So I got to work with Air Force, Navy, some Marines sometimes, civilian sector as well. We were all working in conjunction, and basically we did live scenarios. The last one we did was, let's say a seventy-two-kiloton bomb goes off in Kansas City. How do we mitigate that? Casualties, working in conjunction with local law enforcement, how do we work in conjunction with the hospitals, what do we do to help on the ground? That was a really unique and interesting thing. It's also good to talk about it, because it lets people know that twenty-four hours a day, seven days a week, there is someone working for our defense here, stateside.

What made me enter the military? Prior to that I worked at UPS. It was a very good job, I made very good money, the benefits were fantastic. But I absolutely hated my job. I was like a robot, every day was the same thing day in and day out. And then I get into the military and from the very get-go, the first day of basic training, it was like they come in like you see in the movies yelling, "Get up, soldiers! Wake your butts up!" And I was already showered, dressed, shaved, ready to go. My rack, my bed, was made, so they were like, "What in the world? Did you sleep with your bed made?" But I was totally ready for that, and we went on like a fifteen-mile ruck march. That was the first day. A ruck march is like hiking. You have about twenty-five pounds, if you could carry it, and your weapon, and that's like the initiation. Like, welcome to the military. And I loved it. That's what I was looking for, the challenges. I loved that aspect of it.

"Something I always wanted to do."

Alexandria Smith

Joining the military was something I always wanted to do, from the time I was a little kid. I joined ROTC while I was at TCU, and in August 2006 I graduated and earned my commission as an officer in the Army Reserve.

But I have done a tour in Afghanistan, so I've done some time on active duty since joining in May 2010.

ROTC was probably one of the more challenging things I did in college. To add almost an extra minor, so to speak, onto your degree plan but not really taking into consideration the fact that you know you're going to get up at six o'clock in the morning to go work out. And on Thursdays we always had what was called leadership lab, so

Army veteran Alexandria Smith.
Courtesy of Alexandria Smith.

every Thursday afternoon—which I am sure you guys noticed—there are always students walking around in uniform. That's because they go to leadership lab, which is learning techniques and leadership training skills outside the classroom to help prepare us for when we all become officers in the United States Army, whether we go reserves, active duty, or National Guard.

Right after college, I joined my reserve unit. The unit that I joined was a human resources company. I became what we called the platoon leader over a group of roughly thirty to forty soldiers along with one other person, my platoon sergeant. I led them through training exercises and made sure that we kept in touch with them throughout the month, because on the reserves side we only meet one weekend a month. And I went from there to my officer basic training course, where I learned more about my job specifically in the military. Then I went to officer basic. It was a pretty fast transition because right after I graduated officer basic, within a month's time I was getting ready to deploy to Afghanistan and then did a tour in Afghanistan for nine months, from May 2012 to January 2013.

"I wanted to do something about it."
Chad Lackovic

I was technically on inactive reserve, which means you're just there in case they need you. But when 9/11 happened I wanted to do something, so I found the closest MP company around and joined up for the reserves, hoping to deploy to Afghanistan quickly. But I ended up waiting around a couple of years.

I thought our unit would go to Afghanistan immediately, but our commander wasn't the sharpest knife in the drawer, and most of the people in my company had never seen active duty. I was very frustrated. And right after that I ended up getting a new job, working at the intake at the city jail. That's just fighting every day. It's where the drunks and crazies came in, and I was able to get some frustration out at work. But I was upset, because everyone was pissed off after 9/11, and I wanted to go out and do something about it.

"I'm just being a stupid college kid."
Stesha Colby

My parents insisted that I go to college out of high school, but I was not mature enough. I skipped class, smoked pot, drank a lot, and lost my scholarship. At the same time, my two cousins were in Iraq and getting shot at. I realized, as I was getting ready to go home for Christmas, that I needed to break it to my parents: "Hey, by the way, I'm out of school. I lost my scholarship, I'm on a year's suspension." I'd gotten a letter from my cousin saying that his convoy had been blown up and he and his buddy barely made it out. This is December 2005. I'm barely twenty-one years old. I was going to Middle Tennessee State University. I'm driving from Murfreesboro to Memphis, realizing that things need to change. It hit me: "What am I doing with my life? I'm just being a stupid college kid." So on the drive home I made the decision that I would talk to recruiters.

I decided to join the Marine Corps. It took nine months, because the job that I wanted wasn't open. I was a little on the chubby side. I needed to lose some weight. But in September 2006, I went to Parris Island for boot camp. I passed in the thirteen weeks that it takes. Some people don't pass. They get hurt, or they fail some portion and have to be rolled back. But I passed in thirteen weeks. I graduated in December, almost a year to the day since deciding to go into the Marine Corps. I got to stay home for a month and work for a recruiting station. Mom joked that she should have sent me to boot camp a long time ago, because every time she asked me a question, I'd be right there: "Yes, Ma'am." I was always a polite child, but I was like over-polite now.

"I liked the structure and discipline."

Felicia Lawson

I did Army JROTC for about three years and it was really, really good. It helped me a lot, and I liked the structure and discipline of it. So I knew I was going into the military at some point. I waited a year after high school and just kind of floated through college for a semester. I wasn't really focused because I was working, and I was like, "Yeah, I need to go ahead and join the military." That was the ultimate goal. I was like, "Okay, at least I can go to the military, learn a skill and a job." And still getting paid while I'm learning, and wind up with money for college. That was the big push, the money for college.

"It was a foregone conclusion."

Bruce Cole

Growing up as an Army brat, it was a foregone conclusion that Bruce was going to grow up to follow in Dad's shoes. I had actually joined the Army Reserve at the young age of seventeen. Didn't care for it too much. The reserves is different from the bigger picture of the military, because you're joining a specific unit to fill a position that they happen to have open, so the possibilities are not endless in that regard. There are very few things that you're able to do, and I was a communications technician, and that's not what I wanted to be. I wanted to be an infantry guy or a Special Forces guy or something like that. Then, when I turned nineteen and graduated high school, I joined the Marine Corps, so I entered the Marine Corps in 1983 and retired in 2013. By the time I had graduated from high school, I was just ready to get away from southeast Texas and move on. The Marine Corps was the route that I wanted to go.

"I was born into a unique culture."
April Brown

I was born in Wiesbaden, Germany. As a child, I did not realize that I was born into a unique culture. My dad, Norman Brown, was an Air Force sergeant stationed there at the time. My mom, Anna Marie Brown, was a military spouse, one of the hardest jobs, which often goes unnoticed. My fondest memories are of connecting with other military kids, especially with activities on the base. The base was its own city. It had a commissary, shoppette, movie theatre, bowling alley, swimming pool, and recreation center. Military kids learn early on that the national anthem will play prior to the movie starting and will stand at attention until it's over. In the early years, there was even a dress code to enter the theatre. The military community would be how I would identify throughout my life, and continues to be one of my strongest identities.

"I was born on an Air Force base."
Jim Hille

I was a military brat. My father was in the Air Force. He was a pilot, and we moved around a lot in my youth. I was born on an Air Force base. My father did a tour in Vietnam as a pilot, so he was away for almost two years. That was difficult. I was old enough to remember that. But all that had an impact, ultimately, on my choice to go to the service as well.

"I wanted a career as a mechanic."
Richard Spence

I joined the Marine Corps in 1979, coming from the South Texas town of Laredo, where there wasn't much to do but get in trouble or join the military. Growing up, I didn't have the guidance or the knowledge of attending college. My mindset growing up was to join the military, just like my father and both my brothers. Our father was Air Force, my brother was Air Force, retired Vietnam era, the middle brother was Navy. So you could say military was a family business, and three different branches of service, and me as a Marine in the best out of all of them.

I initially joined the Navy to be like my brother. When he came to visit I would love to see him in uniform. When I was old enough to join, I was going to school in Grand Prairie, Texas, and talked with a Navy recruiter. The recruiter told me that the Navy were integrating their platoons by race, having certain percentages of Caucasian, Hispanics, and African Americans in their platoons. Because they were integrating their platoons, I would have to wait six to eight months before I could go to boot camp.

I decided to get a fast food job during the interim and wait to go into the Navy. While waiting, I met a good friend that told me he was joining the United States Marine Corps. I told him I was joining the Navy and that I was leaving in six to eight months. He said he was leaving in about two weeks and that I should join him. I didn't know that I could switch services and ended up talking to a Marine Corps recruiter. I told him that I wanted a career as a mechanic, and he told me he could get me in that field if I wanted to switch over. So I did, and I could leave for boot camp in two weeks.

"It's civic duty, which means you serve."

Tami Tovar

Why did I join the Army? Nine-eleven had happened, and I wanted to be sure to be able to do at least some military service before I got too old. I had already been married for six years with two small kids. My last job before joining was teaching two-year-olds as a caregiver at more than one church to make ends meet. It enabled zero conflicts with childcare, because I could take my kids to work with me.

More seriously, that motivation comes from four hundred years of family military tradition. It's a thing we do. It's civic duty, which means you serve both in the military and in your local community. You don't have a government, especially not one like ours, which is supposedly democratic, unless everybody actually participates. That realization did not come until many years later. If you really boil it down, it was like my family's religion. It's not the religion, but it would be if there were no other.

The family descends from a group of people in France called Huguenots. It was in an area of land in dispute between France and Germany, called Hasbrouck. That's my family's last name. It's a region in France now—they won! Therefore we're considered French and, thanks to religious tensions being what they were and later the French Revolution, the parents of my specific progenitors didn't make it out, as many Huguenots were slaughtered, but a young son and a daughter escaped to England. The son enlisted in the military, became a Redcoat, came over, built a house in New York, which is still standing. Built of stone.

My great-grandfather was a Union soldier. His picture, in his uniform, still hung on the wall when I was growing up. My grandfather was in the Navy during World War II on the Pacific Coast, but because he already had ten kids, they didn't let him deploy on the boats and kept him stateside. He was always bitter that he didn't "really" get to serve.

One uncle was the sole survivor of his troop that got mortared in the Korean War. Another uncle went to Vietnam. My stepdad also served in Vietnam and was a forward observer, field artillery commander in Vietnam. Another uncle became a first sergeant, Green Beret. Out of the seventy-six first cousins I would say 80 to 85 percent have served, in every branch from Coast Guard to Marines. One of them did the Presidential Detail. He did that for a few years, and it nearly broke apart his marriage because you're on call so much. He gave that up. Another cousin got roped into guard detail at Fort Knox.

I had already worked my whole life in healthcare. My last job prior to taking care of little kids for the church was in the ER, as an ER tech. So when I went to enlist, I wanted to do medical, and the particular field that was offering a bonus at that time was laboratory technicians, since they were short staffed. Turns out it's not a popular job, because they have all the prerequisite education as an officer as well as doing all the same workload with the same level of responsibility as an officer, but they make you enlisted. So they had to do a kicker, a bonus to enlist. That sounded good to me and I thought, "I need a kicker. I need a new car."

"I needed something to ground me."

John Garcia

I'm from here, Fort Worth. Name a high school, I probably went to it. I come from a very poor family. Didn't have a father; he left when I was a child. My mother had schizophrenia, abusive relationship. Jumped around to different family homes. I graduated from Paschal [High School in Fort Worth]. I didn't have any plans. I was actually a good kid for the most part, until I got a little older and got into women and drugs. I got kicked off the football team, which I was scouted at one point. I got into a fistfight with the coach. My avenues were decreased, and I figured my options were either going to jail, dead, or do something. So I looked for a military recruiter, because I had jumped around to so many schools that I wasn't on their list, so they did not look for me. I went to the Air Force, they seemed too easy; Navy, I didn't want to wear the white uniform; Army, I didn't like how the guy approached me at the time and how we interacted. The Marine Corps seemed like the hardest, and I felt that I needed something to ground me, so I chose the Marine Corps.

"I actually wanted to protect America."
Thaddeus Rix

I was just really gung-ho, and I didn't really have any college prospects. I was going to high school in Fresno. I wasn't really looking forward to college. I was just like, "Eh, I'll just join the Marines." I was always excited about serving my country. Which is funny, because that's honestly one of the more minimal reasons why people join nowadays. But I actually wanted to protect America. So I signed the papers when I was seventeen, left on September 17th. Started boot camp. Stood on those yellow footprints. And then I got beat up for three months and got out in December. Then did combat training, which is something that only Marines do, because all the other services are soft, to put it nicely.

In high school I really, really, really enjoyed learning Spanish. I took one year of Spanish, and I learned it to moderate fluency. I really took it up. My teacher was an Ecuadorian woman, like straight from Ecuador, and she had a passion for teaching it and I had a passion for learning it, so it was a really great combo. I would spend at least two hours after class every day just talking to her and learning, getting really into it. I just loved it. Language was really fun, like a puzzle to me. So when you sign up, you take the ASVAB. The "B" is "battery," so it just means it's a test. Every person in the military takes it before signing up. There's no commitment; you take the test and it gives you placement. And it's a percentile type test, so you're compared against everybody who's taken the test in the past three months or so. When my brother took his, he got a 99, which means he was literally the best person who took it in the past three months. He wanted to be a mechanic, but unfortunately you have to have around a 60 or 70 to be a mechanic. They want that level of aptitude, and he was far above and beyond that. And they were like, "Well, we don't really want to give you this job, so how about you take this job which requires more intellect?" Because linguistics, I'm not sure what the cutoff score is, but it's higher, I think 85 or so. They didn't want to waste him on a lower job, because recruiters are the devil and they just want to put you where the needs are. The one time you ever have a choice in the military is before you sign up. But then, even before you sign up, they're trying to direct you where they want you to go. So he didn't become a mechanic, he became a Chinese linguist. He wasn't interested in it at all; he just did it because they told him to. But that got me more interested in it, so I ended up becoming a linguist. I was hoping for Chinese or one of the Iraqi languages, like Arab or Pashto or Farsi or Dari or something like that, because I was hoping to actually contribute to our cause. I got Korean. The needs of the Marine Corps.

"I just got filled with patriotism."

Jake Melton

I was twenty-eight when September 11th happened. Didn't get to see my son a whole lot. Sold furniture, nothing really to write home about. And 9/11 happened. Next day I went to see the recruiter, just got filled with patriotism. And got to thinking: Who should go there and do something about that, the guy that's got a wife and 2.3 kids to come home to every night, or someone like me, that if I don't go home for a week nobody notices? You know? So I went to see the recruiter the next day, they were closed, and the day after they were closed, and the day after that. So I came back like six or seven days later, and they were open. I went to the Marine recruiter, and he said—I'll remember this forever, it was hilarious: "How old are you again?" I said, "Well, I'm twenty-eight." And he said, "Oh, no, you're about a year too old. Anyway, you gotta be pretty smart to be a Marine." It was pretty funny, actually. So I went next door to the Army recruiter and I just walked in and said, "How old can I be and get in?" And they said something like thirty-two. And I said, "Okay. Here I am."

But the funny thing about that was after the ASVAB, they just tell you what your ASVAB is, they don't give you a piece of paper. But I asked my recruiter, "Can you print that out or something for me, to show me what the ASVAB is?" And I went back over to the Marine recruiter and I just slid it to him and I said, "I got a 96 on my ASVAB. Sorry I'm not smart enough for you."

"I was lost."

Rey Soto

I went in in February 2005, to get out of Dallas. My uncle had gotten killed the year prior. He was my father figure, and I just wanted to get away. My mom had gone to prison for dealing drugs and stuff like that. I was lost. That was my bottom of the barrel. They say there's always two ways you can get out of that game: either you die, or you go to jail. It just so happened that of the two people that I loved the most, one had died and one was in jail. So it was one of those things. One of my uncles was talking to me about going into the military and I was like, "I'm not doing that." It just so happened I woke up one day and went to the Marines recruiting. I took my test a week later, and I was gone two weeks after that. Something within me was like, "I have to get the hell out of here, like ASAP."

I grew up in Dallas, then went to high school between Dallas and Michigan. My uncles here were getting drugs cheaper, and my stepdad and my mom moved to Michigan, and that's how they were getting stuff. The price you get for the drugs gets higher, the more north and east you get. I feel like my past has made me who I am today, not being ashamed of that stuff. My mom is the bravest woman I know. She's my hero, to sacrifice and do all what she did to make sure that me and my brothers and my sister were taken care of and well and our bills were paid. Her work ethic is something that is in me, but I'm just going about it a different way. I'm doing that for my kids. I know what I felt when my mom wasn't there because she had to go to Detroit in the middle of the night and me being nervous because I knew what was going on. Knowing that and feeling that is something I don't want my daughters to ever feel. It's a big reason why I chose not to have kids until after I got out of the Marine Corps.

My uncle that passed away has two kids, and they're calling somebody else Dad right now. Being a parent means a lot to me, because I didn't have a stable home. I had a good relationship with my mom, but it wasn't like I wanted, and I didn't have a dad to really talk to besides my uncle. My uncle was my hero, just because I seen what he had. He didn't have a high school diploma, but he made over a million dollars a year. Six months before he died, I was watching him get ready. I was sixteen. He co-owned a nightclub in Dallas, and I was watching him get ready, and he said, "What are you looking at?" And I was like, "Man, I want to be just like you." I was in the door of his closet, and he was getting ready in front of his mirror. He wasn't the typical drug dealer type. He approached it as a business, and I think that's why he made so much money. Because he dressed really nice, took care of himself really well, wasn't really into all that shiny jewelry type of lifestyle. He wanted nice things, so he dressed like he should. So he was getting ready, and I told him I wanted to be like him, and he stopped and put down his comb. And he looked at me and he hit me, and I started crying. And he said, "Don't you ever tell me that. You're not gonna do this, you're gonna be better than me." It's one of those things I'll remember for the rest of my life.

Six months later he got murdered. He had a club on lower Greenville in Dallas. He was with his bodyguard at the time, and it was anywhere between one and four o'clock in the afternoon, and he was sitting in his car, waiting for a person to go to the restaurant to meet with. And somebody shot him through the back window of his car. His bodyguard was sitting next to him, and he didn't get a chance to shoot back. He got shot ten times. The first bullet when he turned around went into the bottom of his ear and came out through his cheek, and he got shot in his neck, and then all along his back. It was one of those things. It's a dog-eat-dog world when you're making that much money. When he died, twenty-some people got indicted within like three months, because he was the top dog. Nobody knew what the hell they were doing after he died. Everybody assumes that they can take responsibility and they can make stuff happen, but when that guy goes down, only he knows how stuff works. His name was Miguel Martinez. One of his partners and a couple of his other friends got life in prison for organized crime.

The whole process after that was tough for me, because people are like, "God is omni-everything, omnipresent, and loving and all sorts of stuff," and I was like, "Why that? Why did that have to happen?" He was the strongest link in my family. Other uncles could be fighting, because Mom has five brothers. The other brothers could be fighting, but whenever Miguel would call, he'd be like, "Hey, we're gonna put aside that BS and we're all gonna get together and have a cookout." And we'd all come together. And when he passed away, everybody dispersed. It's not even near what it was. We're always fighting. Even now, I see stuff now as an adult that I didn't see when I was a kid, and we just don't have that glue anymore. He was the glue, hands down. His character, his demeanor, was always fun and loving. He was real big, almost like a bear. He could be so loving and nurturing. And at the same time, you didn't want to piss him off, because he could kill you, too.

I lived with him almost two years from fifteen to sixteen and a half. And what I learned in that year and a half is something that I still carry today, as far as staying true to yourself and being humble, and what family means. He did everything for his two kids and for his wife. And I do everything for my wife and my two kids now. But what the Marine Corps taught me was more a sense of brotherhood. And I guess I was always that leader, because I was always outspoken and always doing, and my athletic ability would always put me in that upper range of athlete, but I guess they found that monster in me, to give me a sense of purpose to find out what I want to do and execute that goal. That's something I never had. I didn't have that before. I was lost. That's the reason why I went: because I was lost. I didn't know what I wanted to do, and my uncle had interviews lined up for me at UPS and some other company that finds gas lines and water lines. I think they were paying like $15 or $20 an hour. I just didn't know what the hell I wanted to do, and the Marine Corps brought that out in me.

"I didn't really know what I was doing."

Jessica Dawson

I went to college before I joined the military—the first time I went to college. I was maybe sixteen when I started, and I really had no idea what I was doing there. I just wanted to go to college, you know? I started one major, I think it was psychology, and I changed it about five times before I left. The last major was math, and I took Calculus 2, and that's as far as I got in college. I joke that I was so bad at calculus that I joined the Navy.

I realized I didn't really know what I was doing in college and was thinking about changing my major again. I just really felt lost, and the military didn't seem like such an obscure idea, because people who were close to me were in the military, and they seemed to make it out okay.

They had really good heads on their shoulders. So I thought maybe if I joined the military, I would miraculously become this person who knows what they're doing with their life and is an adult, you know?

"I wanted to do something to help people."
William Howe Jr.

I graduated seminary and was working as an assistant pastor when my mom got breast cancer. So I fell out of favor with the church, because I was just mad at God and stuff. I had a wife and daughter, and I needed something to make money and go back to school, because nobody recognized my seminary education because it wasn't an accredited school. The Army would pay for that, and they also offered me a $40,000 or $60,000 signing bonus, which helped take care of my family in the short term. In the long term I knew I'd be able to go to college. So that's why I ended up going in. But if I went in, I wanted to do something to help people, which is why I chose to become a combat medic.

The Marines don't have medics; they use the Navy's corpsmen. I didn't want to risk ending up on a boat for a year at a time. I wanted to make sure that I was actually in the action, and I knew that if I was in the Army as a medic, I would be. I went to basic training at Fort Leonard Wood, Missouri, which was interesting because it was a co-military base; they had guys and girls doing basic training together. We weren't allowed to talk, but that opened my eyes to what exactly women can do. They can do everything a guy can do, because they did all the obstacle courses better than I did. Then I went to Advanced Individual Training at Fort Sam Houston down in San Antonio. I graduated training, went to Fort Hood, and two months later I was shipping off to Iraq.

"Daddy, these guys are awesome."
Paige McCloud

I'm originally from Bridgeport, a small town in the upper northeast corner of Alabama, right where Georgia, Tennessee, and Alabama come together. A little bitty town that no one's ever heard of. But sometimes people will be like, "Oh, yeah, I know where Bridgeport is." It's in the valley. My grandparents lived in Skyline, which is on the mountains, and we lived below. The closest city is Chattanooga, Tennessee, thirty-six miles from my front door. So any time we'd go shopping, it's always to Chattanooga. It's all right, but I wouldn't live there.

When I was six years old, my dad took me to an air show, the Blue Angels. I asked him, "Daddy, these guys are awesome. What do I have to do to do this?" And he's like, "Oh, you have to go to the Naval Academy." So I thought for the next ten years that I was going to go to the Naval Academy. Once I got to high school, I kind of switched and didn't make the grades, didn't do community service, didn't do anything that would help me get into college, much less the Naval Academy. So my parents sat me down and they're like, "You know, Paige, we don't think you're going to get into college anywhere, especially to become an officer, so maybe you should go enlisted." At the time my mom was working at an Army hospital: Dwight D. Eisenhower Army Medical Center at Fort Ord in Georgia. So I was going to work with her every once in a while, volunteering in the Red Cross, because I thought at the time I wanted to be a nurse. So I saw the enlisted guys there and I thought it was pretty cool. So that's what I ended up doing instead of going in as an officer and doing college first.

It was a good, positive experience. It definitely taught me responsibility and how to handle things on my own, in a slower process than I think college would have. All of my brothers and sisters left between the ages of sixteen and eighteen. And after that, my parents had this agreement that they don't help us through college because nobody helped them through college, so it would have been me all on my own. But going into the Navy, I had boot camp for two months and then straight to A School for the next year, and I couldn't dress like a civilian when I wanted to, I couldn't go out when I wanted to. Maybe on the weekends sometimes, but you had to get certain watch qualifications to get to wear civilian clothes or stay out all night. So I had to go through these stages to kind of earn my freedom, and I think earning that freedom helped me realize that you have to be responsible for yourself. It was definitely a good thing for me.

"I received a draft induction letter."

Dan Southard

In late November 1967, I received a letter from the registrar at Buena Vista University indicating that I needed one upper-level course in biology to graduate the following May. I had completed all upper level courses offered in the spring semester related to my major. It appeared that I would not graduate till the following December, and I accepted my fate. However, to complicate matters further, a short time later I received a draft induction letter requiring me to report to the induction center at Omaha, Nebraska, in June. My four-year draft deferment to attend college would no longer be valid. Consequently, I would not graduate before going into the military. I didn't have a problem going into the military, but I did want to graduate first. It was a certainty that I would be drafted before graduating.

That December I was sitting in the student union contemplating my situation, when a Marine captain and a gunnery sergeant walked in and set up a recruitment booth. The sign on the booth read, "Graduate from college and become a Marine officer." For me, "graduate" was the key word in the sign. It was worth a try to determine if the Marines would allow me to graduate prior to my service obligation. I approached the booth and asked the question. The captain's reply was, "Sure, we can do that! First, you have to complete Officer Candidate School this summer. If you make it through OCS, the Marine Corps will allow you to graduate the following fall semester. Following graduation, you will receive your commission and begin your service obligation as a Marine officer." Without much hesitation I replied, "Sold!" and signed the papers. Next to proposing to my wife, that decision turned out to be one of the best in my life. I became a Marine for less than honorable reasons; but being an officer of Marines has been my highest honor.

"I wanted to travel."

Rodney Baker

I joined the Navy right out of high school from Batesville, Mississippi. South Panola High School. I joined in 1982. Went to boot camp in Great Lakes, Illinois, and I also did my engineering machinist mate, what we call A School, there. I excelled in the program, and they had a position where you would stay there for eighteen months when you finished your school. They had some modular power plants there that they trained students on. So I had the good fortune of qualifying there and training other students on how to operate distilling plants at the training facility there at Great Lakes. In 1984 I transferred to my first ship, the USS *Dubuque*, in San Diego, California. There I got qualified on all the operations of the plant and made E-4, which was a really big pay increase, and I qualified then as a machinist mate of the watch, which is a top engineering position.

So I was the senior enlisted supervisor for underway operations for the machinist mate's side of the engine room. The machinist mates are responsible for maintaining the reduction gears, operation of generators, all the pumps that support this equipment, and the distilling plant. I had four other guys under me, and I answered to an engineering officer on watch. That engineering officer would answer to the bridge. My main reason for wanting to be an engineer was an old John Wayne movie, *In Harm's Way*. The engineering chief was Archie Bunker, Carroll O'Connor. The old, rough, rugged guy inspired me, and they made that ship run when it wasn't supposed to run. I used to tell my guys, "If you give me half the parts and two hours, we can do whatever you need to get done."

I wanted to travel. And from all I saw, when you watch movies—because that's what we did, we watched movies and read books—it goes back to John Wayne and Archie Bunker. They were in the South Pacific on these tropical islands. There was Hawaii. The Army, you got to go sleep in the mud. And I'm one of those guys—I'm not going to go sleep in the woods.

Let me describe Batesville. The most successful thing in Batesville, you can look it up online, is South Panola High School football. We play football as well as they play here in Texas. We've produced pro football players. We won six or seven state championships. But academically, a lot of those kids, once football is over, they don't do anything. When you graduated high school in a typical small town, you went to work in one of the factories. You were limited what you could do as far as growth, financial success. And I dreamed. I can say we were poor, but you would never have known it.

Back then they had the FHA [Federal Housing Administration] program. My mother's father left her some land, so she used that as a mortgage to build us a home. So we had a nice three-bedroom brick home in a nice little suburban area. The majority of the people that lived around us were white; we were a few little black families that were in there. So we saw doctors, we were exposed to different things. So we had different desires and dreams. One of my schoolteachers, Mrs. Hopper, lived around the corner from us, and her husband was my coach, and they would pick us up on the way to school and we would talk. So we just got exposed to a different thought process and encouraged to strive to reach our potential.

Mr. and Mrs. Hopper were white. So it was just a different exposure to things. Then we had Coach Abson and Mrs. Abson, and they were black. Mrs. Abson was a history teacher, and she instilled a pride in our ability to achieve great things by ensuring we knew the historical contributions Blacks made to society. These were some of the influences on my life.

My mother had a sixth-grade education, and she was determined that her kids were going to do better than she did. That was instilled in us. You may not get to college, but you make a way for your child to do better than you did and not repeat the poverty thing. I don't know how people are today, but we had to have food stamps. I was embarrassed to have to go to the store with food stamps. And some people say I was arrogant, but I didn't feel I should have to be like that. So we worked hard to get out of poverty. Now I teach my son this: We've laid opportunities out for you. If you choose to go do stupid, that's on you. I don't pay for stupid. You don't have to live like we live, but you know how you're not supposed to live. But if you choose to go live in a ghetto hood area, that's on you. I don't pay for that. These were the type of things my mother instilled in us. And that's part of why I dreamed of doing more and doing better.

I joined the Navy, of all the branches of the military, because I wanted to travel. That was the biggest thing—I wanted to travel. I think it gave me the best opportunity. Matter of fact, it even goes back to my second-grade year. In second grade, Batesville Elementary, in geography class, there was a book, and this family went on a trip around the world, to all these exotic places with little Timmy and Jimmy and their mother and father, and they got to see different cultures. And that had an influence on me. So, education matters. I think sometimes we focus so much on testing that we get away from educating. I was educated in a little, small town in Mississippi that showed me the possibilities of the world, and I took advantage of it.

"I am very stubborn by nature."

Steven Gonzalez

I'm from Fort Worth. I was born here. I'm a first-generation American, both of my parents are from Mexico, my family is from Mexico. So I'm the first out of my entire family—and there were eight children overall and something like sixty grandchildren and another like sixty great-grandchildren—to join the military and to attend a university. It's something that I am prideful of and try to set the example, especially for my two kids. I am married and have two children, a son and a daughter.

I am a dual media studies major and history major. I am very stubborn by nature. I was a football player out of high school, and I wanted to play for TCU, and I applied. I got accepted, but I did not get any of the scholarships or anything like that, so there was no way I could afford it. So my mentality at eighteen years old was either I am going to TCU or joining the Marine Corps. As soon as I knew I wouldn't be getting a full ride or anything, the very next day I got it done. I believe I enlisted in April of 2003.

"I was competitive for an ROTC scholarship."

Jeff Coffer

I am a graduate of Wofford College in Spartanburg, South Carolina. It's a private liberal arts school, like TCU. When I started my studies in 1978, tuition was still twice what it was at public universities, so I was looking for financial aid of some type, and I was competitive for an ROTC scholarship. I got a three-year scholarship, and that's how I got started. I was commissioned second lieutenant upon graduation.

When I graduated with my BS degree in '82, it was the time of the so-called Reagan buildup, and there was a lot of money being spent on the defense side of things. To make a long story short, the Army had more second lieutenants than they knew what to do with, so it was relatively easy to get a deferral to go to graduate school. So they told me: If you want to go on and finish a master's degree first, if we need you at that time we will take you into active duty, and if we don't, and if you want to go get your PhD, we will consider your request. So I finished my master's degree in '85, then I petitioned for and got another deferral until 1987.

I finished my doctorate and went into active duty for six months at

Fort McClellan in Alabama. It was very interesting. Lots of things have changed in the world since then. There were a lot more military installations in the country at that time. I had gotten married the year before, so I was away from my wife for six months, which was hard.

"There was nothing for me here."

Carl Castillo

I was bored, to be honest with you. At a very young age my mother pushed me to excel academically. So, in a sense, I kind of rebelled. I got tired of school, because when I looked at college, I just looked at it as an extension of high school. I managed to still pass with a 3.8, so it wasn't much of a challenge.

My friend went off to the Marine Corps first. He came back, and I saw in him what I kind of wanted, because it challenged him physically and whatnot. I knew it was going to be probably the toughest thing I was going to do. I chose the Marine Corps specifically, because you always heard it was the toughest. I qualified for pretty much everything the Marine Corps had to offer. I wanted the hardest thing out there, that would test me physically, so I chose infantry.

I left everything behind, because there was nothing left where I was at. I mean, I grew up on the north side of Fort Worth. If you didn't do drugs, if you didn't get in a gang, or if you didn't go to jail, you looked for ways to get out of the neighborhood. College being one of them, if you're fortunate enough to be smart enough to go to a college away from the area. If not, then the military is an option, but not too many people in my generation in that area had clean enough records to go into the Marine Corps or any military service. So there was nothing for me here.

"It was a musical fat camp."

Andy Lahey

I enlisted straight out of high school, at eighteen. I was scheduled to march with a drum and bugle corps for that summer, and my recruiter was real wary to let me go, because before they can ship us to boot camp we have to be able to pass certain physical tests, and the recruiting stations generally like to be able to test for that themselves. He was like, "Are you going to be ready?" And I was like, "Let me put it this way: What

I'm going to be doing this summer is a hundred times more intense than anything you'll be able to put me through, no offense, sir." For all intents and purposes, it was a musical fat camp: constantly running around anywhere from four to fourteen hours every day, with an instrument that weighs forty-one pounds [a tuba]. I went there at the beginning of the summer at 172 pounds and lost twelve pounds that summer.

So he reluctantly let me go, and I came back and about two weeks later shipped off to boot camp, MCRD San Diego. Then I came back for about a month, because it was December and they weren't going to send me to combat training over the Christmas and New Year's holidays.

"I had no clue where I was going."

Christa Banet

In 2002 I was attending Indiana University Southeast. I graduated from high school in 2001, and shortly after that we had the terrorist attacks in New York City. I waited until January to enroll in college, but I just didn't feel right being at home. I felt like there was something else bigger going on, and that I needed to go. So I went to the recruiting station in Clarksville, Indiana, and talked to the recruiters, and I asked them how soon I could leave. They had a shipment of women going out in twenty-eight days—in the Marine Corps, the women don't ship out every month like the guys. They do rotations once every three months. I essentially went in open contract, but I had chosen two MOSes [military occupational specialties] that I could have been put into. The recruiter was still working it out. With twenty-eight days going in, it's kind of rushed. I chose legal admin and aviation electrician, and I didn't find out until I graduated from boot camp that I had gotten the aviation electrician MOS. But I had no clue where I was going until after Marine combat training.

"The main problem was the Cold War."

Mark Wassenich

After my freshman year at TCU, I realized that I was going to be drafted when I got out of school. That was true for just about all the men in classes of 1960 to '68. And there were certain categories to get out of it, like ministerial students, engineers, so forth, but I wasn't in those categories. So I decided I did not want to be an enlisted guy working for some tough sergeant in the Army. The alternatives were Air Force enlisted for three years, or Air Force officer for four years. So I joined the Air Force ROTC as a sophomore and had to double up that year and do both the freshman and sophomore work in ROTC, then went on and graduated in '64 and became a lieutenant.

In that period, the main problem was the Cold War. In 1962 there had been the Cuban missile crisis, the closest that we and the Soviets ever came to nuclear war. So the US was building up the military, and then in '64–'65 the Vietnam War started, and I think the military realized even before that it was short of people to fight an intensive regional war like Vietnam, at the same time they were building up this worldwide nuclear deterrent. As soon as I went in they assigned me to air intelligence and photo interpretation, which was really what I wanted to do, and related to my major in geography as an undergraduate.

"He's really smart, he's very well groomed."

Shawn Keane

I have been married to an Air Force officer for over thirty years. Growing up in San Diego and having no military background, I had no clue about military life. I have always been patriotic and admired what little I knew about the military. I did witness the return of many young Vietnam veterans from war, along with an influx of Vietnamese arriving by boats.

I met my husband, Bradley, while I was working at the University of Arizona. Bradley enlisted in the Army in 1967, when he was seventeen. At the age of eighteen, he was sent to Vietnam as part of the 101st Airborne (Screaming Eagles) for thirteen months during a conflict called Hamburger Hill. He survived, came home, and thought, "I'm never doing that again!" Soon after being discharged, he attended UCLA and received an undergraduate degree. He seriously considered applying to law school. However, the economy (in 1980) wasn't doing well and instead of law school, he competed for and was selected to attend Air Force Officer Training School (OTS). He was commissioned an Air Force officer in 1981. He had made a promise to himself after Vietnam, "If I ever go back into the military, I am going in the Air Force, because they live better in wartime and place a higher priority on family and quality of life issues." Also, he appreciated the emphasis on higher education in the Air Force.

Air Force veteran Bradley Keane points to the area he served in during the Vietnam War. *Courtesy of Shawn Keane.*

At the time, Air Force deployments were less frequent than those of the other branches of service.

Soon after Bradley and I met, in 1984, he left for a one-year remote tour in Belgium. When he returned, we dated for a year and then married. When I first met him, I thought, "Gosh! He's really smart, he's very well groomed, and he's very articulate." I had never spoken to anyone in the military and assumed they were more formal than fun. But there was more to him than I realized. I began to meet other military people and their families; it was a great start to a wonderful relationship that has lasted more than thirty years.

"I just kind of got really bored."
Jonathan Ide

It was actually kind of boredom. I got out of high school and I was going to college and working full time, and I just kind of got really bored with it. So I was like, "Oh, I'll join up." And also my family has always been in the military. My dad's side has been here since the American Revolution, and they have always served. So I figured I would go out, have fun, and see what happens.

"The military allowed me to get away."
Megan Morris

I was so immature. I couldn't spend the night at a friend's house until I was thirteen, because I would get homesick. My mom was my best friend. When I was sixteen, we found out she had brain and lung cancer. And when I was seventeen, I held her hand as she passed away.

When she died, my world crumbled. Joining the military allowed me to get away from that pain of being surrounded by my family, who were now at war with each other, because my mom was the peacemaker of the family. The military allowed me to get away from that, but also forced me to depend on myself to make my own decisions. Pre-military, I didn't even like me.

I graduated high school in 2008 and went straight into the Air Force. I entered on August 12, 2008, in San Antonio, Texas, because that is where basic training is. I began tech school at Shepherd Air Force Base in Wichita Falls, and became a dental assistant. I did dental assisting for a little under eight years. I was stationed at Tinker Air Force Base in Oklahoma City, then Joint Base Elmendorf-Richardson in Anchorage, Alaska. I was at each base for roughly three and a half, four years. In Alaska I did a year of honor guard. Ceremonies honoring people or events like promotions, changes of command, and funerals.

Funerals held a special place in my heart, especially because I got to fold the flag and hand it to the next of kin. It's a humbling experience and really makes you view life differently. That was my favorite part of my career.

I was burnt out on school when, by the time I was done with my senior year, I knew I wanted to make my own money, travel the world, just be independent really. I knew I would make my own money and they would pay for my education while I was in and after I got out. And I would have a good skill set. So that's why I decided to join. It's surprising because I have a lot of veterans in my family, like my dad, my grandparents, aunts and uncles, a couple of cousins, but they all did not want me to join. Specifically my dad, because he was scared.

We had a recruiter come onto the high school campus and set up a booth. If you were interested, you could walk up to him. So that's pretty much what I did. I didn't feel pressure. Had I felt pressure, I wouldn't have joined. Once I qualified to go into the Air Force, I had to participate in the Delayed Entry Program. If you're still in high school, or you have a bunch of weight to lose, or you're trying to raise your ASVAB scores, then you do the Delayed Entry Program and they work with you on your fitness, familiarizing yourself with military ranks, customs and courtesies and whatnot, marching, all that jazz.

"The rest were going to watch them on TV."
Tommy Dunaway

I was never prouder or more disappointed to be an American than on September 12, 2001. On one hand, I could not have been prouder to see the renewed patriotism and resolve of most Americans, as they proudly flew flags from their homes, cars, and places of business. On the other hand I was angry, because my own devotion to our country had been unwavering on September 10, when it seemed as if no one else really cared. I was a Marine Corps Reserve corporal with over four years of service, and being on a college campus around carefree coeds only added to my mixed emotions.

In that fall of 2001 I was renting a house with a group of people I hardly knew, and whose names I can't even remember. My planned roommates for that year had all failed out, transferred, or quit while I was away the previous summer at Officer Candidate School. As I drove toward campus on the morning of September 11, I heard on the radio that a plane had hit one of the World Trade Center towers. "Why was someone flying that close?" I thought. "What a shame. There are definitely going to be some people losing jobs over this one." With that in mind, I walked into an astronomy lab and caught up on work until early afternoon. Then I walked to my old dorm to meet some friends who had agreed to fill me in on a class I had missed the previous week. As I walked down the hall toward their room, they came toward me, noticeably upset, saying, "You're going to have to leave!" "Okay," I remember thinking. "Maybe I'll get the notes some other time." Sensing my confusion, they told me just to go look at the TV in their room.

The first thing I saw was a shot of the recently attacked Pentagon. I watched another couple of minutes, thought to myself, "Well, World War III just started," and drove home to pack my gear. On the way home I was strangely excited, in the way only another Marine would understand. My mindset was that astronomy labs and notes from Western Civ are one thing, but deploying to the Middle East as soon as humanly possible would be great! So that evening I sat by the phone—no cell at the time— and waited for the call. Eventually a few calls came in, with instructions to be at our reserve center Friday evening with our gear, and that more details would follow.

I watched the news all night, then went back to campus the next day, but not to class. As far as I knew, I was going to be dropping out in a matter of days anyway, so why bother. I wanted to be around other people who might be feeling the way I was, instead of glued to the TV. But it soon occurred to me that only a fraction likely had the same concerns. For some reason I felt compelled to write down the wide range of thoughts I had about everything going on in my country that day. The flying flags and palpable sense of "We're in this together" had affirmed my faith in Americans, but it dawned on me that only a few people were ever going to be directly impacted by these events. The rest were going to watch them on TV for a few minutes, then resume life as usual.

The Horseshoe at the University of South Carolina campus is a bucolic setting only a few yards from the Statehouse and Columbia's Main Street. The early nineteenth-century buildings there were among the few parts of the state's capital city not burned to the ground in the Civil War, because General Sherman used them as a hospital and barracks for his men during the occupation. As I sat on a bench under a giant live oak tree looking around at those hallowed grounds, I couldn't avoid asking myself, "Why does man keep doing this?"

So I wrote and wrote about everything I was seeing and feeling— mostly questions about things I didn't understand. As a group of sorority sisters walked by smiling and laughing, I wondered how much impact the last twenty-four hours had had on their lives. Then a few tenured professors walked past in deep discussion about some abstract subject, and I wondered if they had even heard the news. Finally, I took in the whole panorama as frisbees flew by, couples chatted, and groups studied on the well-manicured grounds, and I realized that most of my class- mates cared only on a superficial level. I wasn't mad at any of these peo- ple, but some things I already knew finally hit me in a deep, deep way. The truths I accepted were that my priorities were not in line with those of the people I went to class with, and that this country is defended by an incredibly small percentage of its population.

That weekend came and went. We updated our wills but were left in limbo about our fates as Marines, so I finished the semester and pre- pared for my final year of college. By the fall of 2002 I was only a few months away from my degree and a commission. Finally, the rumor of our reserve unit activating for deployment was starting to seem like a real possibility. That created a personal dilemma. I wanted nothing more than to deploy to the Middle East with my buddies. On the other hand, past summers at Officer Candidate School had been far from easy, and I was only a few months away from my dream of a commission and the opportunity to lead Marines. With that in mind, I started to miss classes and planned to postpone graduation by a semester, with the hope that an opportunity would arise soon for me to join my friends in combat.

My USMC Officer Selection Officer's job included monitoring my grades to ensure that I graduated on time, got commissioned, then went off to The Basic School in Quantico, Virginia, to begin an active-duty Marine Corps officer career. After reviewing my academic progress, or rather lack thereof, through the early fall of 2002, he called me into his office to ask why my grades were slipping.

I offered some sort of excuse about senioritis or tougher upper-level classes.

"Don't think you're kidding me," he rejoined. "I know *exactly* what you're doing. You're going to get your grades back up and graduate in December, understand?"

At that point I said what corporals say to upset captains: "Yes sir, understood."

"Look, I get it," he assured me. "But trust me, it's a big shit sandwich, and you'll eventually get to take a bite." With that he dismissed me, and I went about the task of improving my grades and taking the next step in my budding career.

As fate would have it, just as I graduated and checked out of my unit, they were called up and my friends were sent to active duty, some of them to Iraq, while I was sent to Virginia for more training. I was also acutely aware that, at the same time, out there somewhere, also heading to Iraq, were Marines that I would later be tasked to lead. Some of those had surely also already been to Afghanistan.

After nine months of training, in fall 2003 I received orders for the assignment I had always wanted and been working toward: platoon commander. Here it was, fall again, and time for another big change. Sure enough, the Marines assigned to me were just back from an intense combat deployment, as part of the initial push into Iraq in early 2003. Over the next several months we got to know each other as the usual turnover of personnel occurred, and within a year it was essentially a brand new group of guys. And in keeping with the annual rhythm of my life, in fall 2004 our training became more focused: We had orders to Iraq.

Leading the Way

The Story of James Newcomer

Mary Newcomer McKinney

*Originally titled "James William Newcomer: Teacher, Scholar, Soldier."
Newcomer (March 14, 1912–August 25, 2012),
served as Vice-Chancellor for Academic Affairs at
Texas Christian University, 1965–1987.*

James William Newcomer was my father. He came to TCU in 1965 as Vice Chancellor for Academic Affairs. He also held the Trustees chair as professor of English and was director of TCU Press. He played violin in the TCU orchestra (as did I as a student) when time permitted and kept a full-sized harp in his office, which he would attempt to play from time to time. Music was a constant in his life. In college, he played the saxophone in a dance band and directed the Glee Club. At TCU, he helped orchestrate the hosting of the Van Cliburn International Piano Competition on the TCU campus after becoming a close friend of Lili Kraus, the famed pianist, Cliburn judge, and TCU artist-in-residence. In 1997, TCU Press published his memoir of Madame Kraus that documented their close friendship. He titled it simply *Lili*, followed by *Lili Kraus and the Van Cliburn International Piano Competition: A Memoir of the TCU Years*. While vice chancellor, he was instrumental in establishing a chapter of Phi Beta Kappa on campus. In 2013, the TCU chapter honored him for his efforts and his seventy-nine-year membership by naming the Senior Scholar Award the James Newcomer Senior Scholar Award. Dad was a scholar by choice, and a soldier by necessity.

Growing up, I heard stories about some of his experiences during World War II. He only told his children the funny things that happened to him. But I recall, as a child, seeing a photo of a truck loaded with dead naked bodies and wondering about the reality of his war. He would not talk about that side of it. It was just something that had to be done, and he was proud to have served his country. When World War II broke out, Dad was assistant head master and chair of the English Department at a private academy in Elgin, Illinois. Decades later, one of his pupils from the academy came to Fort Worth to interview him for a book he was writing about the war. *Go with God* was published in 2007 and chronicles Dad's student's experience as a World War II pilot and prisoner of war and, as an escapee from the prison, his eventual encounter with General Patton's Third Army. He and Dad talked over the course of a few days about their war experiences. I did not think then to ask, but wonder now, if they encountered each other during the war, since Dad fought in Patton's Third Army. Dad and his student both died in 2012. The academy recognized them in its alumni magazine that year and ded-

> **In his letters home to his parents, he does not talk about the battlefield but rather comments on their family news and news sent about his hometown, along with comments about the sites he was seeing in Europe.**

icated the back inside cover to honor Dad's one hundredth birthday, five and a half months before his death. As a scholar, he was a quiet, reserved gentleman, and I think he was much the same as a soldier.

In his letters home to his parents, he does not talk about the battlefield but rather comments on their family news and news sent about his hometown, along with comments about the sites he was seeing in Europe. He took photographs of many of the places he went in Europe and of himself and fellow soldiers. On the back of one he wrote that everyone in the photograph was laughing because one of them had just received a camera with a time-lapse button that allowed the photographer to set the camera and then run into the photograph. A marvel at the time. Other photos show his troops attending a prayer service in a field before a battle, his fellow officers relaxing, his driver in the jeep, along with the aftermath of battle and him sitting in the bombed-out living room of Hitler's Eagle's Nest. Much of his poetry and many of his short stories describe the cold and damp he endured for months along with the pain and suffering of the wounded and dying, and those who observed it.

A few days after the bombing of Pearl Harbor, Dad went to the local recruitment office to enlist. He tried to enlist in every branch of the service, but each one turned him down. They all said his eyesight was too poor to serve. However, in 1942, at the age of thirty, he was drafted and entered the Army, wearing Army-issue eyeglasses. Growing up, those same eyeglasses came out of the drawer once in a while to be worn when he played the violin. My siblings and I were always intrigued by them and knew they must have seen unbelievable horrors, the ones about which he would not tell us. But as he aged, he occasionally shared more details. He had a trunk full of photographs that he later allowed us to see, and those photographs began to tell a story of this scholar-soldier.

When I was about ten years old, we took a family vacation to California. We drove and camped along the way. One day, we found ourselves in Gila Bend, Arizona. It was a very hot, dry day in the desert. We all complained about the heat, asking why we were in the middle of nowhere. Our car was an old barebones station wagon. Air-conditioning was a contraption filled with water that hung on the outside of the passenger's window, and a burlap bag of water draped over the radiator on the hood of the car kept the radiator from overheating. The car had very little suspension, and parts fell off as we traveled along a remote dusty and rocky road that led to our destination—Dad's first Army training camp. It was not really a place he ever wanted to return to, but since it was on our way, we took a side trip for him to revisit it. He actually wanted to see if it was as horrible as he remembered. It was. The temperature that day almost reached the 120 degrees that he wrote about experiencing in his tent as a soldier. He did not say much about the camp, other than how miserable it was and how desperate everyone was to get enough water to drink in that godforsaken place. They had to raid the locked train cars at night to get that water.

We did not stay long that day, just long enough to have someone repair the car so we could continue on to California. Dad was sent to Gila Bend to train for desert warfare in Africa, where he was told the Army was going to send him following that training. But the Army changed its mind, and in one letter he wrote that with so many changes it was all like a game of chess and he was a checker. He was sent to Florida, California, New England, and eventually to the Quartermaster Officer Candidate School at Camp Lee, Virginia, where for thirteen weeks he was trained as one of the first of the "Fighting Quartermasters in Modern American Military History," as the title of a roster booklet found in his trunk indicated. There he attended trucking school, training to later lead a troop of truck drivers in General Patton's Third Army. Dad, the scholar, was no mechanic and panicked at the thought of driving and having to fix those very large troop trucks. But as luck would have it, he was partnered with a man who earned his living as a mechanic in civilian life, and who helped get Dad through trucking school.

Upon graduation from the Quartermaster School, he was next sent to Fort Dix, New Jersey. There he was made a first lieutenant and put in charge of a troop of young African American soldiers who did not want to be there any more than he did. In fact, because of prejudices of the times, other white officers refused to lead this troop. As a product of a very small Midwestern town, Dad was unaware of the prejudice against African Americans and the anti-Semitism that overshadowed the war. During World War I, he had witnessed the hatred shown toward a German immigrant who owned the local clothing store in his hometown. He did not understand such hatred then as a boy, nor later as an adult. There were no African Americans living in his town so, at the age of thirty-two, he met his first one and became the proud, although a bit intimidated at times, commanding officer of the 4051st Quartermaster Truck Company, composed of all African American soldiers. Some came from the urban north and some from the rural south. Many were teenagers who had learned to drive on tractors rather than cars on their farms, but nevertheless, they were able to drive the large trucks. He worried that those inner-city New Jersey and New York boys who had grown up in the dangerous black ghettos would not take this meek, soft-spoken white teacher seriously. He soon solved the dilemma. Dad was on the small side, 5'10" tall and weighing 135 pounds. He decided to look over his charges and pick out the largest man there, an ex-barkeeper from Newark, New Jersey, who stood over six feet tall and weighed in at 250 pounds. This was the man Dad ordered to always stand beside and a little behind him, looking as menacing as he possibly could every time Dad, most likely in a quivering voice, had to give an order to his troops. According to Dad, his troops always obeyed his orders, and he had nothing but respect for and fond memories of his men.

But he learned quickly about prejudice. He and four other white officers were in charge. He often had to defend one or another of his troops in a court martial and lost every time, although he declared the innocence of the soldier. He was dismayed by the consistency of the outcomes and punishment handed out by the white officers of the courts against his men and, later, by how often his troops were denied needed supplies and support because of their skin color. Eventually, in order to avoid unfair punishment of his men, he and his fellow officers came up with a plan. He wrote on page seventeen of his book of short stories, entitled *Hell: Stories Out of the Wars* (Editions Le Phare): "Toward the end of the eleven-day voyage to England we five white men made the best decision of our lives. We agreed that no matter what crime our men committed, except for murder or rape, we would not punish them. For six months in England the circumstance of being without a resident white superior officer permitted us to pursue our desperate, idealistic plan."

Before landing in Normandy, Dad and his troops spent six months in England, preparing for the invasion. In *Hell* he wrote, "For the duration of the European war, from the invasion of Normandy, through the Battle of France, the Battle of the Bulge, the Battle of the Rhine, the Battle of Germany those black men personified bravery, reliability, courtesy, and endurance. They gave us not one cause for punishment." He also wrote in that same book that by the end of the war, he "ended the war hating white men" for their treatment of the African American soldiers. On the sixty-fifth anniversary celebration of D-day, Dad happened to be in the office of his financial adviser, who asked him if he was going to celebrate the occasion. Dad responded negatively and recounted how poorly his troops had been treated after landing in Normandy on D-day plus three. The Allies had pushed back, and his troops began to flood the beach with supplies of food, water, ammunition, and fuel, while being strafed by German planes. Under such circumstances, the drivers were trained to drive the trucks into a ditch, jump out, and seek cover. All those years later, Dad was still appalled by the fact that if there were white soldiers in the bunkers, they would not let his soldiers in. They were different times, but that did not make it right in his eyes.

Once they were ordered to leave New Jersey, it took eleven days to cross the North Atlantic. It was bitter cold and stormy, the seas were rough, and most everyone was seasick. Inside, the stench from vomit was sickening. So Dad stayed outside wrapped in a blanket, with his back to the smokestack to keep warm, and crossed the ocean reading Shakespeare, Dickens, and the Bible from tiny two-inch red leather-bound books that fit in his pocket. He continued his scholarly pursuits as much as possible while in the Army. In his Army trunk today remain many notebooks where he wrote poems, short stories, and ideas for stories or articles. Although he was a soldier, he never stopped being a scholar. Now the scholar-soldier was off to war and, unbeknownst to him, off to his destiny. (Nearly fifty years later, my husband was called to captain one of the many World War II troop ships to carry supplies to the Gulf War. Supposedly, those ships were to have been maintained by private companies all those years as the Ready Reserve Fleet. Unfortunately, that was not the case for many of them, and they were anything but ready to cross the Atlantic again for another war.)

In the European Theatre, Dad fought in the major battles of General Patton's Third Army. Years later he wrote in *Hell:* "Before General Patton was in the Third Army I was in the Third Army. Together Patton and I invaded Normandy, fought our way out of Normandy and across France, liberated Luxembourg on September 10, fought every day in the Bulge but did not get killed or freeze to death, crossed the Rhine, and drove Germans deep into Bavaria. For a few hours I controlled—I laughed—a million German soldiers in their redoubt."

But it was in England where he had his first non-encounter with General Patton. Dad took advantage of being sent to Europe and liked to sightsee between battles whenever possible. He was particularly fond of antique shops and churches. During down times, his driver would take him along country roads to visit a church whose steeple he saw in the distance. Sometimes he came out of a church only to find that the battle lines had changed while he played tourist, and that he was now behind enemy lines. On these occasions he became quite nervous about getting back to his troops. He was not good with sports trivia, and worried that he would not know the answer to the latest sports-related security questions to get through the Allied lines. But he always managed to return safely. One day in England, he had his driver stop at an antique shop and wait for him in the jeep while he went inside. While he was there, General Patton drove up and demanded to know from Dad's driver whose jeep was parked there. The driver responded that it belonged to

Lieutenant Newcomer. In a menacing tone, Patton instructed the driver to tell Dad that he wanted to see him at 0900 the next day in his office. Dad, always a rule follower yet fearing the wrath of the general, enjoyed ending that story by saying that that was one appointment he decided not to keep. However, he was faced with another problem. In the shop he purchased a large painting and worried over what to do with it. He solved the problem one day on the battlefield, asking a soldier for an empty cartridge shell in which he secured the rolled-up painting for the duration of the war. He also skipped out on another appointment, this time in Normandy, where he was arrested after leading his forty-eight trucks, each pulling a loaded two-wheel trailer, the wrong way on a one-way road just as the Army was moving out in the other direction. He thought it in his best interest to ignore the order to report to Third Army Headquarters, and he thereby remained free to drive his convoy of trucks and five jeeps through many major battles yet to come.

A story he told often about these trucks took place one Christmas Eve. I like to remember it being Christmas Eve 1944, during the Battle of the Bulge. My brother remembers it more accurately as Christmas Eve in New Jersey while monitoring the coastline for enemy submarines, ready to go to battle should there be an invasion. Either way Dad felt sorry for his young troops, some of them still teenagers away from home for the first time. Because he didn't think they would see much action that particular night, he let his men go into the nearby town to celebrate the holiday. No one returned to camp on time, and many were drunk. As he and two others stayed behind, he was not worried until he received the unexpected order to move out. Fearing the worst and not knowing where his men were, he did the only thing he could think of. To his advantage it was bitter cold that night, with snow on the ground and a hard frost. As the three men started up all the trucks, steam began to fill the air, camouflaging the fact that there were no drivers in the trucks. They moved the first three trucks ahead a few yards, ran back to move the next three, and so on throughout the night. When his commanding officer (in my memory of the story it was General Patton) drove by to ensure that Dad's unit was moving out, the officer could not see in the dark and through the steam that there were no men in those forty-eight trucks. To him everything looked in order, and Dad was told to carry on. Fortunately for Dad, his trucks were not needed for a battle that night.

On another occasion, he was traveling on a scenic road with his trucks when they encountered General Patton driving in the opposite direction. Maybe the 4051st read the map incorrectly, or maybe they were just lost, but an officer yelled to Dad and his troops that they were in Patton's way and proceeded to drive past Dad's trucks, running them off the road into the ditches, where they once again got stuck in the mud. His trucks often got stuck in the mud. He also lost trucks while driving on ice during the Battle of the Bulge. They slid off cliffs because they had to travel with their lights off in the dark and could not see the edge of the road. With his head bowed sorrowfully, he told us that in the midst of a battle he could only continue on, leaving them behind and hoping they made it out.

Although many of Dad's stories were humorous, we cannot forget that he and his men faced death daily. They transported thousands of men and supplies to and from the front lines of battle. They were all alive when they went to the line, but when they were carted back, many were dead. He hated having to carry his men into battle. Each time he got the order to move out, he worried about them, not knowing what to say as he looked at them sitting on their helmets, playing cards, talking or napping while waiting for their next command. A chaplain often held services for them before battle. While the trucks readied to be loaded, Dad wondered what the chaplain could possibly say to offer comfort before a battle. He knew those same trucks that were about to carry his men into battle would be returning with body parts of the dead from the front lines. After the Bulge, his trucks carried dead bodies to be buried in the cemetery in Hamm, Luxembourg. They also carried out POWs after liberating camps. Our family still has a portrait of Dad drawn by a colonel in the Luftwaffe who was taken prisoner by the Allies. It used to hang outside my bedroom door as a child and often gave me nightmares if I stared at it in the dim light as I was falling asleep.

Along with staying alive and defeating the Germans, food, warmth, dry clothes, water to drink, enough ammunition, and fuel for the trucks were among the many things the soldiers worried about on a daily basis. Dad stashed water and blankets for survival in different trucks, in case he lost his jeep. He melted snow in his helmet to wash. Like every soldier, he followed his orders but took precautions to better his chances of survival. He did survive and, in August 1945, he learned that he was recommended to be an instructor, of what is not mentioned in a letter in which he states that he does not wish to be considered for the job. His reply underscored his loyalty to and respect for his troops when he wrote: "Having been with my present organization throughout the war, I should like to remain with it, for there is still work to be done here."

As horrific as the war was, it also introduced Dad to what would become his lifelong passion, Luxembourg. He was involved in the two liberations of the Grand Duchy and spent some months there, where he and his fellow officers lived with local families between battles during the Bulge. In a café in the home of one such family, he met many Luxembourgers whom he questioned about the history, culture, and literature of Luxembourg. He was told countless times that Luxembourg did not have its own literature, because there was no consistent grammar or spelling in the native language. But Dad did not give up. He wanted to know everything about this country and its people. He was fascinated by everything he saw and everyone he met. Dad stayed in touch with his hosts and years later returned to Luxembourg to visit them and this country that he came to love. Some of his friends also visited us in Texas. There was a close bond between our families. I met more of them when I was eighteen and visiting Luxembourg for the first time. They invited my family into their homes with joy over seeing Dad again so many years later, and with gratitude for what the Americans did to rescue and free them during the war. They laughed at the memory of Dad's routine coming home after particularly difficult days, witnessing the horrors of the war, walking through the front door so fatigued that he immediately would drop his "steel helmet and liner, carbine, .45 caliber pistol, submachine gun, web belt carrying cantine [sic], two hand grenades, bayonet, bullet magazines, map case, compass, coats, galoshes, boots" and seek the refuge of hot water and a warm clean bed. On New Year's Eve that year, we all went together to a country inn for dinner. Once seated at the table, his host parents told more stories and, remembering how Dad would sing in the shower, asked if he would please entertain everyone at the inn with a song. He announced that because it was my birthday, he would sing "Happy Birthday" to me. When he finished, every male in the inn came to our table to shake his hand and give me a birthday kiss. We were both embarrassed.

Eventually, Dad discovered that there was no complete written history of the Grand Duchy of Luxembourg in English, so he set about to make one a reality. Upon his retirement at the age of seventy, he spent the next several years researching the tiny duchy, collecting data, books, and anything written about Luxembourg, as well as interviewing countless native citizens, until he produced the first complete and most thorough history of his adopted country in English, which is also considered the best one-volume history of this nation in any language. His work was praised by the government and, fifty years after the Battle of the Bulge, upon the release of the second edition in 1995, the consul general of the Grand Duchy of Luxembourg came to TCU to confer on him the rank of Commander in the Order of Merit. There were also receptions in Luxembourg upon the publication of this history, with many interviews with Dad appearing in their local press. His collection of books, pamphlets, art, recordings, and all things cultural from Luxembourg is one of the largest in the United States and today is housed in the Special Collections of the Mary Couts Burnett Library at TCU. With the aid of his friend Aggie Pate and Pate's widow and brother, they were able to create this gift for TCU, known as the Pate-Newcomer Collection. Dad helped this nation preserve and protect its history for future scholars.

In 2011, a year before he died, the TCU Veterans Task Force invited Dad to the Veterans Day Luncheon on campus. I was asked to persuade him to attend. Never being one to dwell on those horrific years of service, yet silently so proud of his role, I did not expect him to accept the invitation. He never wanted to draw attention to himself. He was of the generation that, when asked to defend their country, rose to the occasion and, when they were finished, did not let it define their lives after the war. But, to my surprise, he did accept the invitation. On the day of the event, he arrived at the TCU Brown Lupton University Union in a van from his retirement home, wearing his best suit with an American flag pin in his lapel. He was rolled in in his wheelchair and seated at one of the front tables, where my three children and I joined him. Now feeble, unable to walk unassisted, and mostly mobile only with a wheelchair yet fiercely loyal to his country, he was determined to stand and salute his flag when the color guard entered the ballroom. A physical strength none of us believed he still had took over, as an inner pride and devotion flooded his consciousness. When the soloist began to sing the national anthem, Dad's voice joined in. The solo became a duet of sorts.

Soon introductions were made about special guests in attendance. The speaker noted that there were two World War II veterans in attendance that day and asked that they raise their hands to be recognized. As Dad was hard of hearing, I leaned in and told him to hold up his hand. He did, asking me why he was raising his hand, noting that no one else at his table was doing so. I explained that it was to recognize him for his service during World War II. He immediately tried to put it down. As I tried to force his arm back up pushing under his elbow, he kept resisting, trying to lower it. When I asked him why he wouldn't raise his hand so people could see who the World War II veteran was, he simply yet firmly replied, "I didn't do it alone!"

No, Dad, you did not do it alone, but you played an important role. You gave yourself over to your country, you served when needed and called upon to do the unthinkable. You were one of the lucky ones to come back home, marry, and continue your life as a teacher and scholar. You were a member of the greatest generation ever and, yes, you were a soldier and a veteran.

The Journey's Lessons

"It was rather spooky and uncomfortable."

Harold J. Leeman Jr.

I entered the United States Military Academy at West Point in 1972 at age seventeen, when the draft was still at full force. My draft number was either two or three, and it was obvious that I was going to be drafted. However, I did not go to the draft board, because I entered USMA before I turned eighteen years old. I arrived at the Academy on July 2, 1972, and I graduated June 2, 1976.

My first assignment upon graduation as an engineer officer was in Karlsruhe, West Germany, a very cool city which sits on the French-German border. The Russian hordes were just about a two-hour drive from where I was stationed. There were a lot of things going on in the world during that time. By 1976 we were no longer in Vietnam, though we still had many soldiers at my station who had served in Nam. You might imagine what it was like for me, as a young twenty-one-year-old second lieutenant, commanding these men who had been in war, some who struggled with drug issues. I had been introduced to a lot of traumatized young men during that time, but it was a very quick learning experience for me.

I was stationed in Germany for three years. We were worried about the Russians attacking. Some of our jobs were to put in minefields and prepare roads to be blown up, to keep their tanks from coming across. Though we were not permitted to get within 1,500 feet of the border, now and then we would go right up to the border. Across the border on their side were open fields with barbed wire and guard towers, and we could see the guards looking down at us the entire time as we walked the border. Even though we had a purpose for being there, it was rather spooky and uncomfortable.

Once I got past the first year or two in Germany, several of our Vietnam soldiers left, and those who remained were those who wanted to be there. We worked well together with great purpose and focus, therefore it was very easy keeping soldiers motivated to do the tasks at hand.

That time in the Army, and certainly in our nation, was a period of unrest, and we were tired of war and things relating to that war. Maintenance of our vehicles was very difficult because we didn't have the proper equipment, for example, but we worked through those things, and all in all it was a good tour.

The barracks in which my soldiers lived had been SS barracks during World War II. Walking down the corridors, one could almost feel the lockstep of those Gestapo soldiers. Our post was in Ettlingen, Germany. Ettlingen was a little town outside of our base. One year the creek overflowed and we sandbagged it and saved the city from a lot of damage. German/US relations were rather good. When we traveled closer to the western side, the Germans would tell us that they had fought on the Russian front. They said: "We didn't fight the Americans, you know, we fought the Russians."

"Doc's down, Doc's down."

Michael Washington Sr.

Fast forward to November of 2010, after I completed my MOS training, I was assigned to the First Cavalry Unit at Fort Hood, Texas. Then I was told that our unit was being deployed in ninety days to Iraq. One year later to the exact date I joined the Army, my boots were setting foot on foreign soil. Our unit was taking over a local airport to ensure flights in and out of Iraq. Three months later, we got information that another unit in Baghdad got attacked by an IED. So, the units were advised to change our current Humvee vehicles to MRAPs (mine-resistant ambush protected vehicles). By the end of June our whole unit was upgraded to the new MRAPs. Once we changed to those vehicles, things started getting worse. There were only two platoons on our small FOB [forward

Army veteran Michael Washington Sr.
Courtesy of Michael Washington Sr.

operating base], Alpha platoon (Infantry) and Charlie platoon (Tankers).
July 12, 2011, was the start of our battles with Iraqi forces. Alpha platoon
got attacked with grenades and small gun fire on a routine mission. The
officers wanted to do something different than just going through town
on our normal routes. That same night, we changed our routes going and
returning to our FOB.

On the fifteenth of July, my world would be turned upside down. Earlier that week, our general and the Iraqi general came to an agreement about not going through the city for our missions. "We are going to let the local police govern the city" was the information we got back from our commander. Charlie platoon was on our last mission to traverse through the city. On that morning, we went through the city to finish setting up the forensics and medical labs. This time at the lab, it took longer than expected. Our mission was to last around five to six hours, but we stayed until late evening. As we were getting ready to leave, the platoon sergeant briefed me that medics had a bounty on them, because if you hurt the medic you hurt the unit. I didn't think anything of it because everyone that I was around loved me. So I overlooked what he was telling me and thought nothing of it.

As we were leaving the labs, there is always one person from each truck to place down the signal blocker to stop cell phone usage as we traverse the city. In my truck I opted to let it down. It was a normal thing for me. I did it every time we went to the city. My sergeant wanted somebody else to do it, but I stated, "I got it, it's the last time I'll do it." I got out of the truck, walked around to the front, placed the signal blocker, hopped back in the truck, and closed the back-door hatch. I sat down in the middle seat on the passenger side to catch my breath. I put on my headset to listen to everyone on the radio, already making jokes about the Combat Action Camera guy—about how he never shot a real photo in action before—but we were about to be wrong that day. I got on the radio and said, "I'm good, we're ready to go." We were the fourth truck leaving the compound. There was a roundabout to get through so we could leave the city and return to base. The platoon sergeant wanted to take an alternate route instead of our typical way. As we started moving on this route, I heard my gunner saying, "Somebody is videotaping us." My sergeant responded, "Don't worry about it, just keep your eyes on him. They're always videotaping us."

The gunner replied, "I actually see two people . . . " I was curious to see what was going on. The question in my head was, "Why are you videotaping us?" As we were turning, I raised the blinds to see what the gunner was seeing. At the same time as I was looking out the window, I saw a guy in all black running towards the truck with something in his hand. I tried to warn everyone on the truck. I said, "Sergeant, somebody is . . . " BOOM! We . . . got . . . hit. He had thrown a Russian RKG anti-tank grenade at my window. I'm on the ground, I'm knocked out. As I come back to consciousness, I hear on the headset, "Doc's down, Doc's down, Doc's down." The gunner gets out of his hatch and runs towards me as I'm lying on the ground. Grabs me, sits me up, and posts me on the seat to start checking me. I responded, "I'm good, I'm good." But it felt like it was in slow motion.

I look up at my seat, I see a hole at the top of the truck. The RKG had pierced the top of the truck and blown the hatch above me. It scraped my helmet and went to the seat next to me. Once I found out that I was okay, I checked on the gunner, because half of his shield on the turret was blown off. As I was checking on everyone in the truck, the other trucks turned around to provide cover, as we were getting smoked out by the fire blast in our truck. We had four or five miles to go, and this was just the first two hundred meters. Now we must navigate back to our base from the city, but we were taking small gun fire from everywhere. We weren't allowed to shoot back in the city, because of the innocent people around and the damage it would cause. It took us just under three hours to get back, which is usually a thirty- to forty-five-minute drive, and we were already down a truck. That week was the worst week I ever felt in the military, but that week was just the beginning of the countless times we were attacked.

On July 17 our unit were Quick Reaction Force (QRF), and we hear on the radio that our reserve unit that was helping us with missions gets contact in the red zone. As we are getting ready and leaving the base, I wanted to know the situation so I could be prepared to assist the medic who was already there. I tried to speak with her, but all I could hear was yelling. As we arrived, I wanted to bring our truck back to back with the other truck so I wouldn't be in danger going from truck to truck getting supplies. I get in and look at this guy, and half of his head is gone. This disturbed me mentally. My promise to my unit was: "None of y'all are gonna die on my watch." He was still breathing. So I attended to his wounds and requested help to put him on a gurney and do everything I could for him. We already got word that the medevac was on their way and was going to fly him back to base. As I hear the helicopters, I spoke to him and said: "Stay with me . . . they're coming." We placed him on a stretcher and took him to the landing zone (LZ). I briefed the flight medic on the injuries and treatment. He took over and loaded him on the helicopter. As we were heading back to base, our unit received confirmation that he didn't make it. There was a great sadness around base. I don't think I was ever the same after that. I feared for my life from that day on. I had the fear that I was not coming back to my family. We got attacked several times after that over the next two months.

"All he had to do was shoot some Scuds over."

Chad Lackovic

We went to Fort Hood in January of '03 for two months of intensive training, and then we went to Kuwait and Iraq. We landed in Kuwait on March 4. There were thousands and thousands of troops there, just waiting to go. It was pretty crazy. We spent most of the time getting in and out of our MOPP gear, which is our chemical gear. We spent a couple of weeks eating and sleeping in our chemical gear, because Saddam knew we were there. All he had to do was shoot some Scuds over, but it never happened. March 19 we didn't know what was going on, but that night a platoon of us slept on cots at the fence line between Iraq and Kuwait. It was cool. We were watching stuff go over our heads, and it was crazy. That next morning was March 20, the official start of the land campaign.

"They couldn't make me quit."

Bob Doran

I was at Fort Hood for sixteen weeks of basic and advanced infantry training, and then was transferred to Fort Bragg, North Carolina. While there I went through jump school and became a parachutist and a member of the famous 82nd Airborne Division. In those days, in the 1950s, there was no such thing as "political correctness." The Army jump school instructors, mostly master sergeants, basically could do anything they wanted to do to their students. In particular, they could be tremendously mean to those of us in their charge. They used profanity, called one's mother terrible names, made you run laps, and did whatever they could to make you quit. For example, one day it was raining heavily and I was told to get down in the mud and do thirty pushups. When I got to twenty-nine, the sergeant put his foot on my helmet and pushed my face in the mud to make sure I couldn't do the last pushup. Again, he was trying to harass me to see if I would quit the program. I was just a kid, but I had already made up my mind that they couldn't make me quit, no matter what they did. Later on, when the Army was looking for people to recruit for the new Special Forces program at Fort Bragg, they appreciated this "don't quit" and "can do" attitude, and they also wanted candidates to have some college. I'd had that year at Cornell College in Iowa, so I was eligible, and I took advantage of the opportunity when it came.

Anyway, after completing jump school at Fort Bragg I was sent to Fort Sherman in Colón, Panama, for jungle survival training at the US Army Jungle Survival School. This unquestionably is one of the most difficult schools in the military, and it is often referred to in the literature as the Green Hell. The training is immensely difficult, and the jungle terrain is extremely hostile. Most foliage has needles and spikes, aggressive insects are everywhere, and the daily heat and heavy rain are almost unbearable! In other words, the jungle seems to attack you in every way possible.

At the end of the training, I took a comprehensive final exam and did extremely well on it. I received a coveted Jungle Expert Patch for my uniform upon graduating. At this point I fully expected to leave Panama and go back to the States, but instead I received orders to remain at Fort Sherman as a Special Forces Instructor at the school. Of course, instructors are expected (in fact required) to take part in the exact same training as students, so this was not particularly good news. It might have been wise not to have done so well on the comprehensive final exam!

"I didn't want a war."

Jim Hille

I never went to war. I fought the Cold War. It was what we were in training to do. Our enemy was the Russians. It wasn't Iraq or Afghanis or ISIS or whatever. Although we did a lot of training for what might occur there. We were in the desert, and we were training for the desert. Russians weren't in the desert. So what were we doing there? It was because of what people saw might happen. And it ultimately did. We were well trained for that. But I got out in '89, before the first Gulf War.

I went into the Ready Reserves, which means I could've been called back up to serve. I was in for six years. If you go into the Ready Reserve, you're not training, you're not Active Reserve. You're just ready to be called up. So I was willing to do that and came within a whisker of getting called up for the first Gulf War. I went to work in manufacturing, which is something that a lot of military guys do. Operations for a company—it's kind of military-esque. You're moving equipment around, and in this case I was building missiles. I was a quality engineer for Texas Instruments. It was a similar culture to the military. A lot of the guys I served with did go into manufacturing. It's not to say I liked it. I didn't like it.

I got my business degree in finance here at TCU. You take stock of your career typically at five-year points. Is my career going like I would want it to go? At the time we'd had actually more officers than the military needed given the threat. The Berlin Wall came down, and the Cold War basically was ending. So the threat went way, way down. It didn't really, because the threat subsequently went way, way up. Just a different kind of threat. But at that time the threat level seemingly went down, so I didn't feel at all guilty about getting out. So I just used my options and went back to school.

Marine veteran Jim Hille.
Courtesy of Jim Hille.

It was one of those generals who said any military person who wants a war is an idiot, right? And I didn't want a war. I'm not embarrassed at all about my service, but my service that I had in no way compares to the guys that have served in this generation. Because they've had a series of these wars. My classmates that stayed in, they're now in charge basically, they're generals. And they've seen three wars, and I saw the Cold War. I don't have any shame about that at all, but is that a lowlight? I don't know. Except I didn't go to battle, test myself under those conditions. So there's that.

"You learn how to get along with people."

Ed Adcock

I was in the United States Navy from 1970 to 1977. I wound up as the lead reactor operator on a fleet ballistic missile submarine, the USS *John Adams*. We maintained the nuclear reactor, and it generates steam to run the propulsion system. A fleet ballistic missile submarine goes out on patrol for three months at a time. We went out on patrol from Guam for a couple patrols, and we went into the shipyard in Portsmouth, New Hampshire. My last patrol was out of Holy Loch, Scotland.

I joined the military because, during the draft, I "tried to major in theatre" (as a technician) at a college that didn't have a major in theatre. My roommate had talked me into joining the Navy Reserve, and when I flunked out I just went on to the regular Navy.

On watch, it's hours of boredom interrupted by moments of sheer panic. We had drills to make sure we knew what we were doing. Guam was good when we went on shore leave, had a great time there. It's not like anybody who was in combat. We basically bored holes in the ocean as we did our patrols. There was no real excitement in that sense. We just did our job.

We ate chow at normal times. We were on Greenwich Mean Time. The ship's work was ten-hour shifts, and the boat would quiet down at what was normally nighttime. During the day it was busy and noisy. It was kind of interesting, even though we couldn't see the sun or anything like that. We had our normal cycle. You played pranks on people, watched movies. I read a lot. Other people slept a lot. You just did your job.

I wasn't claustrophobic. You get into the cycle of the watch stations, and there's always something to do. Either you're qualifying for the next watch station, or you're helping other people get qualified. I had to qualify on the whole boat, because that's how I got my what's called dolphin. You get qualified as a submariner. So there was always something to do, always somebody who wanted you to do something else. We had a thing called field day, which was to clean up the ship once a week, scrubbing the decks down, wiping things down. You just get into a routine and keep on doing it.

You learn how to get along with people. It's too tight a space to get into an argument or anything like that. You get used to getting along with people and just doing your job. You learn not to discuss sex, religion, or politics, is basically what it boils down to.

"I was a motor transport operator instructor."

Richard Spence

I became a motor transport driver for the Marine Corps. It was the best decision I ever made. I was scared before going to MCRD, San Diego, not about the physical aspects of being a Marine, but about how to be a Marine. I was an athlete—I ran track and played football and basketball—so the physical part was fairly easy for me.

What was difficult was learning the marching, shooting weapons, and tactics. Those are the things that had me worried. But I succeeded and graduated boot camp from Platoon 3071. After graduation, I had two weeks' leave before going to my assigned school to learn how to be a motor transport operator (driver). While in school I learned how to operate jeeps, two-and-a-half-ton trucks, and five-ton trucks. It was one of

Marine veteran Richard Spence rappelling.
Courtesy of April Brown.

the best times I had, learning how to operate this machinery in support of my fellow Marines.

While in school, that's when reality hit about being a Marine. We were put on alert to deploy to Iran. We packed all our uniforms and equipment and waited for two weeks to hear if we were going to deploy or not. It was one of the longest two weeks I have ever spent, just going to classes and back to our rooms. We were restricted to the barracks only.

The Marine Corps has taken me to a lot of different places throughout the United States: West Coast, Midwest, East Coast, San Antonio,

Kansas City, Long Beach. It has also shown me different countries, such as South America, Korea, Thailand, and Japan. I've served in elite units such as Force Recon, Recon, 3rd Air Naval Liaison Gunfire Company, and MASS-6 in San Diego. The Marine Corps also has shown me a lot of different vehicles that I learned how to operate such as converting over to the seven tons and Logistics Vehicle System (LVS). I also was a motor transport operator instructor at Camp Johnson in North Carolina, teaching our future Marines how to operate these vehicles. (Camp Johnson, formerly Montford Point, is where the first black Marines went to boot camp when the United States Marine Corps was integrated.) I was able to switch over from a 3533 to a 3529, which is a mechanic. I could say I was one of the few Marines that were motor transport on both the operator side and the mechanic side.

"You got to practice leadership."

Joddy Murray

I went to the United States Air Force Academy as an undergraduate. It's considered active duty while you're there. It is a military institution. In a time of conflict, cadets can be called up for wartime mission, though this is rare. But otherwise, it is more like a combination of college and military. I graduated four years later and then went to pilot training for about half a year, at which point they were reducing the number of pilots in the Air Force. I got about halfway through before they decided that I would take a different career path. So I went on to intelligence training from there, and I was a military intelligence officer for five years, four of which were in Germany. I was discharged from there. So I was in the Air Force, in total, for just under ten years.

The Academy is very different than most other people's college experience, pretty much in almost every way, including how to get in. It is very selective. It is very difficult. You get nominated by a senator or representative from your state; you have to show a range of various skills, attitudes, and abilities, including physical tests. So you start early. I think I had my first meeting about getting into the Academy when I was in eighth grade, and then you work with a liaison for several years before you get selected. You need both an appointment and a nomination and then, if you get in, you start the summer after graduating high school.

You have a military job the whole time that you're doing academic work. In fact, you have an MPA, a military performance average, as well as a GPA. You march to every meal, and you wear a military uniform the whole time. You are either training or being trained, because, as you advance, as an upperclassman, you start taking over the duties of running the place. So you are in leadership, and one of the best things about it is that it's often called a "leadership laboratory." You practiced leadership while you were there. I was in charge of an element of twelve to fifteen other cadets at one point, and at another point, I was the XO (Executive Officer) for a squadron, the number three person in charge of about a hundred people in the squadron. So you have opportunities to not only learn about, but also exercise leadership while you're there. Then there's survival training and parachute training, and I soloed two different kinds of planes while I was there—a glider and a single-engine prop plane. So there's a whole bunch of training that's going on the whole four years that you're there. It's really exhausting to go through it all, but that was some of the best parts of the Academy: the variety of experiences that you would get.

Air Force veteran Joddy Murray.
Courtesy of Joddy Murray.

Most people who begin in the military will go to someplace like San Antonio or another base, and you go through boot camp for three to six weeks. We had that at the Academy, the six weeks of intense boot camp, during our first summer. But then the whole first year that you are a freshman (we called them "doolies"), that whole year you're hazed—that whole year. You're not free to roam, not free to talk. You can't even eat your meal the way you would eat your meal. Everything is very regulated. You have to memorize a bunch of military trivia. The first year is a kind of a weed-out process. It also proves that you really want to be here. When I use the word "haze," it's not really the way it's used nowadays, where you think of people dying. Certainly people died in the Academy, but it was more a regimen of induction, and that regimen of induction goes back since the Academy was founded. It was borrowed from West Point, which goes back to the 1800s and the Civil War. So there is a long, historical tradition to a lot of the things that we did every day. This was the worst part, when people end up leaving—when people end up discovering that they might want to go somewhere else and have a normal college experience.

The transition into the military was very difficult, of course. And nobody else I knew who went through that process would say anything else. It's difficult for everybody. But for some it might be a little bit more difficult. I was not a star by any means. I was just barely making it day by day most of the time. I was hanging on by my fingernails. And then what you realize—when you become an upperclassman and you have a lot more freedom—is it's just difficult in a different way the next year. After that, it's difficult in a *different* way the following year. And then you just want to graduate. You have to graduate in four years. There's no option. You must graduate in four years or they kick you out and you have to pay the government and go into the enlisted ranks. I graduated with something like 210 credits. You take a lot of course work. Most semesters for me were between eighteen and twenty-seven hours, so each year is challenging. It's academically challenging. It's militarily challenging.

"Sometimes guys don't like to listen to women."

Christa Banet

When I was at A School in Pensacola, so October-November 2002 time frame, our instructors told us, "Hey, just so you guys know, as soon as you hit the fleet, you're meeting up with your units in Iraq." That was kind of like, "Oh my God, what am I doing?" Because we weren't at war at the time. No shots had been fired yet when I went into the Marine Corps, so it was kind of like a sinking gut feeling. I had gotten to Yuma, and I was waiting to check in, we were on leave, my husband was there before me, and we were trying to find a place to live. I was staying at a base hotel, we didn't have a car, we didn't have anything. So it was a little difficult, and he wasn't able to take leave because his entire unit was deployed, and he was just waiting for someone to come back. But I was in a hotel room watching CNN, and I saw President Bush come on and officially declare war on Iraq. Then the TV screen flashed over to like night vision, and you could see tanks, and then you just saw a bunch of bombs going off and Baghdad being blown up. I was like, "Oh, crap." So I hurried up and threw on my camis and went and checked in, and I was shaking all day long, like, "Oh my God, we're at war, what's going on, what do I need to do?"

I'm here to help, for whatever needs to be done, and I walk into my work center and they're playing "Bombs over Baghdad," which is a Ludacris song. It was all guys, and they were singing and dancing "Bombs over Baghdad." And they were all excited, like, "Yeah, fuck yeah, we're going to war!" And I'm like, "What do I need to do?"

When I first started out, I had the guys that had a negative impression of women. I was the second girl that they had worked with ever, and the other girl that was there before me got pregnant. She never deployed, and she really didn't get to do much, because whenever you're pregnant you're not allowed to work because it could kill the baby. So you don't do anything besides paperwork. So they were like, "You're gonna learn how to do your job, and you're gonna work." And I was like, "Well, that's kind of why I'm here." The guys were really mean all the time, but at the time I understood it. I didn't really appreciate it, I think every day for the first year I was in the Marine Corps I called home crying, like, "Why are they so mean?" My dad usually laughed, and my mom was really emotional about it, so I usually didn't talk to her about it. But I would talk to my dad, and he would just be like, "You have brothers, you know what this is like, just suck it up."

I went back to work in what's called production control. Instead of working hands on, on aircraft equipment fixing stuff, that's more of like the planning. You have a list of things that need to be done for the day, and you prioritize the list. I would typically give it to the work center supervisor, but he was like, "Don't give it to me, give it to the sergeants." So I give it to the sergeants, and sergeants would either get it done or they wouldn't get it done. If they got it done, then they wouldn't have to hear from me. If they didn't get it done, then I got to complain to them all day long about, "Hey, why didn't this get done?" And eventually if they kept gaffing me off, I'd just report them up line. The guys handle things differently. They'll argue and fight each other to get stuff done, but I found that to not be very useful, but they don't listen anyway. Sometimes they get it done, but sometimes guys don't like to listen to women, especially in the Marine Corps, so it was kind of tough.

Being put into a leadership position, I would really have to assess the situation and be like, "Okay, are they going to listen to me and do what I tell them to do? Or am I just wasting my breath? Do I need to take this up the chain of command?" I would have to assess personalities and test the waters to see like, "Okay, are they going to listen to me, or are they going to be like, 'Screw you, you're a female, I'm not going to listen to you'?" It could go either way, so if it came down to it I would just report it up line and eventually one of my bosses would come down and lay the hammer down, like, "Hey, this is going to get done." And that would make them mad because they were like, "Ugh, I hate working with females." You get called every name in the book, but it is what it is. You just got to do what you got to do to get the job done. Just do your job, guys.

But the last unit I was at with the infantry guys, that was my favorite. We were really a close, tight-knit group. You see all this stuff about women in combat and all these comments from male Marines, like, "We don't want females in combat," but the best I was ever treated in the Marine Corps is whenever I was in an infantry unit. The most professional men I have ever worked with. If I had a daughter that was going to join the Marine Corps, I would rather her go to an infantry unit than go through all the crap that I went through at the airway. All of the shit that I had to put up with for so long, I would not want her to go through that. Yeah, she would get a lot of shit for going into the infantry and have to hold her guff, but they're going to respect her and treat her with respect, and treat her like a lady, essentially. They let you do your thing, but still they're very protective.

"We went out on the last Pan Am plane."

Shirley Beck

We got called up at the end of October 1990. I had to go and stay in Oklahoma City, and we did some training and planning, and we went to Otis Air Force Base when we flew out. We went out on the last Pan Am plane. Remember, they filed bankruptcy. And we were on the last plane that flew for that company. But those people were so good to us, they gave us all this fruit they had for when we got off, all this good stuff that we took with us when we got off the airplane. But I'll tell you, that was a sight to behold. That runway we came in on, this long runway, and here's four hundred people standing there. And we all watched that plane go to the end and turn around and fly back to the States, and there we were.

The advance party was supposed to go ahead to plan and get the land identified where you're going to set up, and measurements, and where you're going to put a bunker and all this good stuff. We were at King Khalid Military City, but we were out away from the main post, and they had airplanes that they hid underground. This was Iraqi stuff now. They just drove all over the area looking at the scenery and going to the Gulf coast, instead of getting everything planned for us. I mean, they thought they were on a damn holiday. The chief nurse from Army central command came to see me once every two weeks. She'd come in and she'd say, "Well, tell me the latest." I could sit down and kinda vent to her, which helped me, because that meant I could really control my feelings, and I never talked to anybody in the unit. She was really a good person.

We were fifty kilometers from where all the bad stuff was going on. And we were set up right next to an Air Force group called Med Base America. They were the ones that, when we evac someone out, we take a stabilized patient to them and then they put them on the airplane and send them back to Germany.

"The people are awesome."

Steve Weis

Right out of high school I was appointed to the Naval Academy and went there for four years, graduated, and went to the fleet for five years, and that pretty much was my Navy career. I did all that during peacetime, and then I got out. I never got shot at. I tried to avoid that.

To compare a Naval Academy grad to an ROTC grad to a grad that came through Officer Candidate School is difficult, because each one brings something else to the table. Graduating from the Naval Academy, I knew a lot about the Navy before I ever was part of it. Whereas a guy from OCS, if they came through OCS or NROTC, had been a normal person. So they would say we were "better prepared." But at the same time, we'd had—and this is gonna sound silly, but bear with me—we had our laundry done, somebody else cooked, all we had to do was show up. So from that point of view we really didn't take care of ourselves;

Navy veteran Steve Weis.
Courtesy of Steve Weis.

someone else was looking out for us. There's been a case made that the
NROTC students are better, because they're managing their own lives
and going to school and doing the Navy. So which is better? I don't know.

Historically, the Naval Academy grads stick around longer, so they tend to rise to the admiral levels. Does that mean that they're better prepared? Maybe not. I taught Navy ROTC at Georgia Tech for two years, and those guys were really good.

I considered submarines, but I just didn't want to spend part of my life under the water. I spent a month, and that was really enough. You just get used to it. It's a different reality. The hard part is coming back, when you go, "Wow, that's the sun!" And that's when I went back and thought, "I'm not doing that again." But the people are awesome. If I had to say anything at all, it'd be that the guys that I worked with, for the most part, were really awesome. When I was in, the guys that worked for me, or with me—I prefer to say with me—some of them, if you were an E-4 or E-5 and you had two children and a wife, you actually made so little money that you qualified for food stamps. I was furious about that. So that was a downside. But to think that those people are giving up the comforts of home and having a decent job to serve the country, how could you not like those guys? To me, that was the best part by far.

It's true you get benefits if you stay in for twenty years, and it's true they provide health care and dental care and things like that, but that's the same as any other job. And usually they're just great people. Every once in a while you get people, and I had a couple, that joined the service rather than going to jail. It's like the judge says: "You can either enlist or you can enlist." I had a couple of those guys. And one of them was fantastic, and the other one we got rid of. But for the most part it's really patriotic people who just want to do something, and they were great.

Ronald Reagan is one of my favorite presidents, because I got a 20 percent raise just like that. I went, I think, from just under $10,000 to almost $12,000 a year. I mean, you wouldn't even think about working for that. And the guys aren't making a whole lot more than that now. You've got to factor in inflation, but we were making nothing.

I think most of the guys that come out of the military come out politically conservative. But seeing part of the world that you never would have seen changes you. I'll never forget some of the things that I saw. I was on a ship named after a French admiral—the only ship in the fleet named after a French person. He saved George Washington in the Battle of Yorktown. So when we went to France, we were treated like royalty. It was great. But we saw parts of North Africa that you just can't imagine the poverty and the smells. It was horrid.

"Doing your hair becomes a daunting task."

Alexandria Smith

I was a plans and operations officer, attached to a human resource company. Our job was in charge of the twenty-two post offices, making sure that all the soldiers across those three regions, thousands of soldiers and civilians and DOD workers and anyone that was a US citizen, that their mail came through the postal system. We did monthly site inspections and gave briefings to the higher headquarters, making sure they were aware of all the ins and outs of everything when it came to the mail system, also whether there was a delay with the mail. There were a couple instances where we had to destroy mail due to security issues, and of course we were over there during election season, so some of the most important pieces of mail were people's absentee ballots, mak-

Army veteran Alexandria Smith.
Courtesy of Alexandria Smith.

ing sure we didn't lose those. And, should anything happen to them, make sure that it was reported properly all the way up to the United States Postal Service.

The camaraderie that I had, particularly with my warrant officers that I came with, was nice because we had another female, and we had already been in the same unit together prior. Washing our hair and braiding each other's hair was something that for me was a nice thing of camaraderie, because as silly as it sounds, something like doing your hair overseas becomes a very daunting task sometimes. Being able to just have someone else there to help you through it. She had kids back home, so even though I don't have children, it was just nice that she was able to talk to me throughout things 'cause I'm much closer in age to her kids. It was just kinda like, "Oh well, you know as a teenager I was like that too," or "My sister was like that," or "My brother might have been like that." It was just nice to have those types of moments. Even now, even if we're not in the same unit, we still message each other every now and then and make sure everything's okay, and since our units are in the same area we'll see each other every now and then and catch up on everything and make sure and know that everyone's okay.

"I was the first female in the infantry unit."

Maria Brown-Spence

When I was growing up I admired military service members, and I identified the sacrifices my parents, April Brown and Richard Spence, made early on. I knew that I too wanted to follow their footsteps and join the military. And in 2010 I did, signing a contract with the Army National Guard. I would leave for boot camp at Fort Jackson, only a few weeks after signing. Almost not making it to training on time, because I got stuck in a weeklong snowstorm at the MEPS location in Amarillo. While attending boot camp or basic training, I had the opportunity to build lifelong friendships with those I trained with, many of whom I consider family, ten years later (and counting). Something I had been longing for since my youth.

Once I finished boot camp, I would venture on to Fort Lee for A.I.T., to continue my training as a 92F or Petroleum Supply Specialist. For the longest time I was embarrassed to say that I was a "fueler," but I grew to have a sense of pride as I began to meet other fuelers in the Army and in the civilian world. We were able to connect because of our shared experiences and even shared jokes, like, "Hey, better be nice to me or I won't pump your gas." Yes, corny, but funny to us.

After I completed training—I almost didn't graduate on time due to an injury—I would go back to Fort Worth and have the opportunity to work on active duty orders at an infantry unit there. This was right after they made the announcement to let women into combat arms, so I was able to be the first female to work in the infantry unit, where I worked alongside a supply sergeant.

"I didn't want people to identify me as the gay sailor."
Israel Sanchez

The legal aspect was that I would have a dishonorable discharge, or other than honorable discharge, if I was caught, and there were plenty of people that wanted to get rid of me, just because they were intimidated by me. I had to prove myself to be ten times of a harder worker.

When I first checked into my seagoing squadron in 2009, one of my admin officers ended up asking me straight up, "Are you gay?" This was still during Don't Ask, Don't Tell, and I told him if he valued his career he'd probably regret asking me that question. I was not the happiest person in the world, because of the fact that that was asked, but I reflect on that moment. It angered me, because I didn't want people to identify me as the gay sailor. I'm a sailor first. My identity of being a homosexual has nothing to do with my job. Who I love shouldn't have an impact on my career, and that's one of the things that I've struggled with my entire time, is trying to live that double life and show people that just because I'm gay doesn't mean I'm changed in any aspect. I'm still the same person. I'm still professional. I'm still going to provide compassion and quality care. And just because you're coming in for an STD doesn't mean I want to look at your junk. It's that I'm trying to take care of you. They refer to us as pecker checkers, so they think that's what we want to do, and it's like, gross. You're here for an STD screening, because you just walked out of a bar. That's why I think I identify first primarily as a sailor, as a corpsman, before my homosexuality.

Being a corpsman, for me, implies a higher standard, because it's one of those things that you earn your shield. You go through a process of earning the Marines' respect. They don't give it to you. You earn the respect. The moment that I met my Marines it was an instant bond, and since then it's an unbreakable bond, and at that point I knew that I could be myself, and not have to worry about it, because I knew my guys had my back, because they knew I was going to take care of them regardless. I wasn't going to look at them in any other way but as my Marine, my dude. That by far was the best experience.

"I believe I was put in the proper place."

Tim Cole

I ended up having thirty-one total years, some active duty, a bunch of quiet reserve years, and then after 9/11 a bunch of active duty at the back end. That logistics work used to occur inside a unit, and then it started occurring at larger Marine units, so that in 2003 I'm doing that [logistics work] for an entire Marine Expeditionary Force—that's 35,000 Marines—and eventually I did it at what's called the combatant command, or strategic level, for Marine Corps Central Command out of Florida.

I believe I was put in the proper place, because I was actually very good at logistics, for whatever reason. And, who knows, maybe there's a knack for it. So I don't have too many regrets, and even though I'm a logistician, I do have time in the combat zone. I've spent time in infantry units as a logistician, I got to hang around those guys. I just wasn't the point of the spear out there doing combat ops.

You want to show up in shape, so I took that very serious, and I used my time beforehand to get physically ready. What I had no way of understanding is the kind of emotional and mental impact that drill instructors have. They've been training Marines for two hundred years. They can take anybody, and I mean anybody, and they can exert influence on you. They had a way of getting you to comply. They talk about taking you down to the same basic level, so even though this boot camp platoon is made up of every social demographic, economic demographic, racial demographic, no matter what your background, no matter your age range, education range, everybody gets what I call "taken down to zero." It doesn't matter who you were before you came in, everybody is a boot camp private. And once they get you to that level, they help you develop to start working as a team. And those that don't buy into that program and become part of the team, their life is filled with frustration and pain. Eventually, if somebody really was not a team player, they might even be discharged. But for the most part everybody becomes part of the team, and you want to make a contribution. If you show up thinking you're the center of the world, this is a place that changes all of that.

"I wanted to learn Russian."

Stesha Colby

Every Marine has to go to combat training. The infantrymen do really long school, but ours was compact: "These are the weapon systems, this is how you clean it, how you take it apart, how you shoot it." Then three to five days of what I call extreme camping, firing a lot of weapons and sleeping in the woods in ten-degree weather in North Carolina in early January. Very cold. I got pneumonia, but that's okay because I finished and went on to Monterey, California, to start language training.

I wanted to learn Russian. You don't get sent there with a language. You get sent there with a spot for a language. You know you're going to get a language, you just don't know which one. I wanted Russian, but I got there a couple of weeks too late; a Russian class had already picked up. So I got put in an Arabic class. At that time, February 2007, we were really big in Iraq. That actually ended up derailing my career, because the schoolhouse for Arabic is a year and a half long. The other languages, like Spanish, are like six months long, but Arabic is basically a year and a half long. And at the end of my training, the Marines and the Army were discussing how they were going to handle their two fronts: were they going to continue both being there, or were they going to do one in one and one in the other? And they had a lot of Arabic linguists, so they made the DLPT—defense language proficiency test—extremely difficult, to weed people out, and it worked. I didn't pass the test. They gave me an extra three months' training. I did better, but I still didn't pass it, so I got reclassified into administration. That was just the luck of the draw.

I went to the Admin School in North Carolina. It's a monthlong school. I got there right as they were picking up class, so I had to wait for a month before I could get into class. So I was there for two months, graduated there, was a top honors grad, and I think, to this day, I still have the highest GPA, which isn't too much to brag about, not putting admin Marines down but, yeah, I still had the highest GPA. I missed one question on one test and I kicked myself, too, because I knew that answer. I could have graduated there with 100 percent.

We ended up getting sent to Fort Worth, and there was an opening in the legal shop, and they wanted to have the new Marines in there. They knew that they were getting two, and they kind of looked at one, our

ages, and two, our test scores, and picked me because I had really high
test scores and I had spent time at Monterey. Also my age; they assumed
I was more mature because in a legal shop you're dealing with highly
sensitive data, in addition to the fact that I had a security clearance. I
had no training. They're like, "Here's the gigantic manual for legal.
Learn it." I did. I was in there for about eighteen months, then I decided
to leave.

"I threaded the needle."

Bob Doran

Eventually I was transferred back to Fort Bragg in the States, and I left
active duty after my two years were over in 1958. On the other hand, I
still had four years to complete in the US Army Reserves before receiving an honorable discharge. Since Vietnam was heating up in the 1960s
and I was not yet discharged, there was always the very real possibility
that I could be recalled to active duty, especially given the special forces
and jungle training that I previously described. Indeed, it was precisely
the background that was needed in Vietnam. There is little doubt that I
would, in fact, have been jumping out of helicopters and serving in the
front lines if called back.

From 1958 to 1965 I studied mathematics and received two degrees
from the University of Iowa. Then from 1965 to 1968, I was in the PhD
program at the University of Washington. I received my PhD in 1968,
one year before the United States put the first man on the moon. Mathematics was considered a "vital and essential subject area" for science and
defense, so I threaded the needle and was never called back into active
service.

I might add here that, at the same time that I was getting a PhD, my
wife's brother, Bill, was in the Army (regular infantry) in Vietnam at the
DMZ, right on the edge where the worst part of the war took place. Much
of the time he was in a sandbag bunker, explosions happening everywhere. Five of his best buddies were killed. A mortar shell hit them and
"boom," their arms and legs are blown off. Bill was never the same after
that. If you tried to talk to him about it, he just wouldn't talk. I repeat, he
just wouldn't talk. All you got back was silence. It was tough.

"You don't know who you kill."

Jon Lippens

I was in the underground. I was in the Red Cross first, that was the dirtiest job I ever done. Our job was to dig up bodies and pieces of bodies and put them in bags and try to identify which corpse it came from, and it was a terrible job. You had to dig, and there were people under there. We had rubble all over the place. The Germans bombed every day before they came in, and then the Allies bombed at least two or three times a week. They bombed the railroads and the harbor, to aggravate the Germans.

There's a certain joy in seeing the mess you've made, especially a supply train when you destroyed the rails. The train derailed and just kept on going because there's no way to stop, like a roller coaster. We blew up one of those things, about fifty to seventy-five wagons pulled by two locomotives. You can imagine the noise it made. A locomotive would go this way and the other one would crash into another, and the next one into the next one, and then they rolled over and it was all over everywhere. Everything was burning. It was unbelievably good for me, but bad for them. That's what I did for a long time: exploding buildings, railroads, railroad signals, telephone poles. Not one, but ten in a row, so that they took a long time to fix. We enjoyed it. But then I went to the Allies as a combat soldier, and that's when we started whipping the Germans out of our country with the help of the Allies.

I was in the Battle of the Bulge. It was the biggest battle fought in Europe, and they lost hundreds of thousands of men. That's really the one that broke the German army's back. When you go to the Battle of the Bulge, you have bad hearing for the rest of your life. We fought day and night without ceasing for a month and one week. Never stopped. Day and night. No sleep. No bath. No nothing. You didn't have time to take your shoes or socks off. Besides, you were afraid you wouldn't be able to get them back on if you took them off, because of frostbite. The minute your feet were out of the shoes they would start swelling, and you would try to get the swollen foot back in, and you couldn't. It was a miserable time. I had trouble with a tooth that went bad. If you don't get fresh fruit and vegetables, you get scurvy. We had that problem. And our bodies were still developing and we didn't have food. So I started losing my teeth when I was thirty years old, because I didn't have the background nourishment that I was supposed to have.

You should have seen Germany after the Americans got through with them. They took their biggest planes and loaded them with as much ammunition as they could and went every day and every night carpet bombing. Every town was a pile of bricks and concrete. I was happy with that.

Probably in the duration of the war I lost three hundred good friends. It was rough. When you have friends that are gone forever by age sixteen. I'm not proud of what I've done, and I ran around a long time feeling guilty. But it was inevitable. When you fight, you don't know who you kill. You know that's the enemy, so you kill. The only time I was hit was in my clothes. I had my clothes ripped up from the bullets and a hand grenade fragment, and I had several big cuts in my head. I went in an infirmary, disinfected it, and got the pieces of metal out of it. No anesthetic, but they got them all out. But both my feet turned black, to the point that when I got out of the service they were talking about amputation. I said, "No way. We're not going to amputate anything." The leg got better, and I went to some skin specialist and they grafted some tissues.

"It was just luck that I was ten feet behind him."

William Howe Jr.

I entered the Army in August '07, and I left for Iraq in May '08. I was in Iraq proper for twelve months, and in Kuwait for one month, thirteen months altogether. I didn't deploy again after that, and I was retired from the military in April 2010 from injuries suffered in Iraq.

We spent a month in Kuwait, doing war scout patrols and testing out all the gear. I was in a very special unit: the 1st Cavalry. We were always at the front line, out in front of everybody else, exploring new territory, so we needed a lot more training. We needed to get acclimated to the heat, because sometimes we'd be out for weeks at a time. We did that in Kuwait for thirty days, then we went to FOB Scania, which was kind of a truck stop on the way from Kuwait to Baghdad. We spent two months there just doing regular patrols, because it wasn't a high-risk area, and they moved us out to FOB Hunter, which was a brand-new base in southern Iraq. We built that base from scratch. I have videos of just nothing around us. All we have is a truck at night, and we're sleeping beside it in the dirt. Just living, surviving. A bottle of water a day, an MRE a day, and that's pretty much our life for ninety days while we got it built up. Then we got to where we were getting supply runs once a month or so. It was an interesting time.

It was like an abandoned airfield. We built some houses inside the airfield, but a lot of them had bomb holes in them from bombs that we'd dropped. So you never knew whether the concrete was going to fall, but we were getting rocketed all the time. They were shooting rockets at us, and mortars, because we were now maybe fifty kilometers from the Iraq/Iran border, so we were trying to stop the bombs going to Baghdad. We busted munitions plants all the time and arrested people with automatic weapons. I think one raid captured over a hundred automatic weapons and two or three hundred IEDs and EFPs. This was stuff that was going to Baghdad, and we were trying to cut the supplier off from getting there.

We had FOB Hunter and FOB Alpha, and our sister squad was FOB Gary

Army veteran William Howe Jr.
Courtesy of William Howe Jr.

Owen, and then there was FOB Blackhawk. We were all kind of working together. The ones on the border never got shot at, but we were behind the border and we would get attacked a lot, because they were afraid that if they shot and missed the ones on the border, they would hit Iran. We could see Iranian guard towers from where their base was, so we could see where Iran could see. So insurgents didn't want to attack that base, because then Iran could attack them back. We walked a very fine line and had to be careful: Are we in Iraq, or are we in Iran? Our GPS didn't always work over there like it should, and our maps weren't always correct, and there's so much disputed land that some of the borders that we visited would go back and forth from Iraqi to Iranian control, so you never really knew where the border was. But being a scouting unit, that was all part of it. They would drop us off and we would do either small kill teams or observation posts, just watching for people that were trying to shoot rockets or trying to smuggle in rockets or materials.

We did a lot of helicopter drops, but they would pull off in the middle of the night and five of us would get out and just walk for fifteen or twenty kilometers, sometimes thirty kilometers, and camp overlooking a swamp or a lake where we thought people were smuggling. If we found a cache of rockets, we would set our sights on it and see who came for the rockets and either try to tag them and track them or eliminate them, depending on what our orders were. Usually on those missions you'd only have four or five guys going out. A lieutenant or high-ranking NCO would be the squad leader, and they really wouldn't have any other specialization than managing the squad. Then you'd always have a heavy gunner, and then you'd have a grenadier. You were supposed to have a designated marksman. A medic can't carry a sniper rifle according to the Geneva Convention, but a medic also can't carry grenades or machine guns. They gave me an M-16 and put an ACOG (advanced combat optical gunsight) on it. Basically it was a sniper rifle, but it wasn't officially a sniper rifle, and I was set up as a designated marksman, providing overwatch for the grenadier and the others, when I wasn't acting as a medic. But when we were in those situations we were trying to keep our presence concealed, so usually my medical skills were just for normal stuff like twisted knees or insect bites. We would also go on patrols with twenty of us going out and just driving, and that's when you have to worry about the IEDs, the EFPs, and stuff like that, or even small arms or sniper fire. Those missions were when I was more of a medic and less of a Cav scout.

One mission we were tasked with was when they knew that one of the top five guys in Iraq was in this house. They had two direct assault teams assault them from the north and south, and another assault team blocked off his escape to the east, and then they dropped five of us in a field. We had about ten Iraqi soldiers with us, and we split up to cover this huge field. The theory was that in case he rabbited out the back, we would be able to capture him. They cleared the house and he wasn't there, and we didn't see anybody running. It was farmland, and I stepped over this produce thing that was being grown, and I looked to my right and noticed footprints. I hadn't seen footprints anywhere else, so I looked to my right, and there was a little lean-to shack there. So, of course, I fall back into the bush and I'm yelling at him to get out, and I see a cell phone light come on, so I don't know whether he's going to trip something or what's going on. We fire a couple warning shots, and he ends up coming out and surrendering. And we come around the front, and he'd set up a machine gun covering the whole front, so it was just luck that I was ten feet behind him instead of ten feet in front of him. We captured him with his automatic weapon and were able to turn him over to the Iraqis.

When my XO (executive officer) got shot, we were on a mission and the mission was over. We had already raided some houses. We captured about twenty people, I guess. The mission was over and, as happened a lot, one of the Iraqis shot him several times in the legs. I was in the very front truck, and they called me. I was three or four hundred feet away, and I heard the shots, but I didn't really know what was going on, then all of a sudden they were calling for a medic. I'm running back and everybody's standing around in a circle and he's lying on his left side, blood pouring out. I get him flipped over on his back, and the blood almost stops. I pull out a tourniquet but then, when I see the blood stopping, I decide instead to go with QuikClot, a new invention that had just come out. I'm using the QuikClot and the pads instead of the powder, and I get the wound stopped, and then he starts going into shock. So then you have something else to deal with.

He had lost a lot of fluids. It was really cold, though. It was the middle of the night, about twenty or thirty degrees, so we couldn't warm up any fluids, because we didn't have the guardian angels to warm the fluids. We tried warming them on the engine block, but it didn't really work too well, so we just had to keep him as warm as possible until the choppers got there. But they eventually got there, and he ended up surviving, and he's doing well now. Both his legs were intact; and he lucked out with the way the bullets bounced around. One of them went straight through his right leg, but the other one hit him right beside his groin and bounced off his hip bone, then exited out the other side of his leg. He just lucked out. It just happened to miss everything major that it could have hit. They did have to give him three units of blood in the helicopter.

"People would pull out their lawn chairs."

David Grantham

I once read that Civil War soldiers faced boredom more frequently than they did war. As a result, soldiers often found themselves inventing all types of leisure activities during all the down time between battles. During my time in both Iraq and Afghanistan, warfare was much busier. But I also discovered, during my time down range, just how jarring it can be to shift back and forth between recreation and war.

In Afghanistan we had to be particularly creative. Bagram Air Base was a mess of smaller, separate bases that housed special government organizations, foreign armies, and random administrative groups. It was easy to get lost among the array of side streets and the bland-colored buildings. As a result, we largely stuck to activities in and around our specific piece of Bagram. The small volleyball court nearby was helpful, but not creative, and it required shoes. The quasi-sand underfoot felt more like minced gravel, and without shoes you would rather quickly shred the soles of your feet. You could always spot the new arrivals, because they were the ones playing barefoot. Perhaps because I was from Florida and volleyball was familiar, I lost interest. My need to find entertainment led me to an unfamiliar game: darts.

Uncle Sam had equipped our rickety little office space with a fully functioning, government-approved dartboard. There was always a sense of reprieve, a moment of letting your hair down, whenever you finally returned to base from a mission "outside the wire." After taking off all our gear, racking the guns, and loosening our boots, we needed something to do that required little thinking. In the intelligence world, operators are always analyzing, planning, and trying to decipher the enemies' intentions based on hard-earned and often incomplete information. Paperwork is never-ending, and sources constantly remind us that, unless we react quickly, the next threat is at our doorstep. Darts acted as a momentary escape from the constant game of outsmarting our adversaries.

It was also the only thing to do at night. Reading in bed meant keeping the light on, which might bother your neighbor, and the TV programs ran on the primitive Armed Forces Network (AFN). Unless you could obtain a satellite dish from some shady foreign national hawking it on base, you had to suffer with AFN's limited programming and self-promoting advertisements that rivaled the cheesiest infomercials. Darts was a simple, repetitive, mind-numbing task. I quickly became fond of our nightly ritual. During the lighthearted games we would talk, joke around, and learn from each other. Darts kept us busy for hours but, more importantly, I realize looking back that it also settled our nerves.

The hardest time to find entertainment was during the day. Intelligence is never-ending and, because of that, sometimes you have to walk away to clear your head. Other times you're waiting on information to come through. So we often found ourselves pulling away from work for thirty minutes or so for recreational activity. Lifting weights was useful, but not necessarily enjoyable. It was during one of these down times that I and another guy invented "Bagram Ball."

Americans donated toys for Afghan children through a government program that used the gifts to build friendlier relations with surrounding villages. The public affairs group that headed up the project called it "Adopt a Village." We affectionately called it "Adopt a Riot," because whenever a group of soldiers showed up at a village with toys, the kids would rush the vehicles. Sometimes smaller toys would get lost in the packing operation prior to leaving the base. On one such occasion, several medium-sized stuffed balls made of cotton found their way into our office. For a few days, we casually threw the balls around the room. Then, as if the baseball gods had put it there for me, one day while returning from lunch I found a PVC pipe, about the length of a baseball bat, sitting next to an abandoned trailer. I snatched it up, jogged back to the office, and suggested my buddy pitch to me out in our tiny parking lot.

Our small dirt lot faced a road, which ran between us and a two-story building across the street that looked like a motel. Since the balls were filled with foam, we didn't have to worry about breaking a window on a government car or injuring someone nearby. The setup was perfect. We began pitching to each other, and the game quickly evolved into a home run derby. Others joined in, and Bagram Ball became an afternoon ritual. Air Force reservists who were NYPD cops in their real lives, a commander who was a Boston native, a squirrelly fellow from Chicago, a Pakistani linguist—all tried their hand at Bagram Ball. It soon became a full-fledged competition. One guy could not hit to save his life; he would always foul off the ball into a disgusting dumpster off to the right of the makeshift home plate. Following the time-honored rules for deployment sports, we made him go in after it. After a couple of dives into the refuse, he stopped playing.

Bagram Ball also quickly became a spectator sport. People would pull out their lawn chairs or lean over the railing from the second story of the motel-dorm across the street, just to watch. They cheered home runs, which we considered to be anything that hit their building. The rooftops and people in lawn chairs reminded me of the apartments on Waveland Avenue that once overlooked Wrigley Field in Chicago. For a brief moment, we could escape the rigors of war and imagine that we were smashing home runs over the iconic ivy that drapes the walls of Wrigley.

"If the Marines need me, I need to go."

Tim Cole

Back in 1990, when my daughter got to grade school, I would go and give little presentations on Veterans Day, Memorial Day, whatever. And the schools watched 9/11, and they kept talking about how this was an active war. She began to get nervous for her dad. Now this daughter, Robin, is my TCU connection. Robin went to school here and graduated in 2013, and she's a nurse with the Army at Fort Lewis. She was in the fourth grade when this happened. Her teacher sent me an email saying, "Hey, Robin is concerned about you." So I sent an email back, saying, "Well, hey, it's unfortunate, but I'm safe, and things are going to be all right." Nine-eleven, that day, was very sobering. I didn't really have any immediate activation or mobilization until 2002, and they were doing kind of a buildup to get ready to go to Iraq, and some buddies in the Marine Corps said, "Hey, we're looking for some guys like you, Tim. We're looking for logisticians to help us." I gave it some long thought, and eventually had a talk with my family, and said, "Hey, I've been in the reserves for a bunch of years, I go in on drill weekends, I get paid to do that, I go to their training, I get paid to do that, and now the Marines are getting ready to go, and it's wrong for me, in my opinion, to stay here and act as if nothing is going on. If the Marines need me, I need to go." So, at that point, I've got a high school senior, a high school junior, I think Robin was in middle school, and I kind of get their buy-in. I get their blessing to go do that.

I initially think I'm just going to the West Coast. But eventually I get pushed—we call it "pushed"—forward into Kuwait, eventually went up into Iraq. The good news was I never actually saw combat. The closest that came was when Saddam Hussein began bombing Kuwait, and we had some explosions near our base, and we had to go into shelters. Probably the darkest time from that time forward would be in 2005 and 2006. I would go into the warzone and do assessments: How are our armored vehicles? How are they holding up? How is our medical support? Do we need more capability here? Everything was with the intent of getting our war fighters what they needed. Then I would come back to the United States and talk to the headquarters of the Marine Corps and others about us needing more capability here, or better armor.

While I was in theater in 2005, there was a number of times Marines were killed. What happens is, that body is processed and sent to Europe, and then sent to the United States for burial. But for the unit to have closure, they'll have a memorial service for that Marine, even if the Marine isn't there. Those memorial services are very moving, and the most moving was for a female Marine who was part of an engineering unit. She had been killed by a sniper. I had been to a number of memorials for fallen Marines, but this particular memorial was very moving to the unit. And even though I did not know her personally, it was moving, it was heartfelt. It was a dark, low time. Because it was evident that those Marines had great respect for her, and had a great love for her, and were greatly moved by her loss.

Another lesson I learned was that even though I had done a lot of that work and was honored, respected for it, and had been accepted to stay in the Marine Corps, I eventually got out. And I remember thinking at the time that there was going to be a huge impact by me leaving, that me leaving was going to really significantly impact the unit. And I learned that, well, not really. Even though you might think you're doing a really good thing, and you may be, these units that are focused on teamwork and getting it together, they're going to find a way to fill the gaps. And never get too big a head. Really you're just making your contribution at this time, and when you go away, hopefully they'll be better served for it.

"He was a tough kid."

David and Teresa Schmidt

David Schmidt: He was originally assigned infantry. He was walking down a stairwell one time and saw a sign about sniper school. And he said, "That sounds pretty cool." So he applied to sniper school and got in and became a sniper.

Teresa Schmidt: To apply for it was one thing, but to be accepted was something else. It was a tough thing to get into, but it really interested him. He had pretty good math skills and stuff, and it really inspired him to want to be a scout sniper.

David Schmidt: He said that graduating from sniper school made graduating from the Marines boot camp seem like a walk in the park. We came to know a lot of his sniper buddies. Particularly after he was killed, they became dear friends of the family.

Teresa Schmidt: In his eyes, snipers were the top of the military. He aspired to be one, and it was a lot of studying and testing. And he did very well, and he really liked it. He was a tough kid, a hardworking kid. The discipline was not a difficult transition at all. He really enjoyed doing what he was doing. Graduated high in his infantry school class. Was promoted twice in boot camp, so he did very well.

David Schmidt: In his deployments there were times when he was very, very frustrated. He was a very bright guy, and he was frustrated with the inefficiencies of the military. His first deployment was on a Navy ship that sailed into Yemen. It was five months of just spectacular boredom, interrupted occasionally by Thailand, Yemen, Kuala Lumpur, the Maldives. He wanted action, but they were on this ship doing janitor work. It was not what he had in mind for being deployed. He was excited about being deployed. They were on this naval ship, and nothing happened, so he was disappointed because there was nothing to do.

His second deployment was to Afghanistan. He was there for five months, and I think within three months after he got back he got contacted and was asked if he wanted to deploy again. He had just been there for five months. His second deployment, he was in war. He was in battle. But what was very frustrating to him were the rules of engagement. They had their hands tied behind their backs. He told me a Taliban guy was on a rooftop with a cell phone, and he knew that guy was telling the bad guys where our guys were, and he couldn't engage them. And the next thing you know that guy would disappear and our guys would start taking fire. So war is not fun, but you have to go to war to win. You have to shoot the bad guys. When you go to battle or when you go to war, you have to kill the bad guys, and he couldn't do it.

Teresa Schmidt: They were in villages where the whole town was evacuated. It wasn't like there were women and little kids running around. These were villages that had been taken over. And it was apparent who the enemies were, and they had to wait for the chain of command and all this protocol to take place, but on this second deployment, when he got back, I got the impression that he was not eager to go back. And David will tell you why he went back on his third deployment. Before he came back from his first deployment on the naval ship, he was very disappointed and frustrated that he did not get to be a part of any action. He made phone calls and wrote letters to his leaders, saying, "I want to go back." He was very interested in going to Afghanistan so he continued to reach out. He even wanted his dad to make phone calls. Any way he could get back into it. And sure enough, it worked out. He got word he was going. But after that second deployment experience, I felt confident that he did not want to go back again. He had, how many months left? Only six months remained of his four-year service commitment, and he was not planning on being deployed again.

David Schmidt: Shortly after he returned from Afghanistan the first time, an entire battalion was going to be sent to Afghanistan, like 1,500 guys. And because Benjamin had just returned, he did not have to go. The sniper platoon that they were sending had no guys that had ever been in combat. So he decided he would go, because he didn't want to send his guys that had never been in combat before. On the day that he was killed he was the point guy, but he was not the leader of the platoon.

We were very proud of him. That's one of the things I wish I had done. My father was in the military, and I was the one that wasn't in the military. My son was in the military. I was very proud of him.

Teresa Schmidt: Once he got in, we saw the change in him, his fire, and he was very focused on it. I became extremely excited for him and proud of him.

David Schmidt: When he would come home, you could see the change. Before he went to Afghanistan the last time, and he made his wishes known about what he wanted to do for TCU, it helped me understand how mature he was. There's not many twenty-four-year-old guys that have the foresight to say, "If something happens to me, I want to leave two hundred thousand dollars to my university."

You had to have a will in place, the first person of contact, all that. He didn't necessarily have to have a will, but he had to make known what his wishes were should he not come back. So I mentioned to him at one point, "You might think about, should something happen, you might want to do something special." So he wrote everything down and sent me all of the criteria. He chose the TCU history department. He stated it had to be a graduate student, they had to have a GPA of 3.0 or greater, and they had to have some history of community service. I remember asking him on the phone one time, "Why a graduate student?" And his response was, "Because I would not want to invest money in a freshman like myself" [chuckles]. So he had obviously matured.

He was a very driven young man, he worked out hard, took good care of himself, was in excellent shape, but like a lot of college freshmen he just loved to party. He became much more focused. He basically referred back to strengths that he already had.

He was a very personable guy. He kind of took over the room when he came in. He was a natural leader. He kind of utilized that to be successful.

"We were walking into the mouth of the wolf."

Marty Leewright

We were basically a support unit. Combat engineers were there to support with heavy equipment, put up barracks or temporary Quonset huts or culverts or sandbags, build temporary runways, build floating bridges, blow bridges up, minesweep roads. There were times when I was attached to other units, like during the invasion of Cambodia I was attached from my combat engineer unit. There were four of us that were attached to the 1st Cavalry and the 11th Armored Cavalry that were part of the invasion force. The four of us had training in demolitions, heavy equipment, and things like that. I was running a front-end loader at the time, and I assumed they wanted somebody who could tear the top off a bunker, dig trenches, put up protective berms, clear out night defensive positions, things like that.

I was in Phuoc Vinh, which is an old Michelin rubber plantation. There was an airstrip there, and that's where we were based. We would go out in the field for six weeks, come back in for two weeks to stand down and resupply, rest, and so forth, then go back out in the field.

On the first of May 1970, we invaded Cambodia. We moved in one minute after midnight. And the Kent State riots happened as a result, shortly after that. We knew for maybe twenty-four hours, might have been thirty-six, that something big was about to happen. I was a specialist E-5, so I wasn't part of the command that would be apprised of

Army veteran Marty Leewright.
Courtesy of Marty Leewright.

troop movements and things like that. But we knew something big was happening 'cause we were beginning to muster, and we were told that we were gonna assemble on the border. So we assumed that we were gonna go into Cambodia. We were massed on the border and had a long convoy and were waiting for that midnight hour and our order to go in.

We had a lot of tanks with us. That was the 11th Armored Cavalry.

We had tanks with armored personnel carriers. So I knew that we were probably gonna be heading into some pretty hot territory, but we had not been in Cambodia legally before, at least under orders. There'd been little forays in there that probably were not legitimate. And I would say that once we knew where we were going we were kind of happy and glad, because they had been supplying from that whole area along the Cambodia/Vietnam border for a long time.

The North Vietnamese had these caches of weapons and supplies and ammunition, just amazing. We felt like they were coming in and hitting us and going back. It'd be like you got your hands tied behind your back and I go there and take a good whack at you and then I run down the hall and you can't go there. So it was kinda like, "Okay, now we're gonna make this right, we're gonna go in there, we're gonna kick some ass, and we're gonna take their supplies away." Which we did, but we also knew that there was gonna be resistance. We were told shortly before we moved in that there might be as many as three thousand North Vietnamese soldiers along the border where we were going in, which was the Parrot's Beak area. So the tension and anxiety were high.

But as a soldier on the ground, I didn't see the big picture. We read in newspapers about the demonstrations on college campuses. I wasn't a college student. There were people my age that were going to college. And we were kinda resentful, kinda angry, because we were trying to do a job. You asked me a minute ago if I was patriotic. I guess I was, in that I wanted to follow orders, I wanted to serve my country. And that's kinda like the myopic view. I had a narrow view of things as a young soldier, uneducated, unworldly, and frightened. Anybody ever says they were in Vietnam and weren't frightened is lying to you. So we wanted to go in, even though we knew we were walking into the mouth of the wolf and it was gonna be deadly and fierce. And we were willing to take that on. We were only in Cambodia for six weeks. And that was the roughest six weeks I had over there.

And there was shooting going on and snipers, and booby traps and things like that. We were reading newspapers about the demonstrations going on at home, and we felt like they didn't have our backs. We weren't being supported, and yet we were being asked to do this job that to an eighteen-year-old seemed monumental, seemed dangerous. And it made us angry. And we'd read those newspapers, and sometimes when we were moving we would bury whatever we had. We wouldn't leave things out where they could be found; we'd bury stuff. I remember burying newspapers with anger, seeing those pictures of the demonstrations and things like that. I couldn't understand it, really, 'cause I didn't see the big picture.

"There's no reset button in combat."

Michael Blackert

I knew I was deploying. It was just a matter of when and how many times. I was in ten months before we deployed the first time. When there's a war going off, there's heavy training going on. I'm talking to different individuals who had already come back from deployment, picking their brains and learning what it's like. And of course I was scared. There's no reset button in combat. I was married. I didn't have any children. My wife and I had been married not even a year, and I was already leaving, and I didn't know if I was going to be coming home at all. All we were seeing was all the stuff that was going on in Iraq.

Our mentality as ground troops was to go in and question every military-age male between eighteen and thirty-five. And, if they weren't cooperative, then we could detain them and take them down for questioning. I was jumping out of helicopters and kicking down doors. I was always the number-one man. We didn't have blueprints of any house. We could train for how to enter a house, but once you enter a house you don't know what the layout is. So I was nervous and scared, but I'm an adrenaline junkie, and after I joined the Army I became even more of an adrenaline junkie, I think because of that feeling you get, man. I can't explain it. It became almost just like tying shoes for us. But of course you were scared. I'm not going to lie. I'm not going to sit here and say there was not a time, kicking the door down and thinking, "Am I going to see my wife again?"

For the most part, the training was pretty good. I think where they lacked in the training was just how to treat people of the Middle East. There was a little bit taught on that, but not really. I really feel like that's where we kinda messed up as a country. We didn't prepare our service men and women for how to interact with the people. A lot of people joined the military after 9/11, and a lot of them wanted revenge. I feel that kinda hurt us as a nation, because it set up the ISIS that we have today. If you look at their ages, and you do the math, you would come to understand. These individuals have probably been seeing war most of their life. We've already burnt that bridge of connection, so now the rebuilding phase is going to be very difficult.

"They were really, really good."
Shirley Beck

Those artillery guys, we were at Fort Sill with them, and they had never seen a medical unit come through there before. And one of the high-ranking guys said, "We never deal with medical units, but we're going to get you guys ready to go, and you will be trained and you'll be ready." They said, "You can't leave here without knowing how to handle your weapon, how to handle your MOPP gear, and until we get all that accomplished for every person in your unit, we aren't going to let you go." They were really, really good. This was active Army guys that did that.

"There were seven guard stations around his dorm."
Bill Galyean

About six months before I got out of college, I was gonna be smart. I didn't want to join the Army. Foxholes and guns and bullets. So I was gonna join the Navy. So I took the Navy OCS test. I wanted to be a naval officer, because I knew I would have clean sheets at night and some hot meals and so on. So I passed the OCS test, they flew me to New Orleans for the physical, and the doctor that was giving me the physical asked, "So I see you have a history of asthma." And I said, "Yes, I do, but I was a child." "Doesn't matter. We can't take you in the Navy. You can go home, son. Don't worry, the Army won't take you either." Six weeks later I got my greetings in the mail from Uncle Sam, and I was drafted. But a lot of that was going on during that time, because Vietnam was really hot, and unless you were married or working on an advanced degree, you went. So I went in as an enlisted man, and when they found out you had a degree, they try to talk you into becoming an officer. I said, "I think I'll do my two years and go home, thank you."

I never got out of the States, but I did my training at Fort Coke, Louisiana, which is a very nasty place. It's where they were training all the Vietnam folks before they went over. Fort Garden, Georgia, then most of my time was spent in Fort Bragg, North Carolina, which is where the Green Berets are. We were the 1st Battalion, 503rd Infantry Regiment, kind of a strike unit, and we did some MP duty, and we were mainly attached to the 82nd Airborne. Any time they'd go somewhere, we'd go with them. And we were on a lot of alerts, for the Dominican Republic when that wasn't looking so good. We never went.

I was at Fort Bragg when John Kennedy was shot. We all went on combat alert and couldn't leave the base. No one knew what was going on. That was a memorable thing. The other thing was kind of a pivotal thing in the civil rights movement. When they integrated Ole Miss, it took thirty thousand troops four years watching James Meredith on that campus till he graduated. President Kennedy ordered that, and initially there were National Guard troops that went, and the rest of the time it was regular Army. It was a pretty serious thing. There were seven guard stations around his dorm 24/7, whether he was there or not. There was a guard walking outside, two guards on each floor, and one right outside his room. If he went home for Christmas, there were still seven people going in his room and the building. Which was understandable at that time.

They kept us out of sight. They didn't want the media to know we were there, so we went behind the football stadium in this big ravine and lived in tents. The only time we left was to go on duty. We were there for about six weeks, and then another unit came in. That went on for close to five years, until Mr. Meredith graduated. I'm sure the bill on that was really staggering. Inside the office where the commanding officer always stayed was a phone to Washington, to Army headquarters, and there was also a red phone that went directly to Bobby Kennedy. Emotionally, psychologically, it was a tough thing, because I was just six months out of college, and here I am, about nine hundred miles from home and at a similar dorm that I had just gotten out of, with live ammunition, with orders to kill anyone who came through this door that wasn't James Meredith or a federal marshal.

"I did find ways to enjoy it."

Joddy Murray

My particular area was never on the front. Our wartime mission was interrogation, so we were where the enemy prisoners would be. I was in the Air Force during the Bosnia-Herzagovina conflict, and, honestly, I can't really talk about a lot of what I did while I was there. It's all very highly classified. But I can say that our job was a support role, mostly, supporting those who were putting their lives out on the line. That's what we were doing. The better we did our job, the easier it was for them to do theirs.

There were aspects I really liked about the military. I knew, pretty much by the time I finished the Academy, that I was not going to be a career officer—that my interests and passions were elsewhere. But I had an obligation to finish out my commitment, so I did find ways to enjoy it. I really did get to know people very closely, and my particular job was very unusual, some would say highly selective. They don't let anybody who signs up for this job do the job I had. My job was interviewing. My job was to collect information, and that meant meeting a lot of people and being trained in how to assess information and then how to write it up. So I did a lot of writing and a lot of verbal communication. And that is exactly what I do now. I help people learn about writing and about conveying an argument or a message in the most effective way possible.

"Someone pulled out a golf club."
David Grantham

If leisure activities in the middle of the day were hard to come by, then finding an enjoyable way to kill time on long missions "outside the wire" was nearly impossible. We always had to remain alert, especially when meeting with confidential sources. A few guys always pulled security while the others met with sources. In the counterintelligence world, operators take great pains to vet and verify those who supply information. Failure to do so often leads to bad information, and sometimes even to death. In one of the more high-profile and costly examples of poor vetting, the CIA lost seven people in 2009 when a potential source detonated his concealed suicide vest minutes after arriving for a meeting at Camp Chapman in Afghanistan. Scenarios like these are forever in the front of your mind during operations.

On the trip home after one of these meetings, our convoy suffered a flat tire. The road we had been traveling on ran alongside a river, between two mountains. About one hundred yards in front of us, the road wrapped around the mountain and out of sight. Some of us fanned out to take up security positions along the road. Two went ahead to guard the bend in the road, some crossed the creek to take a high position on the side of the mountain, and others guarded the rear. We would rotate between security positions and relaxing near the vehicles.

As the tire was being repaired, someone pulled out a golf club and a handful of golf balls, and we took turns trying to hit a ball into the distant mountains. I failed to hit the ball off the ground, nearly breaking the club, and the owner of the equipment banned me from taking any more swings. This moment of leisure was one of the most unusual. After a very stressful meeting and an equally stressful time waiting for the repair, hitting golf balls into the mountains represented a reprieve, if just for a minute. It also represented home, where regular life went on in our absence.

"Is someone out there with an automatic weapon?"
Shirley Beck

I'll tell you a funny story. When we got over there and Pan Am dumped us on the runway, the Army had three or four small planes that were going to take us in small groups up to where we were going to set up the hospital, up to King Khalid Military City. Everything done in the dark of night by the Army, of course. They were taking people up, coming back, picking them up, taking them up. And we had two GP large tents, huge tents, that we occupied that night. Well, we were lined up like sardines with our sleeping bags, because we only had those two big tents. I thought, well, I'm not going to sleep until I know all these nurses are up here in the tent. Once they all arrived I kept asking, "Are any more coming?" They said, "No, we're all here."

We had the tents, there was concertina wire around our area, our guards were out there. All of a sudden, I hear this pop, pop, pop, pop, pop, pop, pop, pop, and I thought, "Oh my gosh, is someone out there with an automatic weapon?" I nudged a couple people beside me, they were dead to the world, they didn't even hardly wake up. I said, "Did you hear that?"

"I didn't hear anything."

The next morning, we did have hot water, and in our MREs we had this instant coffee, so we're all standing around talking and drinking our coffee, and I said, "Did any of you hear that automatic weapon in the middle of the night?"

They said, "No, did you hear one?"

I said, "I swear I did."

The dental officer comes up behind me and taps me on the shoulder. He said, "Colonel Beck, I need to tell you something."

I said, "What?"

He said, "I was one of the last ones to get in. I went to the trash pile where some of the stuff had been unpacked. I found some bubble pack with bubbles that big, and when I put my sleeping bag on top of it and moved around, that's what you heard."

Every time we get together, that story gets told.

"Seen a lot of morbid things out there."

John Garcia

It was mostly full of excitement, just being away from all the things I grew up with. I was establishing myself. I joined the Marine Corps and did my four years, did one tour in Iraq, the invasion, and got out. I would have stayed longer, but they had a freeze on our promotions, so I didn't re-up. There were a lot of other things too. I was going through a divorce, I had my oldest child in that divorce, and [my ex-wife] moved away with him. I had done some things in Iraq that I wasn't mentally prepared for. I think all of that added up to the reason that I left the Marine Corps.

Originally I was supposed to be legal administration. Before I left to the Marine Corps I got in trouble, so it was either jail time or go to the Marine Corps right now, and that's kind of why I left right out of high school instead of a couple months after. So I lost that and I went open contract and they gave me food service, which was a cook. I tried to fight, but I couldn't. I did food service, and I ended up going to Okinawa, Japan.

I'm just thinking of how to say it without being too blunt. Iraq was probably my hardest deployment. We got into a lot of firefights there. Seen a lot of morbid things out there. That's a hard one. Uh, I'm gonna skip that part.

Afghanistan, I don't know if I can say this, but I'm gonna say it. If I get in trouble, I get in trouble. Our gate guy got ran over by some Afghan nationals—or not nationals, but the Army. And they came on our base and they shot up our base with a .50 cal before the .50 cal locked and couldn't fire no more. They dismounted and proceeded to attack our base, I think it was three of them total, and they killed one civilian woman and wounded several others. I don't know how to say if this was a cover-up, but they reported it as the Taliban and not the Afghan Army that attacked us. And this was all over Yahoo, this was all over CNN, but they wouldn't say that it was them when it was them, when they infiltrated in and got our people. I remember it because I had control of sixteen Afghan civilians, and so they told us not to carry our weapons on us. We asked for pistols. To be qualified and get them, we had the ranges and the assets right there. We were told there was not enough, when there was an army full of them. And where they inserted right into our camp, it was right at our mess hall. They came in, I seen them, I couldn't fire at them. I don't know what could have happened if I had a weapon.

"We didn't know what was going to happen."

Andy Lahey

In January I shipped out to Camp Pendleton for School of Infantry Marine combat training, then to the Armed Forces School of Music in Norfolk, Virginia, where I spent about seven months learning all the basics of being a musician: music theory, some private lessons, how to march in the military style. Most people march at some point in high school or drum corps or what have you, but the military style is a little bit different.

After about seven months there, I shipped off to the Marine Forces Pacific Band at Marine Corps Base Hawaii, Kaneohe Bay on Oahu, and I was there from August 2008 until September 2011. I never deployed to a combat zone. North Korea got a little testy between 2009 and 2010; a small island got shelled just across the thirty-eighth parallel, and there was a period when we were put on high alert, where we didn't know what Congress was going to do or what the president was going to do.

Should they have taken military action, the band actually would have been the first unit on the ground in North Korea, as a security detail. We would have left our instruments in Hawaii. We would have packed up all the combat gear, gone into the armory and checked out our weapons, hopped on an airplane to South Korea. It was over the Christmas holiday, and most of us had actually gone on leave. But they basically told us, "We're going to let you go on leave, but should the call come down, you will get a phone call and you'll have forty-eight hours to get from wherever you are back to Hawaii." Because we're shipping out in two weeks from the time we get the phone call. So it was a little bit unsettling. We didn't know what was going to happen, and it was a different environment from what we'd been training for. All the combat training we had had was for urban-style warfare in the Middle East.

I did get to do a little bit of traveling. You get to go to some really neat places. I got to go to American Samoa three times for the Samoan Flag Day Festival, which is the anniversary of the US flag being raised over the main island of Tutuila. At one point I got the opportunity to go to the governor's mansion. We had essentially a state dinner at the governor's mansion, which was really cool, and got to actually know the governor, not just shake his hand and say, "Thank you for having us," but actually got to sit down and have a real conversation with him and his wife. I still have the ability to contact him today. He gave me his business card with his personal email on it, and I have actually emailed him a couple of times since that day. He's no longer governor.

And we were invited to Tonga to play for King George Tupou V, for his birthday celebration. He was having a military tattoo to celebrate his birthday. The Royal Australian Army Band come in from Australia, the Royal Tongan Marines put on a display, the Royal Tongan Army Band played. It was a really neat experience, and it's another part of the world that people just don't hear about. Unless you follow rugby, you don't hear about Tonga at all, ever.

"Get out there and do the next best right thing."

Tim Cole

One time as a first lieutenant, we were getting ready to do a big exercise out in Arizona, and a general officer came to the room and said, "I'm talking to you lieutenants now, and I'm talking to you captains now." And he said, "If you are not making mistakes in this exercise, it's because you're not making decisions. And if you're not making decisions in an exercise, then that means you're going to make your first decisions in a wartime environment." And he goes, "And then it's going to be impacting lives. So get out there, make decisions, let's see what happens. If there's mistakes, or if these are learning processes, let's do it here." That was the most empowering thing I ever heard. I mean, most times they don't tell lieutenants to go make decisions. It's, you know, "Shut up and color. Do what I tell you." So that was really empowering, and I would say that that's kind of carried through my life. Get out there and do the next best right thing to do. That kind of helped shape the rest of my career. You just step out and do your best work. It doesn't have to be perfect. Just care, and make a contribution, do the best you can.

Like a lot of young men that age, laundry would get done when it absolutely needed to get done. Whereas, in the military, we literally lace our shoes in a specific way. We hang shirts, pants, ties, and coats in a very specific way. It teaches you that some organization and some daily processes, daily disciplines, make your life much simpler. Which frees up your brain to do some of those other things: creative problem-solving, or reading, growing, learning. I did not have that before the military. After the military, I know that I do better in a clean environment. And why? It's easier to find stuff. So discipline was a big part, and I would also say that I learned in the military that physical fitness represented an opportunity to get away from the brain game, to get out of my head. There's a reason the military gets up and goes to PT before you go to work, and there's a reason the Marine Corps gives you an hour and a half for lunch, and it isn't so that you can go eat for an hour and a half. It's so that you can go get your physical fitness in and come back that afternoon. So when I went back to the civilian world, it was like, "When can I get my runs in?" We joke when we go on a family vacation, because I know how to load planes and whatnot, and I know how to load ships and whatnot, so the joke is that I know how to load a trunk pretty well. They paid me lots of money to learn how to pack things.

"The Marine Corps is about leaving things behind."

Richard Spence

I remember a story of a young Marine who was graduating from motor transport operator school. He was wearing his graduation uniform at the time. I was inspecting our LVS trucks and found one that had been tagged inside of the vehicle. I knew exactly who the Marine was that wrote on the truck. I went to his graduation ceremony and confronted him about tagging the vehicle. I knew that it was him, due to the fact that I came from the streets like he did. I proceeded to bring him down, and he admitted that he had written on the vehicle. I had him wash and scrub trucks in his graduation uniform, to show him that writing and tagging has no place in the Marine Corps. The Marine Corps is not about doing things that you did out in the street, it's about learning and grow-ing and leaving those things behind you and moving on to better and bigger things.

Five years went on and I returned to Camp Johnson, MCSSS for school, and they put me in the barracks. The door opened in the middle of the night, and a Marine walked in. In the darkness we were talking, and I asked him where he was coming from. He had flown in from Oki-nawa, Japan, and he was here for NCO motor transport school, and he had so many memories about Camp Johnson. I asked him whether they were good memories or bad memories. He told me there were good memories, but one day when he graduated there was this sergeant that grabbed him to wash vehicles in his graduation uniform for tagging. He went on to say that that was the best thing that ever happened to him, because he never did it again, and he grew from it and became a better Marine because of it.

I told him, "What a great story," and asked him to turn on the light. Once he turned the light on and saw my face, his face turned completely white. We went on to laugh about it. It was a great time.

"Nothing was ideal in this evacuation hospital."

Shirley Beck

Now, I'm going to be real honest with you. Nothing was ideal in this evacuation hospital. I highly respected the enlisted people. My best friend was the command sergeant major, because if I didn't know some-thing or I needed something, I could go and talk to him. Some of the higher-ranking guys, it was like this was a joke to them, which was kind of scary.

The one thing that I thought was probably a real concern: We were supposed to get a big rubber bladder; there's no running water out there. They were supposed to deliver water to fill the bladder. Well, it took days after we were there to get that accomplished, which I thought was a lit-tle bit ridiculous. It was strictly purified water that we could use in the hospital. However, we did get bottled water for the troops delivered. That helped.

When we put our tents up, it was really tough. It wasn't where you could drive a wooden stake to hold up a tent. So we had to use rebar. I tell you what, every morning when I woke up, I would thank the good

Lord that somebody didn't go wandering around at night, trip on one of those rebars, and wound herself. So we started putting all of our empty water bottles over the rebar, so that helped. But I really had a concern about that, you know?

The XO gave my weapon to his girlfriend, who was stationed in town in Riyadh in an apartment, supposedly to do bartering and purchasing supplies that we might need in Iraq. So I had fifty nurses in a tent, with no weapon.

Occasionally I would have a nurse come in the middle of the night. I was on my cot, and she said, "Colonel Beck, I'm scared. Can I lay down beside you?" I said, "Sure." You know, here's a cot this wide. But you know, I had three nurses in that group that had only been to drill two times. They had gotten their commission, and came on board, but hadn't really been involved in a whole lot of training yet. Several of them were working in a hospital on an Indian reservation in Oklahoma. Some of the others worked in the local hospitals. I mean, they were accomplished, they knew how to do nursing, you know, and so did the three that had never been to drill. But you know they were scared.

The hospital dietician and I became real pals. She and I talked and I said, "What are we going to feed people who are on liquid diets?" We were all eating MREs, you know, meals ready to eat. Before we left Oklahoma City we went to the local supermarket, and she and I bought all kinds of things that you could use for liquid diets and packed them up and took them with us. But that should've been in the plan. You don't want to have somebody come in that's got all kinds of injuries and they can't eat food, but you've got to give them some liquid plus IVs or whatever. That dietician, Jenny Roper, I give her a lot of credit, and the cooks. It's so easy to get a bunch of people ill with diarrhea when you go somewhere like that, where it's very difficult to keep everything really, really clean. But we didn't have one bit of problems; those cooks knew what they were doing and did it.

"They told us to go home, pack a temporary bag."
David Ziomek

David Ziomek was interviewed by his daughter Rachel.

I joined the military because I felt it was important to serve my country, and I also thought it would be great to fly an airplane in the military. I

**Air Force veteran David Ziomek, his wife, Susan,
and daughters Rachel and Sarah.** *Courtesy of David Ziomek.*

was near the top and I selected an F-4 Phantom, and that's what I got selected to fly. I got my degree in 1980, then I applied to officer training school and got accepted. That lasted ninety days. Then I came out of officer training school, and I was a second lieutenant in the United States Air Force. From there I went on to flight school, where I got my wings. That took about a year. After that I went on to learn how to fly a specific type of fighter aircraft.

I went to flight school at Mather Air Force Base in Sacramento, California. That was in 1981. And then in 1982–83 I was at Homestead AFB in Florida, where I learned how to fly the F-4. I was then stationed from 1983 to 1987 at Moody AFB in Georgia. From there I went to South Korea, from 1987 to '88. And then from 1988 to '89 I was at George AFB in California, where your sister Sarah was born. And then, in 1991 to '94, I went to Langley AFB in Virginia. That was a non-flying assignment. And then in 1994–95 I went to school with the Army for a year. And then 1995 to '98 I went to Seymour Johnson AFB, which was back to flying. And that was in the F-15E Strike Eagle. And then in 1998–2002 I was at Langley AFB in Virginia. And I retired in 2002.

I had two tours over in Iraq. I've got one hundred combat hours flying over Iraq. I was hoping that I would get shot at just so I could shoot back, but I never got shot at. Both times I was stationed in the country of Qatar, right as Desert Storm was starting to wind down. So I was actually flying over Iraq. Southern Watch was the name of the operation, enforcing the UN-sanctioned no-fly zones in Iraq. It was very strange. We lived in what we called the tent city. There was an international airport in Doha, Qatar. And on the other end of the runway the Army Corps of Engineers built these huge tents, and that's what we lived in.

I spent a year over in Korea, and it was fun, it was good flying. Not as many rules and regulations, flying regulations, like there are here back in the States. It was different in that our airplanes were at a Korean air base and so here I was, an American aviator, flying American jets, and the maintenance personnel were Korean. You can go more where you want, and you could fly lower than you can here in the States, and faster than you can here in the States.

We were stationed in Virginia, but I happened to be TDY, on temporary duty, down in Seymour Johnson AFB, when 9/11 happened. I was actually in the squadron, briefing, getting ready to go fly a training sortie. Nine-eleven happened, they came in and canceled all the flights, told us to go home, pack a temporary bag in case we had to deploy. I came back to the squadron, and they loaded all the aircraft with live missiles on our airplanes. And several of us got to take off. I personally got to fly over southern Virginia, some people got to fly over Washington, DC. Some people flew over New York, and it was just patrolling the skies over the United States to make sure nothing else happened. Typically you only have live missiles or live bombs in certain locations in the United States. Not every location. It's only used for emergencies, like this happened to be.

I was in two different squadrons, one in Moody AFB in Georgia, and a second time was in George AFB in California, where two airplanes had a midair [collision]. In both those instances the aircrew died, and they weren't very good times. The one in Georgia ran into the ground, and we had the funeral for him at the base chapel, and it's very somber and they play Taps, and they have the whole formality of the flag folding and all that to be presented to his wife, so that's not very good. They were squadron mates, and there was a lot of friendship and camaraderie with your squadron mates.

I actually wanted to retire right at twenty years. But 9/11 was happening, so they wouldn't let me retire for a year and a half later. It was a program called Stop Loss. So rather than getting out at twenty years, I had about twenty-one and a half years. So that was a little bit nerve-wracking. It seemed like every six months they would give us official notification that "You're not released to be retired yet." Luckily it all worked out, and I got hired by Lockheed Martin about the time that I was released from the military. It was time to retire because I was due to get promoted again, and I knew I was going to make the promotion, but it would have required me to move three times in the next five years. I retired as a lieutenant colonel. I was going to get promoted to full bird colonel, and your mother and I talked it over, and we didn't want to move three times in the next five years, so we put in for retirement.

"That was a sobering time."

Tim Cole

The dark days for me would be during the first Gulf war. Iraq invaded Kuwait in August 1990. I was with a Marine infantry unit, a reserve unit, and we got mobilized in January of '91 and stayed on active duty until May of '91. We didn't know it was just going to be a three-day war. We thought the war was going to take months to win, and here I was with a Marine infantry unit. It was a sobering time. We had just had our third daughter, she had been born in '90, and this was the beginning days of video. So we began videoing a dialogue with each of my daughters. I held each one and talked about how much I loved them. Prepared for the worst. The good news was the battle only lasted three days, and we never left the United States. So that was a sobering time, and more reserve years followed, and then 9/11 happened.

"It's cool to go to a place completely different."

Nick Sellman

My brother and I wanted to serve the country as part of a family tradition. We were all Army before, then my older brother and I joined the Marine Corps, and my younger brother joined the Navy. Neither of my parents were in the military, but I had an uncle in the Army.

I served for just about fifteen and a half years. Due to the downsizing of the military I applied for an early retirement, so I actually retired from the Marine Corps. I was stationed in Okinawa, Japan, San Diego, here in Fort Worth, back to Okinawa, then Cherry Point, North Carolina.

L-R: Staff Sergeant Jean Colley, SSgt. Mike Hoffman (deceased), and SSgt. Nicholas Sellman (Marine veteran). *Courtesy of Nicholas Sellman.*

I got very lucky being on the C-130 aircraft. I traveled a lot more than a lot of other people. I've been to about sixty different countries and six continents. Our job was pretty unique, normally four to eight guys together in the plane going on two- to three-week trips around the world, wherever we had to take stuff. I was the loadmaster; my job was to take care of all the passengers on the aircraft. We would plan any of the loads, balance out the plane, and make sure it was within takeoff and landing limitations. We also were in charge of all the airdrops. From our planes we could drop personnel, cargo, vehicles, food. We also did in-flight re-fueling of other aircraft.

Probably my favorite place I ever got to go to was the Federated States of Micronesia, which is a small country, like 120 islands in the South Pacific. My first commanding officer when I went to Okinawa was the son of the president of Micronesia, so we kind of had an "in" with them. It's very primitive there, a lot of dirt roads, a lot of places they still wore grass skirts and used rock-coin money. It's just so far off from everything; I don't think there was Internet when we were there. It's cool to go to a place completely different from yourself. We went there for a week one time, and he had some guys take us out and drive us around. We went fishing, got to go see a lot of manufacturing and wood carving for Pacific-type figures.

We went to Singapore a couple times, and it's insane the amount of money and stuff that's there. But I always liked the places that were kind of austere and away from the hustle and bustle. I did three tours in Iraq and one to Afghanistan. Those were kind of not the nicest places.

A lot of stuff we did in the military, people don't talk about, especially with the C-130s. Like when we were stationed in Japan, we did more humanitarian service stuff on that side of the world that I don't think gets talked about. When the big earthquake in northern Japan happened, my unit was one of the main units they sent to do humanitarian service there for days. The typhoon in 2014 that obliterated part of the Philippines, our unit was the first unit down there helping people and moving them out. I always think getting to help people out is so much more rewarding than anything else. There was the Ebola outbreak when I was on my last deployment; we flew all the Ospreys into Liberia to help them out. They were some of the friendliest people. So I guess the best stories are getting to see the people around the world, seeing how friendly they are, having a world perspective.

"It was just a constant go."

Bruce Cole

My last duty was as the division sergeant major for 3rd Marine Division in Okinawa, Japan. It was a tumultuous time of traveling and speeches. I was working for a two-star general of the division CG, General Fred Padilla. At any given time, I had about four thousand Marines in Hawaii. I had another thousand or so Marines in Okinawa, probably a handful of Marines in the mainland on Camp Fuji training. In Australia, I would have any number of Marines there at any given time training. In Korea, I would have any number of Marines there, and in Twentynine Palms, California, going through different training exercises they do in preparation for deploying. It was just a constant go. I earned over half a million frequent flier miles with United alone, over the first two years.

There were almost seven thousand Marines in the 3rd Marine Division. General Padilla and I spent an inordinate amount of our time dealing with designer drugs and other discipline problems. This was long after my own time as a young lance corporal who really had my ear to the ground about what was going on. By the time this came out, I was having to ask lance corporals what was going on. "Tell me about this stuff. What is it really all about?" I don't know, maybe it was cheap or whatever. The only thing we had going for us when I was a lance corporal was beer. Now it was like bath salts, and weird incense kind of stuff that they would roll up and do gosh knows what with. It was crazy, and what I'm getting at is that it was the flavor of the month. Because fast forward two weeks, and that wasn't even something that we worry about. Now it was hazing all of a sudden, and then wait a few weeks and it would be something else. It was Whac-A-Mole, and you had to scratch your head and wonder where the stuff came from.

There were date rapes and stuff like that in the barracks when I was the Camp Fuji sergeant major. It was a very, very small camp, about two hundred Marines altogether. It was a training base, so there were very few permanent personnel there. Units would come, and they would use the camp to train, and then they would go back to their place. It was a camp where everyone there was only on a twelve-month tour. It was unaccompanied, which means your family didn't come with you. So when you got orders to go to Camp Fuji to serve there, you were going for twelve months and your family wasn't going with you. So everyone at the camp was single, so to speak, so that was a challenge in and of itself, just maintaining that sense of decorum with all the married people. If my figures are right, about a third of my personnel there were female.

Sexual misconduct became so frequent at some point that I recommended to the commander that we create a separate barracks for the girls and for the guys. At that point, all the young ladies and the young men were all in the same barracks, just on different floors, but it just meant going up a ladder well and then you were in the wrong place. And when I recommended that, you would have thought I had done just the most evil thing. Everybody was up in arms, because I was going to segregate the men and the women. It was a head-scratcher to me why anyone could construe that as being obstructive somehow. I thought I was fixing the problem and wondered, "Why hadn't anyone ever thought of that before?"

"If they out to get you, you go straight."
Alcee Chriss Sr.

It started when President Roosevelt passed that Executive Order 8802, where any citizen can serve in any service force. He passed that order in 1941. I was in school. And they drafted me for the Army. But in '42, they start recruiting African Americans in the Marines. I said, "Whoa! The fighting Marines!" So I went and changed order to go in the Marines. So when we left New Orleans in October 1942, it was about almost a platoon of us riding on that train. Two of the recruits had master's degrees and were teaching at university. We had a musician. We had a professional baseball player on the team. And a lot of entertainers. And had me on that train.

It was Camp Lejeune before we got there, but it changed to be called Montford Point. At Montford Point we had tent-like huts with canvas and wood at the bottom. We were sort of surprised at that, because right across the bay, white recruits had brick barracks. It sorta struck us. But I said, "We're gonna make it." So we did make it. We had some problems. But we came through. We persevered through that. I thought that was a great bunch, the group I worked with.

And we had some good officers. Now all officers wasn't good now. We had some people who were trying to stop our going. But we were fortunate enough to be having these two officers, and we got training and that, which was good. We split up, and I got in the infantry working with small weapons.

I was in the 7th Separate Infantry. Then went to 51st Seacoast Artillery. They're shooting out in the ocean. I was in five patrols in there, I got moved again, and I'm aware of what's about to go down. But I still persevered. Then they changed me to work with a quartermaster, and that's when I got into trouble. I was platoon sergeant at the time, what you called a staff sergeant. The lieutenant had a corporal, would order me and tell me what to do. And I went to him and said, "I respect you, sir, as an officer and lieutenant. I'm a sergeant, and I did work for my sergeant stripe." From then on, we couldn't get together on that. But I respect his rank.

Montford Point Marine Alcee Chriss Sr.
Courtesy of Alcee Chriss Sr.

On weekends, the staff sergeant could go out at twelve o'clock every weekend. I had a brother in Washington, and he had lined up a party. He said, "Party gonna start at" a hour before I could get there. So I decide okay, to have fun, I said, "I better get there on time." So I left before. See, so that was wrong. [The lieutenant] heard all about that. So he wrote me up for being AWOL. But then I lost that stripe. I wasn't discharged with a platoon sergeant, I was discharged with buck sergeant, three stripes. But know what that did for me? And anybody got to watch out for this. If anybody out to get you, brother, you go the right straight road. Because they could mess with you. So I really learned from that, and that is a good thing to do. If you know you got some problems with somebody and they out to get you, you go straight.

"I had never contemplated Vietnam."

George Wahl

In 1961 I had never contemplated Vietnam, never even heard of it, even though we had special ops working in that part of Southeast Asia at the time. But I never saw it. I was blind to it. I got orders to go to Vietnam in May of 1967 with the 173rd Airborne Brigade. I was the executive officer of the brigade medical company, the frontline medical company in the forward battle, where we would treat the wounded before they went to the field hospitals and the combat support hospitals. That was May 1967 to May 1968, one year.

My reward for completing a deployment in combat was that the Army said, "Major, you're going to graduate school." And I went to graduate school for an MBA program at American University in Washington, DC, thanks to the US Army. The assignments subsequent to that were primarily command staff. I was a battalion commander of 550-plus soldiers at Fort Hood, 2nd Armored Division, another combat unit, in 1979 and 1980, and I was at a large command control headquarters of the Army Basic Medical Training in San Antonio, Fort Sam Houston, as an instructor. I was selected to go work at Camp Smith, Hawaii, which is a joint site of Army, Navy, and Air Force.

I culminated my thirty-year career as a full colonel and as the deputy commander and chief of staff of the Army Medical Department Training Center and School at Fort Sam Houston. The Gulf War was running then, in 1991. We ran a physicians' basic officer training course, which is normally five or six weeks. We condensed it down during the war to two weeks. These were physicians right off the street, never stood in a formation, never fired a weapon: civilian physicians. Guys like Hawkeye Pierce. I liked to get out where the training was going on and, on Saturday or Sunday, I'd go out to the firing range and see them. It was amazing to see the transition from Joe and Mary Civilian, because they had to be able to wear a uniform and deploy in the combat zone. (Now granted, they were working mostly in combat support hospitals, evacuation hospitals, field hospitals. They weren't frontline medics.) That was really exciting. That was an accomplishment.

"I have Saddam Hussein's signature."

John Garcia

One of the coolest things I didn't mention was that I have Saddam Hussein's signature. I just thought of that. We came into Al Kut and we had just got there. They were still clearing hospitals and buildings out, and they had us clear these barrack rooms. So we're clearing these barrack rooms and we come to this office, with thousands of books just piled up. And we're telling everybody, "Watch out, it could be booby trapped." And sure enough, on the wall there was hand grenades in a way that if you pulled something down, they'd explode. But on the floor people were just walking, and there could be something underneath like a landmine or whatever. I wasn't thinking, so I just grabbed a book and flipped and I saw his picture, Saddam Hussein.

And I didn't realize where I was either; they explained to me later where I was. I looked and it was signed in like a gold ink. I said, "Oh crap, I'm gonna see what this is." There was paperwork and stuff like that, so I had to turn it in to make sure there was nothing classified in there. They ended up telling me that that was the Air Force general with all the books on the floor, so I actually found the book that was given to him by Saddam Hussein, and I got it. I mean, I turned it in, but they gave it back. They actually cut out pages in it, though. I don't know what was in it.

"It's all about having the strong mental mindset."

Steven Gonzalez

Going in was a culture shock. It was my first time on a plane, and boot camp isn't a very pleasant experience. The way I saw it was there were people who had done it before, and there was no reason why I could not accomplish that. But during the process, in my thoughts, I'm like, "Man, this sucks. What would happen if I just quit?" It lingers in the back of your mind. They would give us these brushes and we would brush the sidewalk, on your knees, and the sidewalks are very clean in San Diego. But it's little things like that, they sucked. While doing it I was like, "I'd rather be in jail." It's all about having the strong mental mindset and getting through it. Like I said, if somebody has done something before me, there is no reason why I can't do it either.

I was just kind of, you know, do the first four years and see what it could lead to after that. But I happened to get married right off the bat to my high school girlfriend, and she enlisted into the Marine Corps too, so we both went to boot camp at the same time. And at the three-and-a-half-year mark where I was due to reenlist, the plan was to get out. I had a job lined up with the railroad company here in Fort Worth, and it was gonna be a pretty good gig. I was a little disgruntled because I had joined, I wanted to go to combat, I wanted to go to war and feel like I did my part, and I didn't get to deploy my first four years. I mean, I lived in Japan, and the big tsunami that hit in 2005, I got to be a part of that and support the humanitarian effort.

"You had to keep morale going, too."

Alcee Chriss Sr.

We wanted to fight, and I went out with Captain Troup, who was a musician there. He played piano, and he wrote "Route 66." Yeah, he wrote that. And he had a band, and he was in charge of the social activity and recreation activity and the band. He had the marching band, and he had a swing band. I went out in his depot company. And I left, and we got to Guam, and I saw some of my fellow men when we first came into the Marines. I met up with them, because they were in Seacoast Artillery. And I stayed there a while. They put me as property sergeant, making me in charge of equipment and guns and all that kind of stuff. We were there a few months.

When we were on Guam, didn't have any fighting. They had cleared up Guam. Let me see, now. It must've been in '43. If it wasn't '43, it was early '44. I stayed on there a few months, then we went to Okinawa. Well, Saipan. I spent most of the time on Saipan. But one time they hinted that we might go to Okinawa, and I'm glad I didn't go there. I was second in charge of the big warehouse. We handled signal material, battery, radar and all kind of lights. And the captain and I was responsible for fifteen to thirty-five men each day. Even had some of the guys who come from the battle front in the working party. The captain would take orders and bring it to me, and I'd see that the men got them out on time. You had to keep morale going too, now, that is important. A lot of people don't think nothing about that, but that's important.

"The elders said it had been thirty years."

Joel Huffman

Our first mission soon after we arrived in country was to clear Salaam Bazaar, a known Taliban hideout and strategic location along a heavily trafficked route. We were told we would be there for three days, so we packed light. Still there three weeks later, we laughed because some guys' clothes were so saturated with salt from sweat that they could stand up on their own.

Expecting opposition, we mobilized several hundred Marines and

Marine veteran Joel Huffman.
Courtesy of Joel Huffman.

dozens of vehicles to clear the bazaar. However, our initial assault went uncontested. Instead of a suicidal attempt to hold the area, the enemy combatants wisely waited as we established a patrol base and fixed our location, then started lobbing mortars and rocket-propelled grenades from safety. We were relaxing for a minute in our trucks, when an RPG flew about two feet away from my buddy's head and hit the wall behind us. Good afternoon.

Our time at Salaam Bazaar consisted mostly of vehicle-mounted patrols, providing support for Alpha Company as they cleared the surrounding area on foot, and escorting EOD [explosive ordnance disposal] as IEDs were found.

Upon our arrival, our commanding officers met with the village elders. The details of this meeting were relayed to us by our commanding officer's interpreter, Nik, who was college-educated, spoke seven tribal languages, and had previously worked with US Special Forces in the mountains of northern Afghanistan. Nik told us that at the *jirga,* when Afghan officers told the local elders we were here from the national government to help them, the elders laughed and said that it had been thirty years—since before the Soviet invasion—since they'd heard anything from the government. When asked how we could help, one man said that they'd like a clinic for their wives and a school for their children. Nik told us later that this man was beheaded that same night by the Taliban to scare the locals into submission to their mafia-style rule.

Over the course of the first few days of living with our Afghan counterparts, we made good friends with a junior Afghan National Police officer with wild eyes and a huge heart named Takkar, which we were told translates roughly to Car Wreck. We called him Rambo because of his caution-be-damned attitude during combat, which caused him to do things like stand up and march head-on into gunfire during a firefight.

One of the most memorable and historic moments I've ever experienced came a few days into the operation. During a lull in fighting, Rambo mounted an Afghan flag to two long wooden poles and marched the red, green, and black symbol of national pride down the center of the bazaar, shouting a victorious, "Shat the fack up Taliban!" Perhaps not the most couth proclamation to usher in a hopeful epoch for the village, but it was certainly a welcome inspiration and comically appropriate for the setting. We never figured out how all the Afghans knew the same phrase, but every time they yelled it, we laughed like crazy.

"I can follow rules and regulations."

George Wahl

I have an MBA thanks to the United States Army and only incurred another four-year commitment. I finished in a year and a half, started on my PhD, and then they called me from the Pentagon: "What the hell is going on here? You've got more than enough credit hours to graduate." Since it was a two-year program and I finished my MBA, I just thought I'd go on, and I took three courses in my PhD program. And they said, "Major, get your alpha out of the university, and you're going to work." It's a highly competitive school. It's called long-term civilian schooling. All services have it. They like you to have at least a track record. Again, I was blessed. There's no way I'd be getting a master's free, when you're on active duty or in reserves, trying to work and then go to school.

I wore civilian clothes and never had to report to anybody. All I had to do was send them my transcripts. In undergraduate school, I just barely graduated with a C or C+ average. In graduate school I made all As and Bs, because I had a different attitude. It was really funny: when you get out here with people who never wore a uniform and just went from high school to undergraduate school to graduate school, they want to argue with the professor: "Oh, that's not right." They're speaking from a zero experience role. I remember one particular hard alpha professor in economics. He said, "Not only is there a written paper requirement, but your topic must be approved on X date. Here's my office hours." So I got my topic approved, and the very first class after that X date where you have to get your topic approved, here's how he started out the class: "Good evening, ladies and gentlemen. These are the scores for the midterm paper. Miss Johnson, F. Mr. Clooney, F." And about the third name, the young kid stands up: "You can't do that, Dr. Schmidt. I haven't even turned in my . . . " He said, "You did not follow instructions." Thank you, US military, that I can follow rules and regulations.

"I want it remembered."

Shirley Beck

We had several that came through who were foolish enough to pick up ordnance, and then it blew up. We had a lot of the Patriot missile commanders come through, and they were having a lot of anxiety and heart problems, because they were under such pressure and stress. But you had to be careful, because you don't want someone to feel like you're challenging their masculinity, when it's just a normal human reaction to be stressed and anxious about your job. I mean, what a job they had. We encouraged them to stay with us and let us give them rest for a couple of days. Then we didn't really give them high-powered medications; it was just something to calm things down a little bit, let them talk about how they felt. Get it out and look at it and talk about it. They felt they were overwhelmed with the responsibility, and they knew they had to get it organized in their heads, and deal with it, and be careful on how they relate it to their people working under them. I don't think I could really get into their heads and know how they really felt. I could see it physically and mentally coming out, but I wasn't in that position; they were.

Oh, here's something I wanted to bring up, I want it remembered. This was one of my nurses. When they thought we were going to have a chemical attack, they wanted us to take the Pyridostigmine pills, with no consideration of age, what medications people were already on. And the XO says, "When we say take this pill, you better take this pill." Well, this lady already had high blood pressure, that was controlled, and it almost threw her into a stroke. And I had another older male nurse there. Both of them, we had to evac them out. And the troops came one night, the shower tent was open, and a couple of the guys came to me and said, "Colonel Beck, we don't know what to do with Colonel Bob. He's down there in the shower tent, just wandering around and picking up stuff and mumbling." I said, "Well, what do you think is going on?" They were smart guys, they worked in hospitals. They said, "We think he's had a light stroke or something." Whoa, he did. That was from that medication, Pyridostigmine. What blew my mind was, you don't just say, "You take this pill." We had some people in charge I thought were fairly uninformed, I'll put it kindly.

"You were responsible to the service to complete your task."

Leo Munson

I was in the Office of Special Investigations, and we had a tri-part mission: to conduct background investigations for security clearances, counterintelligence, and criminal investigations. I oversaw the detachment's background investigations. I was on a base, Bergstrom Air Force base, but I was not assigned to the command of that base. I was actually assigned to a command out of San Antonio. And I oversaw the background investigations for our detachment and spent the majority of my time in criminal investigations. One of the benefits of the branch I was in was I think I wore a uniform three times during the time I was on active duty. The rationale for not wearing a uniform was to not be recognizable as a member of the military. Well, everyone on the base knew we were military. And two, not to have any sense of who was the superior officer, who was the officer, who was the noncom. The rationale probably made sense, but everybody knew who we were and what we did, and they may not have known my rank, but they had a pretty good idea that I was an officer.

In the spring of 1972, we received notification that because of the wind down in Vietnam, my commissioning class was given the opportunity to release early if we wanted. I had a four-year active duty commitment and then a two-year reserve commitment. I had only been in two years. So I called the staff sergeant that I knew in our command headquarters in Washington. One of the things you do is you meet and befriend people in Human Resources, so they can tell you what's going on with your life. He said, "Give me twenty-four hours." This was in March. He called me back in twenty-four hours and said, "Well, I've got good news and bad news for you, Leo. The good news is you've got a really bright future in the Air Force. You've received perfect scores on your Officer Efficiency Reports, sky's the limit for you." I said, "Well then, what's the bad news?" And he said, "Well, remember this is the military. You are scheduled to go to Saigon sometime in the spring or summer of 1973, to oversee the black market narcotics operation in Southeast Asia." I said, "That doesn't sound like a real good deal to me." *[laughs]* "Well," he said, "That's what they've got you slated to do."

So I went in to talk to my boss, who was a major. He hadn't been in Vietnam, but he had served at one of the bases in Thailand. And I said, "This is what they just told me. What do you think?" And he said, "Just sit down. What do you think about going home?" And I said, "Well, I guess I hadn't thought much about it." And he said, "You want to go home." "Why is that?" And he said, because when he was there—which would have been '69—the guy who was in that position was assassinated on the streets of Saigon by a thirteen-year-old for the equivalent of fifty cents. So I went home, talked to my wife, and said, "What do you think?"

And she said, "It's up to you." And I said, "Well, it doesn't sound like a real good deal to me."

And so, couple-three days later, I went in and turned in my paperwork to get out in September. So I only served active duty for two years. That's why this is not a very exciting *[laughs]* interview.

I had friends from both high school and college who were killed in Vietnam while I was an active duty service member. I didn't disagree with the war at that time. I personally had issues with what appeared to me to be politicians making decisions instead of career servicemen. And it turns out I was pretty accurate on that, from the way history looks at that period of time. But I thought it was a natural progression of things that if you join the service, or if you were drafted in the service, you were responsible to the service to complete your task. I still believe that.

"Some of the rules just didn't make sense."

Jonathan Ide

I did two deployments. I went to Iraq pretty much all of 2011, and then I went to Afghanistan 2012 to 2013. My first duty was eleven months, and the second was nine. All the patrolling I did was pretty much in Afghanistan. You would drive out to one location, and let's say the terrain is not really vehicle friendly, we would just get as close as possible, then we would get out and walk around and meet with the elders, to see if they noticed anybody. For the most part the people there were just trying to, you know, live, and the Taliban or whatever different forces would come in and place the IEDs or pay one of the poor farmers to shoot at us. So basically we would go out there just to show a kind of presence, make sure we talked to the elders to see if there was anything we could do or if there's any complaints, and just kind of control the area and get a good idea of what's going on.

Initially when I signed up I was like, "I'm just going to do the four years and finish and go back to school." But then I wanted to do another deployment, so I reenlisted. I knew that if I went in past the ten-year mark, I would almost have this feeling that I'm obligated to stay in, because of the retirement part of it all. So I wasn't going to do the ten years, because I didn't want to do the full twenty. But it was mainly just kind of getting tired with the atmosphere. There was really great people you could work with, and there was really awful people as well, and some of the rules just didn't really make sense to me. There was a lot of things where I was like, "This just is stupid." Like, "I don't want to do this no more." I enjoyed my time deployed, but in the States, unless you're doing response, it's a lot of boring work, and they find busy work for you to do, and you're kind of like, "Why am I doing this?" I have to go clean, like, this hallway every day for a couple hours. I felt it was kind of a waste of time.

There was a team that replaced me—whenever you go into a deployment area in a country, you go in and get the people going to replace you and you kind of go over for a week of like, "Hey, this is how things go in this certain area." So they sent the EOD team into my little area, and I voiced to my superiors that these guys aren't ready and they shouldn't be in this area, 'cause my area I happened to be in was a little bit more eventful than other certain areas. So I voiced my opinion and nothing happened, and they ended up switching out, and I had like a month at the main base, and we saw some other guys, and they were having some kind of mass trauma casualty event, because the infantry guys thought the EOD team that replaced us was really incompetent. They just stopped taking them out, which when I was there they took us on like 95 percent of the patrols. So yeah, they had one KIA, one triple amputee, and one double amputee, and other various injuries, and I felt like it could have been somewhat avoided, or maybe you don't really know, but I feel like I wished I was out there to help out. That was probably the roughest part for the last one, especially because the guy who got killed, I mean he was a young kid about nineteen, maybe twenty.

But yeah, that was pretty rough. Other than that I had a couple of other friends get killed, but they were EOD guys, you kind of expect you have a pretty good likelihood of getting killed or be some kind of amputee, so I kind of already accepted that somewhat, so it doesn't hit as hard.

"I spent Thanksgiving in the hospital."
Charles Lamb

I graduated from college in 1966, a bad time to graduate from college. There weren't many good jobs available, and I was eligible for the draft and was going to be drafted soon. That meant no good jobs were available for me. At the time, you could join the Air Force or Navy for four years, you could join the Marine Corps or Army for three years, or you could be drafted for two years. I thought: I'm a college graduate, I'm good at math, I can type, I'll be a clerk for two years and be done with it. I was drafted, and it didn't work out the way I had planned. I spent sixteen weeks at Fort Jackson, South Carolina, training to become an infantry-man. In September of 1967, I shipped off to Vietnam.

I was assigned to the 4th Infantry Division and our headquarters was in Pleiku, in the Central Highlands of Vietnam. I was then sent to a combat unit that was working near a village named Dak To, about five miles east of Cambodia. The engagement that followed involved several North Vietnamese units and several US companies. The fighting there was later named the Battle of Dak To. In early November, about a month after arriving, I was wounded in an ambush. I received multiple shrapnel wounds on my arms, back, and elsewhere. A large piece of shrapnel hit my eye. My eye looked like the eye of the Target department store dog; it was the biggest black eye I have ever seen. Fortunately, the wound did not cause any permanent damage. I was very lucky. My company suf-fered twenty-two killed and 122 wounded that day.

I still have shrapnel fragments under my skin. Every time I have an X-ray the technician says, "Oh, you were in Vietnam." The fragments show up in the X-rays.

I was wounded on November 11 and sent to a hospital in Cam Ranh Bay by helicopter the next day. I went back to rejoin my unit about November 20th and three days later was medically evacuated with ma-laria to the same hospital I'd been in before.

I spent Thanksgiving in the hospital. It took several days for me to recover from the disease. My temperature was above 105, so they put me in a bed and packed me with ice and put a fan on me. That was much worse than being wounded. They follow this procedure to try to avoid brain damage. The medical staff wants to get your temperature down as quickly as they can. Oh, that was terrible torture. I rejoined my unit in early December.

Christmas Day 1967 was a hard day for me. I can remember being alone and very sad. It was tough. It's tough thinking about it now, even after all these years. Even though we were observing a holiday ceasefire, everyone was thinking about home and family.

When I went to college, I was sixty or seventy miles away from home. That's not really away from home. But when you're sitting out there on a hill by yourself on Christmas Day, it's hard.

By the end of March 1968, the Tet Offensive was well underway. On March 30, I received two gunshot wounds on my right leg. Interestingly, the first time I was shot, I was shot in my thigh, and the bullet went in one side and out the other. I can remember thinking, "I just got shot. That didn't hurt much." Then about the time I had that thought, I was shot the second time, and that was the worst pain I've ever experienced in my life. It fractured my tibia and I immediately fell to the ground.

I remember people calling for a medic. A medic came up and gave me a shot of morphine. I was on the side of a hill, and we were being shot at from a wooded area at the foot of the hill. Some of my colleagues carried me up to the top of the hill. Another guy in my unit was shot and killed. As they carried us up to the top, the pain was as severe as any I have ever experienced. It probably hurt as much as being shot. After they got me to the top of the hill somebody gave me another shot of morphine, and then they called a helicopter in that took me and the dead guy out. They gave me another shot of morphine. Soon a helicopter arrived that took me to the hospital. On the flight to the hospital I was given a third shot of morphine. To say I was intoxicated would be a gross understatement. I was high and feeling no pain. At the hospital they performed a procedure that they call debriding a wound, which is basically making a large incision and cleaning the wound. The doctors then put a cast on my leg, and a couple of days later I was shipped out to a hospital in Japan. I was on my way home, alive.

I still have vivid memories of that hospital in Japan. It was a horrible experience, but not because of the care I received. The hospital ward I was in was probably close to half the size of a football field. It was full of paraplegic and quadriplegic soldiers—kids. Arms, legs, both legs—gone. It was awful, seeing all those young people that had lost a limb or probably would never get use of one or more limbs. I was one of the very lucky ones.

The last thing I remember about Japan is that the cherry blossoms were in bloom everywhere. I could see them as I was being transported from the hospital to the airport for my flight back to the United States.

"He called: 'I was just shot.'"

Bruce and Charlotte Cole

Bruce Cole: Pretty much the whole tail end of the last ten years of my career, we've been in combat. In 2003, at the onset of the war in Iraq, I was with the 2/5 [2nd Battalion, 5th Marines]. I was a first sergeant there, and I made the initial push into Iraq. We crossed the line of departure and headed up north. I got shot like ten miles out of Baghdad, and I got evacuated.

Charlotte Cole: They let him call. He was the one who got to call me. They didn't call and say, "Your husband's been wounded." He called: "I was just shot."

Bruce Cole: They sent me back to the States. My family was in California. They were going to leave me in Maryland, at Bethesda, to convalesce. I said, "Well, why don't you just send me to the West Coast? I mean, there's lots of hospitals over there." They said, "Yeah, you've got a point," so they sent me back to California.

Charlotte Cole: Wait, let me interject something. He told them that I would take care of the wounds, without my approval. "She'll wash out those large wounds."

Bruce Cole: Which is funny, because our youngest daughter who's not here, Bailey, she was what, four years old at the time? Almost four? I had wounds that needed to be irrigated daily. Neither of these two [Charlotte or daughter Jordan] could even stand to look at me, so here's my four-year-old with saline solution and a swab and water.

Charlotte Cole: Yeah, Bailey loved it. Bailey was like, "I'll do that." She didn't care. But that's her personality.

"Nothing was safe from the sand."

Jake Melton

I went to Korea in July of '02 after basic and AIT, and in '03 I got to Fort Hood in July, and I shipped out to Kuwait in August. I definitely wanted to go overseas again, but not so fast. But it turned out to be all right. I got to Kuwait and was kind of amazed by that place. People there had so much money. You'd see goat and camel farmers or whatever living in a tent, but the tent had a couple of satellite dishes, and there'd be a Mercedes SUV parked outside the tent. It didn't make any sense. And it was August, and every day it was like 120 degrees, and humidity was like 80–85 percent. I'd be exhausted from going outside to smoke a cigarette. I'd come back in and have to rest. It was amazing, man. When I shipped over there I didn't even have an M-16, because all the M-16s were with the unit, so they shipped me over there without one.

We were in Kuwait about three weeks because there were some sandstorms blowing through there—really, really bad. Man, it was just like in the movies, just a big wall of red comin' at you, and it was crazy-looking. There'd be no wind, it'd just be real calm and still, and then the wind would pick up a little bit, and then it would just hit you and, man, it was like gettin' hit with a brick if you were standing outside. It was crazy, and nothing was safe from the sand. You could be buttoned up inside of a tent with everything sealed. You've got floors and you think you're damn near airtight, and when that comes through, sand is everywhere. It's amazing.

We drove straight up and through Baghdad. It took three days, and we stopped a couple of places on the way. I forget where. Somebody said we were close to a river delta, and it was very nice there. Still hot and humid, but a lot of fig trees and stuff like that, and the people seemed to be a lot more prosperous. One of the guys on the convoy, some Sergeant First Class, told us that we were at the Garden of Eden—the Tigris and Euphrates or some dumb crap like that. I don't know, but I thought, man, what a load of shit. There's a bunch of fig trees here, and not one damn apple tree anywhere. So maybe they got the story wrong. Maybe it was a fig tree instead of an apple tree, who knows. But I was pretty tense. Keep in mind, we still don't have M-16s.

So we're riding in the back of these cargo trucks, these deuce-and-a-half personnel carriers, and there's canvas sides, and they've got some sandbags stacked up on the inside. So if some rounds start flying you can dodge bullets behind the sandbags, but we didn't have any weapons. We took some fire a few times, but nothing too serious. We just kept driving straight through, didn't stop and address it. I think one IED hit one of the trucks, nobody seriously injured. Scared the shit out of me. That was my first one, and I was, "What was that? What was that?" And they're like, "IED," and I'm like, "Oh, you mean like roadside bombs?" and they're like, "Yeah." And I'm like, "Oh, that's not good."

Al Taji was a real big air base, and we had a small group of soldiers. There weren't massive amounts of soldiers yet, because we were still halfway through '03, but we didn't have enough personnel to secure the perimeter. So there'd be Iraqis sneaking on at night, some of them trying to set bombs or to shoot at us, most of them just trying to steal shit. They'd come on, and they wouldn't necessarily take stuff from us, but some of the stuff left over from the Iraqi air force that was there before, that we had shooed away.

They'd be walking in with mortars. It would hit way off in the distance, maybe a mile away, and you could hear the next one a little bit closer, and the next one a little bit closer. And man, it was so scary, because there's nothing you could do. There's no enemy here to fight. You couldn't attack anything. You'd just have to sit there and wait for it and at first, I think our first night there, mortars came in on us, and some dumbass who didn't know what he was doin' told us all to get up on the roof in close security. So we're halfway up to the roof and we're, "Wait a minute, why would you get up on the roof when mortars are coming in?" So there's this big argument, so we just put security around the building, and then we realized by the next day that that was stupid, too: why should we be outside? We lived in this concrete building right next to the airstrip there and anyway, it seemed fairly durable even though we'd seen buildings just like it that had been bombed out, had big huge holes in the ceiling and whatnot. But it was still better than standing outside or being in a tent, and by the third or fourth night you would just get to the point where you would take your bulletproof vest and just lay it over the top of you and go back to sleep. We'd catch one right outside the window and some shrapnel would come through the window or hit the roof or something, but that wasn't too frequent.

"We are in a real-world scenario."

Shawn Keane

As a stay-at-home spouse I also dealt often with uncertainty about where my husband was going. Sometimes Bradley didn't tell me where he was going TDY [temporary duty travel], and I would say, "Well, just come home safe, and I love you." One of the most uncertain times for everyone was after September 11, 2001. That horrible event created tension among many of those in the military and their families. At that time, we were stationed at the Malmstrom Air Force Base in Montana. On that day I was the carpool mom, so everybody hopped in the car and off we went. We got up to a friend's house to pick her up for school, but she wasn't coming out of her house. I told my daughter Melissa, "Go see where she is; she's not coming out." Melissa returned to the car and said, "[Her mom] said that she's not going to school today, because we are in a 'real-world scenario.'" I said, "What? You're in fifth grade. What does that mean, 'We are in a real-world scenario'?" My mother-in-law had just flown in from Texas the night before, and my husband had just taken leave. He was currently serving as the deputy group commander for Malmstrom Air Force Base, which was like the mayor of the base.

So, I went up to the door, and my friend was crying. She said, "Shawn, they've hit the World Trade Centers," or at least one of them at that time. I didn't know if they had hit the Pentagon at the time. Then she said, "They may be heading for the White House. I'm keeping my daughter from school today." I responded by saying, "Okay, well, I'm taking the kids to school." The school was right outside the base through a small chain-link fence, right at the end of the street. I went home after dropping the kids off so I could regroup and figure out what the heck was going on. I turned on the TV, and I'm thinking, "Okay, this is real. This isn't a movie." So, I woke my husband up, and he got up and he's going, "Whoa." Then I said, "I think I'll go get the kids, Bradley. And you maybe want to call the command post to see if you're needed for anything." No one was answering their phones, and we were in complete lockdown on the base. Many of the older kids, including my oldest daughter, were off the base at school.

I decided to walk to the school this time, because we were not allowed to move on the base. As I walked back to the school it was eerily silent, dead silence. There were no dogs barking, or birds chirping. Generally on the base there's a lot of activity, with bulldozers, airplanes, children playing. Especially children, because everyone has kids. So I walked the kids back home. Immediately, I could sense that something had changed. The reactions of everyone on base varied. Some people remained strong, or at least put up a good front, while others were panicky. Some were visibly upset with what they had just seen. The whole experience was just surreal.

The guards were at the gates in their tanks, dogs were sniffing cars, and all eyes were on the gate. There was some irony to the MPs facing the gates, because when the national anthem was playing at 4:00 p.m. they turned their backs to the gate to stand at attention and salute wherever the music was coming from or the American flag. Not that a terrorist would come through a gate anyway. I think this whole situation was confusing for many of the children. My son Brad, who was five years old at the time, asked, "Why do we have plastic bags over our signs?" We had signs in our yards that had our rank and names. "So that the terrorists won't see our names or something? Can't they just take off the plastic bags and see our names?" I was thinking—I didn't tell Brad this, because he was only in kindergarten—"These people are the kind of people that fly a 747 right down your street. They're not looking at names." The entire back side of the base was open, and terrorists would probably not be coming through a gate. They were checking our ID cards at this little guard gate by the elementary school.

I think at this point, and especially once the deployments started, people were pitching in to help each other out. My neighbor across the street was the commander of Red Horse, a mobile unit that sets up bases. His squadron was being deployed to Baghdad in the first wave, and bless his heart, he wanted to go with his men. He wasn't selected to go, but he wanted to go to lead his men and women. He left his wife and their daughter and went over to the Middle East. His wife was taking care of the homestead while he was gone. I would help her by babysitting and going over to her house to shovel snow. I shoveled snow for several neighbors whose spouses were deployed. We all did small acts of kindness like this. When you live on base there is a great support network, wives in particular, because we're all in the same boat. You also make friends really fast . . . partially because we all know we're only going to be at this assignment for such a short time.

Right after 9/11, we were at a Walmart in Montana, and my husband was in his blues. We were just getting a rotisserie chicken. The lady at the front counter said, "Sir, do you mind if I shake your hand?" He had never had anybody ask to shake his hand, not during the Cold War, and certainly not after Vietnam. In all those years, from 1967 to 2001, he had never been told, "Thank you for your service." That was a very happy moment for both of us. It was one of the positive things that I remember about 9/11. Later, when the VFW in White Settlement, Texas, had a "Welcome Home Vietnam Vets" event, including a parade, we went to celebrate with other vets. This was another milestone for my husband. It was the first time he had ever been welcomed home, after twenty-plus years of service.

"If they came in we were going to die."
William Howe Jr.

This is how the story went down, and I was there. I saw it. It happened. If you talk to guys who were on the border, it happened. A patrol unit caught fifteen people sneaking into Iraq and they had maps, they had compasses, they had weapons, they had everything. They had charting equipment. They were there from Iran to scout our bases, and we captured them. Iran sent tanks to the border and basically demanded us to turn them back over or they were going to invade. This was about a month after Obama had been inaugurated. We think they were just testing him to see how he was going to respond. He had us release them and turn them back over to them. But we were laying in our beds at night, I remember, and our platoon leader came in and said, "Hey, get out to the trucks right now and get them all ready, get .50 cals on all of them, get Mark 19s on all of them." We never used Mark 19s on them. Those are grenade launchers. There's no reason to use those. It was like, "Get Mark 19s on everything because we might have tanks," and we were in Humvees, and our nearest tank battalion was three miles away. We had an armory division, armored corps, but they could only do so much. So if we have to take this fight, we have to slow them down enough.

And we knew that if they came in we were going to die, but we knew we had to slow them down enough to get armored positions in place to be able to stop them. We had eyes on them on the border, but we gave them the people back, and they backed off, and it was very tense for a couple of days. Things could have popped off if we had kept the guys. No telling, they might have, they might not have, they might have just been bluffing. But either way, they got their guys back.

And the rules of engagement changed. Before, if someone was walking and they aimed an AK-47 at you, you could take them out. You could kill them. If someone was driving a speeding car at you and you had a blockade up, you could take them out. But the rules changed to where now we had this whole progression we had to go through: shout at them, *then* shove them, *then* shoot a warning shot, *then* shoot them. So if someone's pointing an AK at you, you have to shout at them, "Hey, put your AK down!" and hope that they're not going to pull the trigger. The progression you were supposed to follow was so crazy. We followed it as much as we could, but there were times when people made split-second decisions and you have a car coming at you at fifty-sixty miles an hour at the blockade, and your gunner is like, "Okay, I can't really shout or shove, and I can't really shoot a warning shot." He's not going to be able to hear it, so they take out the engine block. We had that happen a couple of times, and we had to make up reasons why it was absolutely necessary to do that.

It became where we were putting the lives of the terrorists ahead of the lives of the soldiers, so it turned into an us-versus-them mentality within the military. We were very strict about chain of command and authority and, although you could argue George W. Bush didn't have much military experience, at least he served in part of the military and understood it. With Obama, we knew that he didn't really understand what we were doing or what was going on. And we saw that the generals who were in war were being replaced by generals that had never deployed. We're like, okay, this is obviously from somebody that's never been here, doesn't know what we're going through. So that makes it hard to follow them, but you still have to, and then that becomes an ethical decision: Do I risk the lives of my buddies that I've been with for nine months to a year, or do I disobey an order from the commander-in-chief? You had to choose, and then you had to live with that decision.

"All four of us were in the military."

Jeffrey Waite

Three of my younger brothers followed me into the Air Force. I'm the oldest of five boys, and the brother next to me, Tim, graduated from high school, and my parents said, "You have three choices: go to college, go to work, go to the military." He said, "Well, I'm not ready to go to the military yet." So he went to work. And Mom said, "You're eighteen. If you're going to live here, you're going to pay rent. You're an adult. You gotta act like an adult." So he worked for two years, stayed at home, paid his rent.

During this time period, I was telling him how cool things were in the military at the time, and it was a good experience, and I'm meeting so many different people. It was really good at the very beginning and for the most part throughout the ten years. So Tim said, "Okay, sounds like I can do this." He got married to his high school sweetheart, and after the wedding ceremony and everyone was back at the house, small community, Mom pulls out a very large envelope and hands him all the money he had paid her over those two years of rent, to give him a boost to get things started as they head off in married bliss. So he went into the military.

While this was going on, the next one down, Rodney, was in dental school at the University at Buffalo. There's two of us in now, and he's thinking, "This might be something interesting to look into." He looked into becoming an officer and a dentist within the military and applied and got accepted. So he joined. So there was three of us in. We were all stair-step kids, two years apart. So the next brother, Barry, went into ROTC in college and liked it so much he said, "I think I'm going to continue, too." So for a very brief period of time all four of us were in the military at the same time, and all in the Air Force. Tim retired at twenty-two years. Rodney, the dentist, went into the reserves, and now he's a hospital commander and has two more years to give. Barry retired a couple years ago right at twenty years. I think we counted up, and we have like seventy-eight or seventy-nine years of total service amongst the four of us.

"I became what they needed me to be."

Jarrod McClendon

I was a combat cameraman. We would have to take pictures of different events, whether it was training or actual missions themselves, and it's not always a firefight. A lot of times we would take footage of domestic interactions. I was in Psychology Operations, and we dealt with civil affairs as well as special forces, 76th Ranger Regiment, and I think even a little bit of CAG, Combat Application Group. Fort Bragg, North Carolina is the home of the 82nd Airborne. I got there in October 2008. I built my career at Fort Bragg. You had two options there: You become a soldier, or you start the out-process. It's just whichever way you take it. I became what they needed me to be while I was there. Right before bin Laden was killed, I was gearing up to go to Pakistan with the 7th Special Forces Group, and the mission got cut the night of his death.

One of the things I would cover was actual border patrol here in Texas with the US military and drug cartels. It was a Psychology Operations thing, but we still had to talk to the people who lived in those areas to make sure that they understood: "Hey, if you're interacting with these people, it could make you an enemy as well."

I never really had a real full mission. The whole time I was on active duty, I never saw combat. I never got to deploy. I regret that a little bit, because I actually made it to the rank of sergeant. There's kind of a boys' club, where your rite of passage is your deployments. I could say I earned my stripes, literally, as a sergeant. But to others, you haven't earned the other stripes, the deployment stripes, and it feels almost as if I was black-balled to a certain extent. I think I got caught up in the construct of training. I was very influential with the younger soldiers, the junior enlisted, specialist and below, and my command took note of that and kept me at home, because I had a loud voice and I was very proactive when it came to training for other things.

I did two things before leaving Fort Bragg. I went to SERE School, which is Survive, Evade, Resist, and Escape, at Camp McCall in Special Forces. And all these other joes have to go through it to be qualified in their select fields. I went to the school before the possible deployment to Pakistan, in hopes that I'd be on the next plane. And when I came back, because I was not going to Pakistan, I started to be the instructor for the Combat Water Survival, which is the drown-proofing test you have to take before actually going into SERE School. And I ended up training 450 soldiers on that. But that was because my command felt I was better at training than I would be at deployment.

I loved the concept of being a part of leadership development, which in turn has made me successful in part here at TCU. I feel like the cadet environment has been great for me to a certain extent, because I can communicate with someone who might not completely understand what it is they're doing. Even if I don't completely get it, we can figure it out together, but we can do it positive.

"You can go any direction."

Jessica Dawson

We all join with a rate, and mine was an AT, an Avionics Technician. So I worked on plane parts, specifically radars in P-3 Orions, until those were phased out. In my entire military experience, I probably worked on radars all of three or four months. When you get to the fleet, you get pulled in so many different directions. A lot of it is kind of what you choose to do, which is kind of cool. So you do all this training for a job, but when you finally get to the fleet you can go any direction. What I ended up do-

Navy veterans Kevin Dawson and Jessica Dawson.
Courtesy of Jessica Dawson.

ing with most of my time in the military was that I was a physical trainer and an artist and a travel agent. There's a name for it, but it's pretty much a travel agent. But most of the time I was a physical trainer.

I never quite mastered the position like my mentor, Smile, as much as I tried to be just like him. He was so good at getting in touch with people and listening to them and hearing their needs and actually helping them on more than a physical level, actually helping them with their lives. You can't help but get close to the people you're training, because you see their struggle. Every month we would weigh them in and measure them and get their body fat percentage and watch them progress. For those who had a harder time progressing it was really emotional, traumatic, because you see how hard they're working. And you know that, for some of them, it's their last chance. It was really traumatic, because they were about to get kicked out. And whether they'd been in for nineteen years and were about to retire or they'd just joined, it didn't matter. They were going to lose their retirement benefits and get kicked out. It had nothing to do with their merit as a sailor or anything. They just couldn't stay within the Navy fitness standards.

Me and another artist made a mural for the command, which went in the command stairwell. And after that I had a bunch of little projects here and there. I promoted little clubs with posters. Even though it wasn't a huge part, I was constantly working on those things in the background while doing everything else. There was never a point that I wasn't doing art while in the Navy. As much as I loved doing the art and feeling I was valued in that way, it kind of hurt me in other aspects of the Navy. Like when people see you doing art, they view you as not doing your job. It was like, "Oh, she's out there painting. She's not here doing her job." I tried to do it in my spare time, and most of the time I would come in after work. But when people did see me painting, it looked really bad to them. Like they thought I was just lazy: "She's not doing what she joined the military to do." Even though working on plane parts isn't really anybody's passion, you know? I joined for a lot of reasons, but none of them were that I wanted to work on plane parts.

So the art that I found fun also made me look—I don't want to say made me look bad, but to the people who weren't pursuing the things that brought them fulfillment, they sort of looked down on it. And I can kind of understand that. So my favorite part was the Fitness Enhancement Program because I felt useful, like I was actually making a difference, and I felt trusted.

Anyway, Smile came to me and said, "Hey, here's an opportunity. You should take it." So I was like, "Okay, I will," and so I did. And the position was DTS, which is Defense Travel Systems. Basically you plan the travel of people going to school or overseas or on little professional Navy-related things that they had to do. I made sure they were getting paid, that their flights were arranged, and that they had rental cars and hotels. I was basically their travel agent. Everybody who went anywhere who was still a part of our command, I planned their travel and made sure that they were taken care of.

I had a romanticized view of the military, and my parents, who were both Air Force, didn't really do anything to dispute it. When I got to Jacksonville and got in the fleet, I felt like a lot of the leadership liked that I tried. I got a lot of respect from the leadership and people like Smile who were above me and tried to promote me and put me in competitions for sailor awards and things like that. But my peers, I don't know if it was competitiveness or something, but the hard thing was finding the balance between doing really well but also making friends. I did make friends, but it was kind of hard.

The hardest part was finding out that the Navy wasn't full of adults, that there were no adults, that "adults" don't exist. I just expected everybody to be perfect, but I wasn't perfect either. I was extremely not perfect at all. The Navy was just a bunch of kids doing the best they could. So I sort of grew up in the Navy. That was the hardest thing: that it wasn't this romanticized image that we all have of it before joining, these crisp uniforms with perfect military bearing. Just finding out that, yeah, they're really just regular people, just in uniforms.

"I really loved being at sea."
Elyana Ramirez

I realized I really loved being at sea. Like, the way the ship rocks back and forth in the ocean. I love the constant, I really like the structure. Even though some days were kinda like *Groundhog Day*: you wake up the same time every day, you do the same things, you eat the same shit, and when I say shit, I mean beef stew from a can. Eggs made from, like, crystals? You just add water and it's egg. It's disgusting. Stale bread. Every once in a while you'd get maybe some fresh fruit or an avocado. That's if you were lucky!

"I got to do everything that I wanted to do."
Bruce Cole

I had so many great adventures. Like I said, I got to do everything that I wanted to do. I was a high-altitude parachutist, an oxygen diver, a combatant diver, a scout sniper, an infantryman, a rifleman, a machine gunner, a mortarman. Everything that started with an 03 over the last thirty years, I got to participate in that.

There's basically two types of military divers. You have combatant divers, and you have salvage divers. Salvage divers go down. They find stuff or they fix stuff. A combatant diver is just a means of insertion to get someplace. They call them oxygen divers, because we dive a rig that's an oxygen rebreather. You breathe pure oxygen, and it's a closed circuit so there's no bubbles that come out. It's a bit dangerous because oxygen becomes toxic under pressure, so you really can't go very deep. You've got a max depth of less than thirty feet. Clandestine insertions into a benign water, like a harbor or something like that. The Draeger gives you the capability of staying under water in excess of a couple hours, whereas with the SCUBA, if you're really disciplined with your breathing you might get forty-five minutes.

"The Air Force shaped me."

Megan Morris

For the first week of basic training I cried. It was terrible. I actually went to the TI and told him I was thinking of committing suicide, to get out of basic training. I really wasn't; I just knew that would get me out of basic training. He was like, "Just give me one more week, and if you still feel like this, then we can let you go." But during that next week I decided I really liked it there, and I was kind of getting used to it and decided to stay. So training was really hard, but at the same time I have some of the best memories there because I was in one barrack, full of forty-eight women, and we did everything together. It was fun and really rough, but overall I enjoyed it.

Coach Gary Patterson and Air Force veteran Megan Morris.
Courtesy of Megan Morris.

In tech school I developed strep throat. No biggie, I took the meds and got better. I got to my first duty station and, about six months after that battle with strep throat, I started developing these really weird symptoms where I would wake up in the morning and be exhausted. I would go to work and be sitting there at lunch, looking at my coworkers in the break room, just feeling like I'm going to fall asleep out of nowhere. But the rest of them are wide awake and I'm just sitting there thinking, "Why am I so exhausted at noon, when everyone else is okay?" I would drink Red Bulls and Monsters and do thermogenics every day just to stay awake. When I would get home from work, I would crash for three hours, wake up, eat dinner, go back to sleep for twelve more hours, and wake up and do it all over again. I complained for years, like, "I'm exhausted, I don't know what's going on." And they said, "Oh, it's your bedtime hygiene. Don't watch TV, don't be on your cell phone, get a new pillow," whatever. Tried everything.

When I got to Alaska I told them, "I'm not getting good sleep. You've got to do something." So they did a sleep study and found out that I had narcolepsy, which was brought on by an autoimmune response I developed when I contracted strep throat in tech school. I was in the middle of honor guard, and they told me narcolepsy is one of those things you cannot have in the military: "We're gonna kick you out." I was devastated. Fortunately they were able to keep me in because we were able to control my symptoms with medication, but two years down the road the medication was ineffective. My symptoms were so bad that while I was cleaning people's teeth I was falling asleep. I wouldn't trust myself. So they ended up "med-boarding" me—if you're medically unfit to serve, they either separate you or retire you from service. So in August of 2015 they started my med-board, and by April of 2016 I was out of the Air Force. I didn't plan on getting out, but because I had this condition that will never go away, I couldn't deploy, I couldn't handle weapons, I wasn't able to work around sharp instruments. So pretty much my whole point of being in the military was gone.

When my ten-year anniversary passed, I was reminded of how incredibly unique my journey was and how much the Air Force shaped me into the person I am today.

"At high temperatures, aluminum would burn."

Jake Melton

I had three [concussions], fairly close together, of different severities. The first one was moderately severe. We were riding in the back of a Bradley, and we were on this Quick Reaction Force, and this QRF would respond to enemy fire, would respond to IEDs on passing convoys going down the highway, going to Kuwait or coming back from Kuwait. If they got attacked, they would phone it to us. They would keep moving and we would respond to the attackers, and a lot of times the insurgents were pretty smart. They would figure out what we were doing and how we would respond to stuff, and then they would attack the responders. It wasn't strange to see them just shoot a couple of rounds at passing trucks just to watch us come off post, see what our SOPs were, and then the next time they'd be ready for that because they knew how we were going to respond. There was eight or ten 115mm artillery rounds buried in the sand, and we drove right over the top of it. The first one went off; they were daisy-chained together, so they set each other off, and it goes in a circle, and we were pretty much in the middle of that circle in the Bradley. The Bradley was supposed to be bulletproofed, which it pretty much was. We had taken some rounds and nothing ever penetrated. You could see the holes on the outside, but not on the inside.

However, it was dense aluminum, supposed to be a hardened aluminum, and unfortunately at high temperatures, aluminum would burn. So those first three IEDs, when they blew the 165mm artillery shells, they caught the front right portion of the Bradley on fire, and there was a driver and the truck commander uptop, hanging out of a hatch. The truck commander has a .50 cal or a 240 Bravo machine gun, and the driver just drives, but their heads are sticking out. So this goes off, and they really threw the Bradley. It lifted the front end up, and I don't know what my head hit or something hit my head, man, I was fuzzy. I didn't know what was going on. I heard a lot of screaming coming from the front of the Bradley. It started to fill up with smoke, got hot in there real quick. It was already hot in there, but in the back there's me, Nick, two other guys, Hispanic dudes, and Sergeant Alvarado. He's this black dude who would kinda respect us, he seemed pretty hardcore, he talked a good game. There's a lot of screaming going on after the explosion, smoke and whatnot, and then the hatch on the back where we could all file off the ramp, and I didn't know what was going on. I was still fuzzy about the whole thing, and Nick kinda just grabbed me by the handle of my bullet-proof vest and carried my ass off.

We get about 100–150 meters away from the vehicle. Alvarado's with us, the two Hispanic dudes are with us, the driver and the TC never got out. They were in their compartments, in the TC and driver compartments, and that's where the IEDs went off, and they never made it out. Man, we were 100–150 meters away, and aluminum burns hot, and it was almost too close for us to stand. And it was fuckin' terrible, because you could hear them screaming. And it's like, "Man, how are they still alive?" And you couldn't go anywhere near it. There's no way to get anywhere near that Bradley. And it didn't take too long, the screamin' stopped, but I remember later in the same day pullin' guard outside the TOC, Tactical Operation Center, and the wrecker brings the Bradley in. It was burnt to a crisp, and the two dead guys are still in the fuckin' Bradley, and they parked it right next to the TOC and we had to pull guard on the damn thing. Pretty insensitive, I think, but it took them a day or two to get the bodies out. Pretty shitty.

My concussion was severe enough that, sitting on my bunk the next day, Nick was talking to me about going to eat at the DFAC and I just couldn't understand what the hell he was saying. I knew he was saying words, but I couldn't put 'em together into a cohesive sentence. It just didn't make sense to me, so it was fairly bad. It took like a week.

"It's how you get around the wall that matters."
Michelle Johnson

In the Navy, the word "striking" means applying for a job. And I wanted to stop being a non-designated seaman and get a rate, a job. So I put in a special request chit. I love the Navy terms, especially the term "request chit." It's about this size piece of paper. It's a Navy thing. At the top of it you write your name, then you write "Service Member." You refer to yourself in the third person and call yourself "Service Member." You say, "Service Member respectfully requests permission to strike for . . ." whatever job you want to do. So, I wanted to do cryptology, to go to language school at the Defense Language Institute in Monterey and learn a language. I had taken the DLAB test, and I wanted to work in the intel unit on base here at Carswell. I made my request, filled out my

Army veteran Michelle Johnson with her dog, Poe.
Courtesy of Michelle Johnson.

application packet, this forty-five-page-long application that goes all the way back to before kindergarten. It's all about you. And all your friends and where they are and all about them. And where are they now, and what they do, and if they did anything wrong. They go all the way into your life. I had done all of that.

And while I was waiting for the results of my request, I still reported for duty one weekend a month for drill. And I was studying all the IT manuals and taking the online correspondence courses, preparing to promote. Part of the promotion process includes taking the rate exam. I had a Leading Petty Officer who would always send me away on "special tasks" whenever the time arrived for me to take my rate exam. Eventually the Navy started reviewing all its sailors, how long had they been in the Navy thus far, and how far had they progressed in their careers. I hadn't gone any farther in my career than from when I first started. I was still helping in Manpower and Finance. And the military has a general rule, that if a service member has not progressed past a certain point after being in the military for a certain amount of time, he or she can be administratively separated for failing to progress. And I had gotten to that point in my career, because I had been in the Navy two and a half years and was in the same position as when I first enlisted. A lot of my shipmates had already been promoted and moved on to their new jobs, their real jobs. One day, after hearing that yet another rate exam had occurred while I was elsewhere, I asked my supervisor, "What's going on?" And he said, "Well, you missed your rate exam." And my response to him was, "But you sent me to the Skipper's office to help decorate and do stuff." And his response was, "Don't worry about it. It'll come up next time." But he'd been in the Navy almost twenty-something years already. He knew the drill. He was just messing with my life. So I started thinking about going to another branch.

One of my jobs included picking up mail. One drill weekend, while picking up mail in the mailroom, this wonderful man, that I hope is still alive, Lieutenant Commander Bracy, a Navy officer, passed by me and said, "Hey, how are you doing?" And I said, "I'm doing all right." I didn't sound convincing. He asked if I was having a good day or something, and I said, "No." And then he asked me why. Most officers don't talk to the junior enlisted people, because they're officers. But for some reason, Commander Bracy talked to me like I'm talking to you two ladies. And it scared me, because I was taught in Navy boot camp that you're not even supposed to look at them. But he was so friendly and genuinely open, and genuinely kind, and he asked me why I was having a bad day. And I told him what I just told y'all. And he said, "What! Let me see what I can do." Now, in the Navy, when anybody with that kind of power says, "Let me see what I can do," that's the best phrase you ever want to hear. And when they pull out their cell phone, you know something nice is getting ready to happen.

He contacted a friend of his, Master Chief Bonds, who just happened to be coming down the stairs near the mailroom. They were good friends. Lieutenant Commander Bracy told his friend about what had happened to me regarding my career. He was just as displeased and said, "How dare they treat a sailor like this! This is not how you treat sailors." All I did was just stand there listening. You know? Kinda like when you know you don't know anything, and you know you have no power, so you just stand there respectfully, waiting on permission to be acknowledged, like a child. And then they both looked at me and said, "What do you wanna do, Johnson?" And I told them what I wanted to do. I said, "This is what I wanna do. I've been studying, and I've been working really hard." And Commander Bracy said to me, "A brick wall is always gonna be a brick wall. It's how you get around the wall that matters." And that has stuck with me all these years. To know that, no matter what obstacles come up, the obstacle's always gonna be there. It's just how you get through it. Or what can you do to make it go away? The wall's not gonna move. Can you climb the wall? Can you blow the wall up? Can you go around the wall? What can you do to still get what you need? That stuck with me. I'm so glad I met him.

And that motivated me to start looking. I went to the Air Force first, to see if they were taking any prior service people. They were not. And right next door were the Marines. And I said, "No!" Because the Marines and the Navy are sisters. We saw the Marines training all the time at Carswell. I had a firsthand look at how Marines act and thought to myself, "No, I don't wanna go that deep. It ain't that serious." So I went to the Army and talked to a recruiter, SSG Jones. He took me to Dallas MEPS, I did the process and became a soldier.

"You're just driving in madness."

Jason Mendoza

I also got to deploy to Afghanistan, and that was an interesting place. Kandahar, specifically. Basically what I did there was what we do stateside but just a little bit different, you know, people trying to kill you. Regularly we would have to watch out for IEDs, which are improvised explosive devices. The other thing is small arms fire. A lot of times we're driving and they're shooting at us. Basically show of force. We are the guys you see on the ground, rolling through, patrolling the streets.

Let me set a picture for you. People look at Afghanistan and they're like, "Oh, it's a desert, there's nothing out there." No, these are bustling cities. Kandahar is a massive city, and it's full of vehicles and cars, with no laws whatsoever. So you're just driving in madness. We specifically were there, in the heart of Kandahar. Let me backtrack a little bit. ANPs are Afghan National Police. And basically we taught them how to police themselves. We would take these guys, train them, and teach them how to police their own people. And we would patrol with them and tell them, "Look, this is how you do it. This is how you conduct law enforcement in your city." Then we would oversee them, and make sure they're doing their jobs. If there's anything they needed to change, we would tell them that. They would say, "Well, you know, you all say do this, but we think this." So we worked in conjunction with them. But, basically, just a show of force.

"You have no idea what's out there."
Elyana Ramirez

They sent us up to the Black Sea, because Russia had just bombed the crap out of a small country called Georgia. Because Georgia wanted to join NATO, they didn't want to stay under Russia's rule. So they blew up their entire coast guard. It's a small country anyway. So we went up there to kind of support them. We anchored out off the coast and this whole time that we were up in the Black Sea, we're the only US ship up there. And the Russians have these communications ships and submarines following us. And we can't do anything. We're just there, sitting ducks, watching them while they watch us.

So we anchor out off the coast because we can't pull in because of all the ships that are down and sunk off the harbor. And everybody has to stand on watch, everybody has to monitor something. They put us outside in the middle of the night, with like a .50-cal machine gun, an M-16, a 9 mil, and you just have to walk around the top of the ship, for like five hours, to make sure that nothing goes down. The thing is, we have lights on the ship and we're anchored, and you can't see anything out there past those lights. It was terrifying. You have no idea what's out there. The other ship could be sitting forty feet off from us and we wouldn't be able to see it. I'm sure the other people, deep down in the insides of the ship in our combat information center, were monitoring that stuff, because every time you turned on the radio, you can pick up those frequencies, and that's how we can tell what kind of ship is what, by the type of frequencies it puts in the water. That was pretty terrifying, but luckily nothing happened to us, and we just kind of hung out for a couple days. We went in and did some community relations projects, like we sodded a soccer field for a school that had been kind of bombed up and stuff. And we spent

Thanksgiving out there, so we didn't pull in any ports or anything, we just spent it on the ship.

And then we came back down from the Black Sea into the Mediterranean. We also went to Bulgaria. That was kind of cool. I mean, who goes to Bulgaria? We went to Ukraine and then Turkey, and then we came back home.

Another time we had to go back into the Mediterranean, and this is when they were looking for Gaddafi's son, so it's kind of like a repeat from 1984 when NATO was looking for Gaddafi himself. But now we were looking for his son, and he was in Libya. So we come out of the straits and head north out of the Red Sea. Right there in Egypt there was a lot of unrest at the time as well, and when you go through the Straits of Hormuz, they're literally just lined up and down with the guys with their M-16s or whatever machine guns they have, and they're just standing there in the sand dunes, and you're just standing there manning your gun. And it takes us maybe four or five hours to get through there, just trying to keep the peace and move on through. So we go to the Mediterranean and get all kinds of permissions to start monitoring closer and closer, we finally get the order, and we ended up like blowing the shit out of Libya. There was us, one other ship, and two submarines out there, and NATO gave us permission to fire on them. So we sent off like a total of fifty-five Tomahawk missiles into Tripoli. You would've thought it was a Fourth of July party, because everyone that didn't have anything to do with like combat and stuff like that, they opened up their lawn chairs, they opened up the little ship store. You could go buy basic essentials, snacks, Monsters, all the bad stuff that you really don't need. "Ship store having a sale, come on through!" People would be lining up outside, so we'd have a countdown, and every time we shot off a Tomahawk they'd just be like, "Yeah!" You know? Cheering, "Fuck yeah, USA!" It was pretty funny stuff.

"We had all kinds of things going on."

Martin Ruch

Martin Ruch was interviewed by his granddaughter, Rebecca Ruch.

I went to a state university, and the state universities were required to provide two years of military training to all the men. So when I went up to register at the University of Illinois, the agricultural side, which was my major study, had the program pretty well laid out, and we got those courses in a breeze. Then the counselor said, "Now, you gotta do one more thing. You gotta go over to the armory and sign up for ROTC." And I said, "What's that?" Well, then he explained to me what the program was.

And I said, "Well, do I have any options?" Because I had uncles who had been in the Army, and I didn't like their stories. So he said, "Well, they do have a Navy program over there. You can go up to the professor of naval science, and see if they have a slot." Well, they didn't have, but I convinced 'em that maybe they should get me in, so they did. I was one over their quota. And I was probably the only one, out of the class of '53, who stayed in for thirty years.

Navy veteran Martin Ruch.
Courtesy of Rebecca Ruch.

I did the first four years in the Navy, because I had to. It wasn't a two-year program when I signed up for it. It was a four-year program. Commissioned as an ensign. And then went to a destroyer out in Pearl Harbor. It was actually the destroyer escort, the USS *Whitehurst.* Our deployments were to the western Pacific, which included Japan, Hong Kong, and Korea. I had two years on the *Whitehurst,* and then I was rotated to sea duty staff. I think I did a year on staff duty. And then was picked as XO of a Landing Ship Tank in Pearl Harbor, the USS *Stark County.* I think I put that LST on the beach more than a lot of people did during wartime. After two years on the LST I got into Sub School and went from reserve to regular Navy. Six months of Sub School in New London, Connecticut, and then I went to my first submarine, the *Sea Poacher,* down in Key West.

Q: *Had you met Grandma before this?*

Yeah, we got married in '55, while I was back here in San Diego on a training, six-week period. We met as part of my recreation program, 'cause I was a folk and square dancer. Had been for a couple of years in Illinois before I graduated, and then I continued, wherever there were folk dance or square dance programs. We met in Balboa Park. We probably met in '53, and then we met up again in '54, and I had two weeks of school before Christmas, and four weeks of school after Christmas. When school was out on the eleventh of February, we got married that evening, and then went up to San Francisco to be transported back to Hawaii. Transportation in those days was a little different than it is now, because a plane flight across the Pacific was anywhere from eight to fourteen hours, just out to Pearl Harbor.

Q: *What made you decide to go into Sub School then, after you'd been on the destroyers and the LST?*

Well, essentially, I didn't like riding rough water very much. And there was the pay bonus, which wasn't much in those days, but it is considerable now. It was only fifty dollars. And the quality of the recruits on subs was considerably better than those that came onto the destroyers. So we had less disciplinary problems, and then we also had a little better food allowance on the subs. We got an extra dollar and a half, or dollar-eighty, a day to feed the troops, over what the destroyers got.

Q: *You went down to Key West and were stationed at a sub base then?*

Yeah, they had a sub base at Key West in those days. And there was a shipyard in Charleston, and then we had other submarines up in Norfolk, Virginia, and New London, Connecticut. But I chose Key West because it was the warmer clime, and they had one of the GUPPYs that was down there, just finishing up an overhaul. I was the supply officer for a little while. He's the guy who handles all the logistics of getting the food, the supplies, the spare parts, and all that kind of stuff onboard. I moved on through several positions in submarines and was soon the operations officer, because I was a pretty senior guy.

Our deployments in Key West were either to the North Atlantic or to the Mediterranean. I much prefer the Mediterranean. After Key West I went to the Navy Yard in Brooklyn, to take over a reserve training center. After that I came to San Diego as the executive officer of the *Redfish*. The submarines here in San Diego then were in a transition period. They were trying to establish a submarine base out at Ballast Point, but we were anchored out in the bay and operated from a support tender that provided us with food, repairs, and spares. We were here for two years, and then I went to Washington, DC, for a tour, as operations officer of the Naval Oceanographic Office. It's a big organization. We had all kinds of things going there, hurricane hunters, research ships, ocean mapping ships charting the ocean floors, trying to find the peaks and valleys and what have you. After that I was scheduled to come back here for command of a submarine, but an officer had failed out of survival school, so they tapped me to take his position and go to Vietnam. So I was a year late getting my command while I served a year in Vietnam.

I was stationed in Saigon on the staff of Naval Forces Vietnam, the operations officer and primary contact for the coastal surveillance forces, which consisted of Destroyers, LSTs, Squadrons of P2Vs, and then we also liaisoned that with the coastal patrol boats, PCFs. We had everything from the shoreline outward. Anything inside of that was riverine patrol. And that was to prevent the infiltration of enemy forces from North Vietnam into South Vietnam.

Actually it was a rather boring assignment. There aren't any particular highlights from there that are important. We lost a number of shipmates out of the office. Their plane got shot down. And we had some investigations to do as to the cause of the accident and civilian casualties. We were there in the build-up period. I visited all five of the provinces either by boat, plane, or ship. Got to fly a couple or three times to the Philippines, to brief incoming P2V squadrons and their crews. Really not much there, just day-to-day, count the numbers, figure out what was going on. What's the tide? What's the moonlight? What's the likely infiltration point? Where's the likely origin? Where are they coming from? A lot of time just looking at maps, plotting all the contacts that we'd had, and drawing conclusions from that list of what was going on.

Q: Was it hard being away from Grandma and your children during this time?

Well, yeah. You forget about that. There were times when we didn't communicate for months in the early days. Later on we had a lot more communication capabilities, so it was easier to get messages in and out.

Q: How did your deployments to the North Atlantic and Mediterranean compare to the one in Vietnam?

Well, the deployments to the Mediterranean and North Atlantic were not in a hostile environment. Vietnam was a hostile environment, so you had to be much more alert. And they don't exaggerate at all when they say that the Viet Cong hired ten-year-old kids to take a bike and park it by a recreation facility, and then they sometimes blow the bike up before the kid can get away from it. So you watch for all kinds of things like that, that do happen, and hope that you're not there. And when you see something odd like that, you start moving to get away from it.

After Vietnam I took command of the submarine USS *Raton* for two years. You can't have better duty than being in command. I was Executive Officer and Commanding Officer of the submarine base at Pearl Harbor for four years. That was a really good tour! We returned to San Diego for four years as Executive Officer of Fleet Training Center. Then I served two years on the Sub-Board of Inspection and Survey San Diego, then two years in Washington, DC, on the Navy Personnel Review Board for the Secretary of the Navy, and finally retirement.

All in all, I loved my active duty years. True, they were sometimes hard on the family. I believe that I have lived through the best one-third of this country's life. That makes me sad. The core values of love of family, love of country, and love of God keep me going.

"You have to make time for your spouse."
Carl Castillo

After boot camp, what surprised me most? That I wanted more. The structure was something that I enjoyed. Maybe not the micromanagement aspect of it, but having to find goals and points I needed to reach, because everything is structured in a very accomplishable way.

When I came back to Fort Worth, actually it was Dallas, Garland actually, I became a recruiter, not the most glamorous of jobs. But the Marine Corps said, "You're going to do it." Do I get a chance to object? No, you don't. Okay, well, I'm going to do it. And recruiting is really hell. It's really one of those jobs that you make it what you want of it, but for the most part it's really a shitty job. It's just hard. It's back-breaking. It can enhance your career, but it can definitely destroy it.

It was the middle of the week. As a recruiter, you put in an excessive amount of time, to the point that sometimes recruiting consumes you. It is, other than being deployed, one of the worst, worst jobs for Marines, especially married Marines. When you're deployed, the Marine is going to be gone in say Iraq, or Afghanistan, or wherever the heck the Marine

Corps is going, for six or eight months. So the only communication you have with your spouse is giving them a call, writing them letters, or pictures, postcards, whatever. As a recruiter you wake up, and you're at the office, and you come back from the office.

Usually, that whole time, my days started at 6:00 a.m. I would go on a run, and I would come back to my apartment, shower about seven o'clock, work, then come back, then go to lunch and do all the normal things you do during the day. I usually wouldn't get back to my apartment until nine, ten p.m. I would have to come home, shower, sleep, wake up and repeat, day in and day out. That was pretty much the life of a recruiter, at least a recruiter that wanted to be successful. They were always pushing themselves, always trying to find somebody who wanted to be in the Marine Corps. So imagine that now with somebody who has a spouse. Most married Marines, their families basically become roommates, because they are never there. You have to actually actively make time for your spouse, and some Marines can't. But point is, you put in a lot of hours. I was beat. My typical day started at 6:00, basically running off six or seven hours of sleep at the most if I was lucky. Usually, it was around five.

One day, I was just sitting there waiting on my guy to complete his testing, and the sergeant major, which is our highest enlisted rank, came to me and saw me just sitting there and was like, "Castillo!" And I was like, "Yes, Sergeant Major." And he goes, "What are you doing?" And I was like, "Aw, I'm just sitting here waiting." And he goes, "You look tired." I'm like, "Aw, it's been a busy week already, Sergeant Major." And he was like, "You're tired. Why are you tired?" And I'm like, "Oh well, Sergeant Major, just having a long day, you know, long week, you know, long few weeks." And he stops me and goes, "You want to know something, Castillo?" And I'm like, "What's that, Sergeant Major?"

And at the time I was like, "Shit. What the fuck did I just get myself into?" I was already thinking of ways to get out, maybe my phone is going off, maybe I need to take a call, something. Actually, he made it kind of short and simple, and I was kinda glad I actually went down this route with him. He was like, "You wanna know something?" And I'm like, "What's that?" And he goes, "I've been in the Marine Corps for like twenty-five years, and I've never worked a day in my life." I looked at him, and I'm like, "Fucking liar." There's no way. If he does half the stuff I'm doing, he has to work. But, then he put it into perspective and was like, "I've never worked a day in my life, because if I'm having fun, I can't consider it work." When I heard that, I was just like, "Shit makes sense." Sorry. I cuss a lot. I tend to do that just randomly. I have actually been trying to curb my cussing speaking to y'all. But he told me that, and it made sense. It truly made sense. After that I started looking for ways to make it fun, because that was the only way to survive.

"It was surreal."

Chad Lackovic

I'd only known this female for ten or eleven months, and I made the brilliant decision to get married. Which a lot of troops do, thinking that if I do get taken out, at least someone will enjoy my SGLI [life insurance policy]. We got married in December, went to Fort Hood in January, and right before we shipped out to Kuwait, she said she's pregnant, and I was just floored. I didn't want that. It was definitely an accident, and I tell my son that, just to give him a hard time. Around the time she was due, I requested to go home, and initially they told me no. My company commander said no, the battalion commander said no. I don't know if it ever went up to higher levels than that, but they told me to go talk to the chaplain. I was really mad, and the chaplain eventually got it to where I came home for two weeks for my son's birth.

Army veteran Chad Lackovic.
Courtesy of Chad Lackovic.

It was surreal. I finally got to see news about what was going on, and it's hard to explain, just looking at it from a different perspective. It was painful to watch, because I knew my guys were over there, and I felt guilty that I was home and they were still there, but it was really important for me to see my son born, and we didn't do a whole lot. I stayed mostly at home when we got back from the hospital. I didn't want to go out anywhere, but when we did, it's just like business as usual. It kind of pissed me off to see civilians going about their daily lives and troops getting killed every day, and it wasn't even like the opening of the news broadcast. It was pretty shameful.

"For her it's been harder than for me."

Michael Blackert

It was rough, man. The first five years of our marriage, I was gone forty-two months. Three of those years were to Iraq. And then training. We would have to do certifications. We would be gone for months, six weeks at a time doing training, basically acting like we were deployed. We wouldn't contact one another or anything. My wife even told me if I had gotten a fourth deployment, she said, "I don't know if I can do this anymore." And I didn't blame her, because our whole relationship was built on great communication. Skype came along on my third deployment, so we were able to Skype a little bit. Internet connection wasn't all that great, but we communicated through phone calls. Our phone calls were all recorded, so if we said certain things, they would cut the phones on us. Or if individuals got hurt or killed, we would lose all communication to the outside world. For the first month I wrote letters and stuff like that, but it was rough, man. For both of us. I think the thing that made it positive for us was our communication skills. We can talk about just about anything now.

We are still married, but where it hurt us was we were just a newly married couple, and you're still kinda establishing all your couple stuff. So it was pretty rough, like I said. What I've noticed in the military is that the ones that divorce or things happen are the couples that got together after they were in. My wife knew what we were getting involved with. We knew I was deploying. It was just a matter of how many times and when. But I think for her it's been harder than for me, because I was always the one to be able to pick up the phone over there. She just had to wait by the phone for those three years, and even during those training exercises. We had people getting killed in training exercises before we deployed.

She probably would have rather me chosen a different job, instead of combat. But I wanted to see the front lines. I wanted to see the people. I wanted to see how we impacted them and how they impacted us. And they offered me a great signup bonus. We were dating then, and that kind of money can start a couple, and I knew I was going to ask her to marry me if she stayed with me after basic, so that would have helped me purchase a ring.

"Being a gay man in the military was a struggle."

Jeffrey Waite

I spent ten years in. I came out when I was in Montgomery. Being a gay man in the military was a very major struggle, because at that time it wasn't allowed, and I was developing my self-realization while I was in the military, and it was challenging to mask that. When I left Scott and went to Maxwell, I said, "I am going to be who I am. I'm not going to hide anymore. There's no reason for this, except from a military standpoint."

There was an underground segment of society, you might say, at the base, where friends would introduce you to other friends and you would just meet for dinners or whatever but very quietly and secretly. It was just crazy that there was this major secret life going on and the OSI—Office of Special Investigations—would monitor where vehicles were parked, if they were at a gay bar. We had stickers on our bumpers that are assigned, that told everybody that we were military. And they would be down there, and they would be writing down things. So you got onto a list. You were on this hit list. During my ten years there was opportunity, unfortunately, where I had to do discharge paperwork on other people. And it was other gay servicemen and women. It was just so contrary to how I felt.

So I finally decided I could do better than my boss. I finished my degree, I can't do any more time. I can't live looking over my shoulder anymore. So I went in to my commander and said, "I'm not reenlisting." And he said, "You're an excellent troop, but I understand." We've had informal but revealing conversations, but he knew. What a relief it was, that sense of relief of you can be who you are without somebody trying to get you, throw you in jail, and discharge you.

"I will always remember that day."

Joe Vera

My first deployment was to Afghanistan in November 2006. My deployment to Afghanistan was not long. We conducted missions to try to help the people build a better community, but learned quickly that the people were either too afraid to talk with us or did not want our help.

I will never forget the day I first saw action in Afghanistan, two weeks into my deployment. It was a routine patrol. We were going to a small village to talk to the locals, and I was driving the lead truck in a four-truck convoy. In my Humvee I had my squad leader, SSG Brown, SPC Romaskin (gunner), CPL Jackson (dismount), and SPC Sullivan (SAW gunner). We usually rolled out together in the same truck, and always on point in every patrol. It had snowed, and the roads were slushy. The roads were empty, and no one was out looking at us. Usually people will come outside and just stand and look at soldiers as they drive by their houses, but this time they didn't.

The only person in my truck who had deployed before was SSG Brown, an Army Ranger. My unit was new and full of new soldiers fresh from boot camp. As I continued down the road we were going to make a left and head towards a village. I missed the turn, and my squad leader said to make the next left turn. That was a mistake that I will always remember and live with. As I made the left turn my truck went into a pothole, and the next thing I remember was feeling a concussion and seeing the front windshield turn black. My truck had hit a pressure plate improvised explosive device. My buddy in the truck behind us told me later that our truck flew up in the air and all four wheels left the ground. My squad leader, SSG Brown, was thrown from the vehicle and landed outside the truck, but his left leg was still inside the truck when it came back down. The armored door had slammed on his leg. We medevacked him out, and I learned later that they had had to amputate his leg. He was never the same again, and we hardly talked after that. Throughout the rest of the deployment we did little but count the time until we went home, in February 2007.

"You have to believe in what you're doing."

Rodney Baker

I am an HVAC technician, and I maintain and treat the water heating and cooling systems on [TCU] campus. Basically, every building you're in is either heated or cooled with water. I maintain the water chemistry to limit corrosion and disease, and maintain the health of personnel in the buildings. My Navy experience got me the position. In the Navy I was what you call a machinist mate. I worked in the engineering department and was tasked with maintaining the engineering propulsion equipment, heating/cooling equipment, electric power generators, and the distilling plants to make the drinking water on board ship. Not only did we make the water, we had to test and treat it and maintain the quality in order to maintain the ship, as well as make sure we didn't get anybody sick.

In 1984, we took the *Dubuque* from San Diego and changed the home port to Sasebo, Japan. I'm something of a history buff. That's the Navy base where the radio message was sent to the Japanese fleet to bomb Pearl Harbor. I lived in Sasebo for four years. The *Dubuque* was a Marine transport, so our duty was to go throughout the western Pacific, pick up Marines, and take them to Mount Fuji or Korea for exercises. Basically a Marine Corps shuttle service. I stayed on the *Dubuque* from '84 to 1988, and during that time I made E-5, and I also qualified engineering officer of the watch for the very first time. As an E-5, I was qualified to supervise an entire engineering operation.

In 1988 I was up for shore duty for the first time, so I transferred from the USS *Dubuque* to shore duty as a Navy recruiter in Atlanta, Georgia. In Atlanta I was pretty successful as a recruiter. You have to believe in what you're doing. I believed in the product that the Navy was selling, and what it did for me. I recruited everybody. My motto was "butts on the bus." I had southwest Columbus, Georgia. We had Baker High School, which is right outside of Fort Benning, Georgia. I also had Spencer High School. They were both predominantly black schools. We had Kendrick, which was fifty-fifty, and then I had several rural area schools, which, depending on the county it was located in, could be predominantly white, could be predominantly black. And I recruited them all, and I put kids in from all over. It didn't matter to me. Butts on the bus.

Finished recruiting in Atlanta. I was married then, and we took orders to Guam. My son was born in Guam; I served on two ships out of

Guam. My son will tell you he's Guamanian. He was actually born at the Naval hospital in Guam. We've had a really, really great life, and it was partly because of the military. As a child I used to read and dream, but the money wasn't going to be there for me to travel to the Philippines or Hong Kong. So how was I going to get there? I had to make a decision as a young man, and the military gave me the opportunity. So that's what I did.

Guam, like I was telling you, I served on two ships. The *San Jose* was a store ship. We supplied other ships and did what we called underway replenishments. If you see those old movies, again, where ships pull up alongside each other and shoot lines across and send cargo back and forth, I was the senior enlisted machinist mate for that division. By this time, I had made first class. I had about ten guys who worked for me. We operated all the hydraulic equipment, all the elevators and refrigeration systems. And again, the Navy sent me to school and trained me how to do this. What happened with the *San Jose* is it got decommissioned. So since I had only been on Guam eight months, I couldn't automatically transfer back to the States, so I had to take another ship that was there in Guam, a submarine repair tender. But the basic principles of hydraulics are the same. You exert force on an object; it's going to be exerted equally in all the areas. That's hydraulics. So I started working on the sub repair. We left Guam in '97.

"You can hear the ocean."

Elyana Ramirez

So my job as a sonar technician is to put sound in the water. The submarines navigate using sound, so you put sound in the water, like you ping, and it bounces off something, and it comes back and tells you how far away that is. It gives you a range. The only bad thing is that when you put sound in the water and it comes back, it gives away your exact location. So typically you just listen in the water, like you're just passive in the water, instead of putting the sound in the water. There's different frequencies for different things. One of them is to navigate through a minefield. When you do this, though, the ship has to go a certain speed, and sonar is all the way at the very front of the ship and three decks down. So when you go through a minefield, if you were to hit one, you would be the first one to go. So they said, "If you ever see a sonar tech run, you might want to run too." It's the only kind of funny joke we ever had.

We were typically just made fun of like we were stepchildren, because no one uses torpedoes anymore, it's all about missiles and stuff you can drop from a plane. But we had to get the ship close enough so that we could shoot from the ship onto land. You had to go a certain speed, and it was the most terrifying thing we'd ever had to do, because you're three decks below and there's no windows, it's just metal and then ocean, and you can hear the ocean; it's not that thick. It's maybe a couple inches between you, the hull of the ship, and the ocean. So here we are, navigating through this minefield, and everything we do is based on what we tell them. Like, "Turn the ship this many degrees to port or starboard." Somehow we made it through and blew up Libya some more, but I don't think anybody breathed, just kind of held our breaths, you know? Like, any little like thud or anything. Oh, we were so on edge. It was just terrifying, you know?

"You had to look good in a uniform."

Rey Soto

James Dever happened to be in town and he's like, "Let me get with 1st Marines." So he called, and I was one of the people that got selected, and we went in and did one scene. After that, they took pictures of us.

This was for [the television show] *Heroes*. They called us and took some pictures and asked some questions. And it was me and another Marine that got called back. And he wasn't able to, because he was getting ready for deployment. I was the only one that was there, so they're like, "Hey, would you be willing to go out again?" And I was like, "As long as it's cool with the command." And I went out there, and just the fact that I was able to communicate well with the guys, and I guess we looked good in our uniforms, and stuff like that. So they weren't sending pork chop Marines out there to represent the unit. You had to look good in a uniform and represent the unit well. My sergeant major and the gunnery sergeant loved the fact that I was out there representing the unit. So they called me out there for the second one and it just happened that I was in ten episodes, I believe.

I was out there from when I first started, three or four hours, to doing like golden time, sixteen hours. You want to get to golden time. It's time and a half after eight hours, and then after sixteen hours, or maybe fourteen hours, you get double pay plus an extra $200 or something like that. And mind you, food is free, drinks are free on set, everything is there. Of course we're not eating as well as the stars, but we're eating really good. I got invited to do a couple pilots for some military shows, and I eventually got to the point where I was one of James's head guys that was kickin' in doors or having to do stuff, because you start building relationships. So it was cool, I liked it a lot.

I actually got to work with Ali Larter. She's anemic, so there was only a few of us that got to work with her, because we had to pick her up a certain way or else she'd bruise real easy and stuff like that. So that was pretty neat. That's a different pay bracket. We get residuals now. I did everything because I was in my last year in the Marine Corps so I was like, I think I could do this for a long time. I was actually thinking about it. But it's not stable. I mean, it's stable for a few months and you're getting paid really well, but at the same time, when you're not working, you're not working. It's all based on your boss. When he gets the gig, he has his budget, and the film has the budget for military advisers, and it goes from there. You want to be one of those top guys. They called me for *Iron Man 3* and *Battle: Los Angeles*. My boss, James Dever, did *Chappie* and *American Sniper*. Now he's getting to where he's getting a lot of big-name films. His company is called 1 FORCE Entertainment. He's the first guy that you see on *Battle: Los Angeles*. Just watch a trailer. He's the guy that they show, older-looking guy, an Italian guy. He's probably about 6' 5". He's a big guy.

"The world is bigger than us."

Rodney Baker

Q: *Of all the places you went in the Navy, what's your favorite place?*

I would have to say Japan. I like the Japanese culture. I like how they respect their elders. I like the tranquility of their society; there's a certain harmony to it. As far as food, I love Mexican food. But the one thing the Navy did for me is I can adapt to any situation, because we travel. We could pull out of port on a Monday. On Friday we could be in Hong Kong. We could leave Hong Kong the following Tuesday, and by the next Saturday, we could be in Australia. You could leave Australia, and then a week and a half later, you could be in India. Along the way you learn phrases, you learn culture.

And I think one of the things all military people learn, that I think our society fails to realize, is that the world is bigger than us. Sometimes we as Americans think the world revolves around us, and in so many aspects it does, but there's a whole world out there not even thinking about us, because there's people trying to survive, trying to make a living, trying to take care of their families. We have to learn to respect that, and I think a lot of military guys learn to respect other cultures. I lived in Japan for four years. So I had neighbors in Japan that invited me over, I invited over, and that cultural exchange. I learned to enjoy *lumpia,* which is basically a Filipino egg roll. And at the same time in Guam, I can eat calamari made Kelaguen-style, which is raw with mixed peppers, onion, and lemon juice, along with Finadene sauce. So you learn to adapt.

"Every day was a good day with a dog."
Brad Murphey

After basic training I went to the Security Police Academy. It was a combined school with the Marine Corps and the Air Force at the time. From there I got selected for the Department of Defense Military Working Dog Program, to become a dog handler.

The best police partner is a dog, because they're loyal. You ain't gotta worry about them lying to you; they're always going to be there for you. But I started off in patrol. A patrol dog is a dog that attacks and bites and holds, and they can also do searches for lost children and suspects. From there they sent me to a new school and I learned how to do narcotics. I learned how to work a dog that could find narcotics, and I did that for a few years, then they sent me back to school to learn how to look for explosives. Wasn't something that we did on a daily basis, look for bombs, but we train a lot. And I was assigned a couple times to the Secret Service, and the protection of President Bush and Vice President Quayle.

I had a German shepherd, and his name was Teddy. He had a really bad disposition, sorta like me. And he was an explosive detector dog. So he found bombs. And he's the one I traveled with the couple times I went out with the Secret Service. Every day was a good day with a dog. I did lose a dog to cancer, and I guess that's not a good story, but it was always good. I always had fun with my dog.

I have a couple of funny stories. One was I actually lost my dog. I was out in the field and they would send the dog handlers out by themselves, and we'd be on what we'd call LPOP, it's Listening Post/Observation Post, just looking for bad guys. It's during an exercise and I'm out in the middle of the German forest, and I'm scared anyhow because I don't know what kind of animals they have out there, I'm not sure if I'm gonna get attacked by a boar or a bear, or what. I'm unfamiliar with German. And I have a dog named Volt, and he's a long-haired shepherd, jet black. And he's about thirteen years old by the time I get him, and it's my first time in the field. And he was always sleeping. I mean, he was just old, and his time was just about up, and he was always sleeping.

Well, I heard some bad guys comin', well, what I thought was bad guys. It turned out they were inspectors and they were coming around trying to find people, and they would quiz us on the spot about our orders and stuff, like what we were doing, who we are. Well, I didn't feel like taking Volt all the way over there to where they were at, 'cause he's sleepin', so I just tied his leash to a tree, and I took off and I talked to the inspectors. They asked me the questions and I answered, and they said, "All right, have a good night, airman," and I said, "All right." Well, they leave, and it's the middle of the night. And it's dark in the forest in the daytime anyhow. I mean, it is unbelievably dark in the forest. So I turn around, and I'm going, "I don't know where my dog's at." And it took me twenty minutes to get back to him. I would take a few steps and listen. And I finally followed the snoring back to him.

Unfortunately Volt passed away, and I got a new dog. Her name was Sheba, and she was sort of a mix coon-hound-type mutt dog. And she was a bite dog, a patrol dog. And every night on patrol we'd have to go to different places to make sure they were locked up for the night. And we had a quality control department in our squadron. They would put these sticky notes on doors that were like way far away, that a lot of people wouldn't go check. They'd say, "Yeah, the building's secure," and just pencil with their paperwork. Well, they put these little sticky notes there, so I was always afraid I wouldn't turn in one of those sticky notes at the end of the shift, and I'd get in trouble. So I'm going around this radar site, and I'm trying to get to this door. And my dog, she just stops. And I said, "Come on," and she won't budge. Oh, I get mad and I jerk the leash and I said, "Come on!" And I fall face down into concertina wire. Concertina wire, it's like barbed wire, but it's razor blades. It's the stuff you see on top of prison fences. And I had to call for help to get cut out of that thing. Yup, so that was embarrassing. So what I learned in that, always trust your dog. She could see it. I couldn't.

"I was completely unprepared to do what I wound up doing."

Leo Munson

The service grew me up. I was completely unprepared to do what I wound up doing, at the emotional maturity level. After I had made my intentions known to get out of the service, we had under investigation an airman. We thought he was one of the major suppliers of drugs into the base. We had all kinds of intelligence that said he was the guy, but we could never develop a criminal case. I'm the officer, a twenty-three-year-old officer, who worked with a grizzled chief master sergeant, who had seen it all. One day he said, "Leo, we're going to call the airman in and interview him." I said, "Based on what?" He said, "We have nothing, so what have we got to lose? Call him in." First thing I know, the airman is confessing. Bottom line was he gave us his source of marijuana. He was involved in about everything near as we can tell, except for heroin. Pills, amphetamines, marijuana. He told us that this large truck was coming in, carrying four hundred pounds of weed. And if we would help him get out of the service, he would give us everything.

Well, we had to go to command, and command said if in fact his story holds up, yeah, we will transfer him out and work to get him out of the service. He bought it. We called the police department and told them what was going on. They came and interviewed with us. All the while, both of us were thinking this is far too easy. This guy is pulling our leg. So the time comes, and we couldn't participate in the bust because of jurisdiction. The deal was that the airman would go into the house, dressed in jeans, looking like a college student with short hair. He's wearing a black cowboy hat and was like, "If I come out and take the hat off, there's drugs in the house." So it's about eight o'clock at night, and my chief master sergeant and I are sitting probably a block and a half away, but the street was lit up enough we could see when he went in and when he came out. And he came out and he pulled his hat off, and we saw the police descend on the house. I mean, this is stuff you see on TV! Next thing we know is a whole bunch of people coming out with their hands over their heads. So we got out of the car and went in.

Well, inside this house was a pickup truck, literally a pickup truck was inside the house, with about a third of its bed empty, with the rest of it filled with marijuana. And I don't even remember how much money, twenty or thirty thousand dollars in cash. So, here's all this cash, here's all this weed, and my chief master sergeant and I look at each other and think, "You've got to be kidding me." *[laughs]* It turned out that at that time that was the largest drug bust by the Air Force in the continental United States. So I held a record *[laughs]*.

But it gets even more amazing than that. The dealers didn't know who had rolled on them, had no idea, and went to court, and the deal was the airman would testify, and we would have him on a transport plane to an Air Force base in the US. We had a transport standing by. After the testimony we took him from the courthouse, back out to the base, put him on the airplane, and saw the airplane take off. I get a call about two o'clock in the morning. "Leo, this is Special Agent Such-and-such. Uh, where is your prisoner?" They couldn't find him. To this day I don't know what happened to him. Truly, I believe he realized his life was in danger, because we did find out that a price was actually on his head, and somehow he managed to hide in that airplane and disappear *[laughs]*. That's my conclusion, but this was in June and I was discharging in September, and all of us had prices on our heads, and it's like, "Where is this guy?" Never heard. Never found him. At least while I was in.

"I was one of the guys that shook the rope."

Rodney Baker

I missed Thailand by three days. It was a typhoon, and we couldn't pull into port. Typhoons, storms, they try to get the ships out to sea because they're safer out in the ocean than getting beat up on the pier. One of the biggest things that I was a part of, the USS *Dubuque* failed to pick up Vietnamese refugees in the South China Sea, and some died and [some] resorted to cannibalism. June of '88. We had left to go be the support ship for the minesweeper operations in the Persian Gulf, because we were trying to keep the channels in the Persian Gulf open during the Iran-Iraq war. We were Saddam Hussein's ally back then. So en route to take over this command platform, we came across some Vietnamese refugees who had been out to sea. The captain at the time was Alexander Balian, who was court martialed for his actions.

This is public record. I'm not disclosing anything that's not in the public record. Basically, what transpired is we came across the ship. There were actually three ships in the battle group, but he was the senior officer, so he told us we should stay off. He took the lead and determined that their vessel was seaworthy, through an interpretation failure. They say he made the wrong decision. And we just gave them some food and some charts and sent them on their way and would not bring them on board, when actually our transit to the Persian Gulf would have taken us right through the Malaccan Straits, near Malaysia and Singapore. And we had a helicopter on board where we could have flown them off if we had taken them on. We could've left them off in Malaysia. But instead we left them in the middle of the ocean, and we went on our way, and they were stranded for an additional two weeks, and that's when some people died. They resorted to cannibalism, and it came back to bite us. One of the chiefs that I served with, Chief Bill Cloonan, has a video online describing the captain. The captain was a very hard man. He was one of those guys.

That was one of the most unusual situations for me while I was on active duty, and to this day I think about it. We lowered the boat in the water. We stayed back out of the way. One of them dove into the water to try to climb one of the ropes to get up on the ship. We were directed to shake him off the rope and not let him up on board, and that person actually drowned right there alongside the ship. I was one of the guys that shook the rope. Did what I was supposed to do. It was the right thing to do as far as not just letting people come up on the ship, but it was the wrong thing to do not to provide proper assistance. That guy didn't have to jump into the water. So that was the decision he made. But us not providing proper care and service for these people was a decision our captain made, and we all have to live with that.

"I made sure things got done."

Gabe Merigian

I was playing football and bouncing around from college to college, chasing scholarships because my dad had lost his job. I was trying to get up to a full ride so I could afford school. I ended up getting injured and losing the scholarship I was promised. That loss hit me hard, and I decided to change things up. This was 2010, and one of my best friends (also named Gabe) was experiencing the same kind of situation. I told him I was thinking of joining the Navy SEALs. He told me that if you don't make it in the SEALs you're going to end up being a seaman, but if you don't make it in MARSOC (Marine Special Operations Command) you'll still be a Marine, and that's better than being a seaman. Hard logic to argue with.

Me and one other guy from comm school ended up at the Pentagon. It was a difficult duty station because it came with a lot of stress, politics, and there was a serious issue of depression rampant in the barracks. For one thing, it was the absolute opposite of what I joined for initially. Although it has been attacked and there is constantly some form of espionage happening in the building, it's also the opposite of the front lines. My job involved communications (IT, cyber security, etc.), so I would constantly see videos or info intel about Marines down range, and I was tantalized every day by the thought of getting out there. I didn't have the opportunity to do what I joined to do and, although the work was important, I didn't feel like I was able to help Marines in combat, and that frustrated me. When I joined I didn't even know there was a Marine Corps base out in DC or Virginia other than Quantico. One big reason I joined was to go out to Japan or California and never see snow again. I grew up in southeastern Michigan, so I was pretty much done with winter, and they put me back on the East Coast with pretty much the worst weather in the United States.

I also didn't really care for the medium I was working with. I didn't know what a hard drive was before I joined the military. I was a jock, and I was smart, but I didn't know anything about technology other than an iPhone. I had issues with some of my initial superiors, and for a year and a half it felt like an extremely hostile working environment, a lot of backstabbing and people gunning for each other. I got a break when we got a new master sergeant and staff sergeant. Those guys really took care of me! They quickly realized that if they let me go out and do my thing fixing issues in my own way, I did really well. I'm more of an independent thinker, and I ended up getting really connected to all the different offices, to the point where my office realized I was a big asset. After a while, if we needed something from a different office, it became, "Just ask Merigian and he'll go up and get the hookup." So that's what I found out was my strength. I was really good socially, I was technically savvy enough to get something done, but the main thing that enhanced my role with the people was that I made sure things got done. In DC there is a lot of just shoving issues off to someone else or giving the classic "That's not my job." I hated that attitude.

"You just couldn't make a mistake."

Mark Wassenich

I went to Denver, to the Air Intelligence Training Center. I was called in by the colonel near my graduation and he said, "First of all, you're being upgraded to a regular officer. And second, I've got two sets of orders for you. One is to go to Germany. The other is, because I'm short of training officers here and because you're first in the class and because you got a degree in geography, I can keep you here as an instructor." And Denver's darn good duty. But I called my fiancée, who was a senior here at the time. I said, "Linda, what do you want? Do you want to go to Germany or do you want to go to Denver?" And she said, "Let's go to Germany." She loves Europe. So we went to Germany, and we were there for nearly three and a half years. Unbroken duty, never came home. It was a front line, nuclear attack fighter base, about a hundred miles from the Iron Curtain. The United States had three bases there, very close together and all just alike. We were set up to throw the first nukes in case the Soviets attacked Western Europe. So we were on alert twenty-four hours a day, seven days a week, forever. We kept a certain number of aircraft on instant alert. I was one of the intelligence officers there supporting that unit.

If I had stayed at the intelligence school, I would have gone to Vietnam for sure. Instead we were right in the middle of Western Europe and thirty miles from the French, Luxembourg, and Belgium borders. So on the three-day weekend we could go to Brussels, Amsterdam, Paris, Frankfurt, Zurich. We saw essentially all of Western Europe in the three and a half years. And Linda got to go to the Holy Land. I was supposed to go with her, but there was an emergency in Czechoslovakia in 1968, so I had to stay on alert. I went down into the bunker for those few days instead of going to Jerusalem.

I don't think I ever relaxed in the whole three years. I was always edgy. The nuclear work had to be perfect, and human beings are not perfect. We make dumb mistakes. We'll add two plus two equals four, two plus two equals four, two plus two equals four, 120 times. Then we'll add two plus two equals six. That's just the way human beings are. So the service, to its credit, had all kinds of safeguards built in to double-check everything related to nuclear war. In most cases there were three and four levels of checking going on. Everything you did, somebody else was doing it with you or just after you or just before you.

And then there were all kinds of spot checks or tests. The most famous was the ORI: Operational Readiness Inspection. They were very
intense and nerve-wracking, because if any critical part of this very
complicated system broke down, then the whole wing failed. If we got a
digit wrong in the target number, then we would be attacking the wrong
target. If we didn't have enough fuel to get the airplane to the target and
back, if we had a route that was over bad territory, if there were map
pages missing in the pilot's packet that he would take to fly the mission—
if any of those things were wrong, then the entire wing would flunk because one mission was wrong. And then we had to carry code words
around in plastic cases. We rarely trained with real code words, but used
exercise ORI code words which would not allow a nuclear weapon to
get armed and off the ground. We were always armed, two officers or
NCOs carrying a code word or a group of code words down to the flight
line so the weapons officers could arm the weapons and the pilot could
see it. Then the pilot would know that he was released to take off with
a real, live nuclear weapon. Carrying those code words around, if they
were cracked, if it was the wrong code system—and there were several of
them—if anybody messed up anywhere along that line—BAM, failure.

There was a concept in the Air Force, it was very important, called
zero defects. It applied primarily to the mechanics and the people who
worked on the flight line, but it was equally important to those of us
in operations: the pilots flying the planes and those of us planning the
missions. You just couldn't make a mistake. A "broken arrow" means a
nuclear weapon with a malfunction. Whenever there was a broken arrow, the word would just informally get all the way across the base in a
few minutes. They didn't ring an alarm or anything. It was just really the
technicians and weapons officers who had to deal with it. But if anything
untoward happened to a weapon it was all hands on deck, fixing it. And
if it didn't get fixed in fifteen minutes, then a report had to go up to
headquarters, and another report when they got it fixed saying what was
wrong. I think we had half a dozen broken arrows in the three years, only
one of which was really serious. Most of them were minor, like technicians trying to hook a weapon on the wing of the airplane and they didn't
get both the hooks fastened, and clunk, one end of the bomb would fall
down and hit the ground. So you dented the fin, okay. You take the fin
off, put a new fin on, and hook it back up. It's no big deal. But that would
be a broken arrow.

Nobody below three stripes could open a nuclear weapon to do maintenance. One time there was this three-striper, senior airman, and this sergeant. One guy did the work, and the second guy had to watch it and log the work. And they both had to sign the maintenance log. So, I don't know what they were doing, but they opened the hatch #2 or whatever, and one of them reached in and tightened the screw that needed tightening. And they wrote down, "Tightened the screw," and they put the lid back on and wrote, "Secured lid on #2," and they both signed it. And then the next ORI happened; the headquarters inspectors were going around opening up nuclear weapons to check them. They found this screwdriver lying inside the weapon. This was serious. They cashiered the airman and the sergeant, and demoted the officer in charge for leaving a screwdriver inside a nuclear weapon. The officer wasn't at the scene, but he was the supervisor. That is the sort of pressure in which we worked.

"You think about what could happen."

Felicia Lawson

I deployed four times in the first four years. With my first command I was in an aviation command, it's called a squadron. We were attached to a group of squadrons called an air wing that went to a specific ship to go out with the ship, because the aircraft carriers had the planes on them, of course. I was on the USS *Ronald Reagan,* and we went out for the first four deployments, which was awesome. We were mainly deployed to the Gulf. It's called a WESTPAC, and you go around to specific countries, and you stop on your way, but you spend about three months of it in the Gulf launching, doing flight ops, protecting troops on the ground. It was fun. I enjoyed it. It was hot, though.

In the Navy you work some variation of twelve hours on, twelve off. Not a lot of down time because during that twelve hours off you want to sleep, eat, shower. And then we do a lot of distance learning, if you want to go to college while you're on the ship. Sometimes they fly professors out there, but that doesn't always work with your work schedule. And they proctor exams and all that fun stuff. I did a lot of my humanities distance learning on deployment, which is really easy and breaks up the monotony of the deployment, 'cause you get out there and you know you have six months, and somebody immediately starts a countdown, the first day. And you're like, "Oh no!" So you have to get into a routine.

In the Navy we do a thing on the ship called mass casualty drill. The whole ship's ops stop for a day, and they hand you a piece of paper, and different people are doing different things. You get hired basically as an actor for the day, and I got hired as a dead person. So I got to ride down on an airplane elevator 'cause technically I was one of the people that got killed on the flight deck, so they put me on one of those little wired gurneys that you see in the old Army movies. I'm on the elevator with thirty other people, and they take us down to the hangar bay level, and then they tell you, "Get up, because nobody's carrying you into the hangar bay," and you get up and you lay down in your gurney on the hangar bay floor and the chaplain came by. And he started talking to me. I'm dead, but he's talking to me, and he's like, "So this is the point in time where I would find out your religious beliefs, whatever they are, Baptist, Catholic, Protestant, Muslim, anything. We would find that out, identify the bodies, and then I would say a blessing over you, and I would write a note to your parents telling them how you died or 'I'm so sorry for your loss.'" I was like, "Wow," because when you go out you don't think about it. You're in the Navy.

I went in during the war after 9/11, after the USS *Cole* had been hit. You don't think about the gravity of the situation, you don't think we could really be bombed. We're not protected out here, even though we're in an air wing on a ship in a carrier group, and there's other ships that are designed to take that hit before you. But then you have to think about how you lost other sailors, other brothers and sisters in the military. It just brings it back so you understand that this is serious, you're not just playing, this is real life. You could potentially die in the military. And like I said, I had never lost anybody and we didn't have anybody lose any limbs or anything.

Sometimes things happen, like we had a pilot hit the back end of the ship. His tailhook hit it and dented it when he was landing, so he was coming onto the aircraft carrier like this, but his tailhook hit the thing that catches him and lets them stay on the ship when they come back. The tailhook didn't catch the resting wire until the third wire. They have three wires set up; he caught the third wire. His plane split in two. The front half, that he was in, went into the ocean over the side, and the back half actually stayed on deck and stayed in that spot where he caught the wire. So we got him out of the water, he was fine, but you think about that stuff. You think about what could happen. Flight ops hadn't ended, so we still had jets with engines on this side of the aircraft carrier. Had that plane veered into that area we would have had a literal mass casualty, and jets would have been blown up all over the deck.

"I did some fun stuff I would pay to do now."
Jeff Coffer

You learn a lot in a short time. You meet people. The military complements the university experience, because you meet lots of people from very diverse backgrounds. That's one of the biggest things you notice in the military. Starting when I was an undergraduate, I went to summer training in Fort Bragg, North Carolina, and in later years saw some rather unglamorous (but still rather picturesque) places: Fort McClellan, Alabama; Fort McCoy, Wisconsin; Camp Grayling, Michigan. You typically don't send postcards to Mom and Dad from those places.

Every lieutenant is assigned a branch of the Army based on degree and experience. I had a degree in chemistry, so I went to the Chemical Corps. The Chemical Corps doesn't really do that much chemistry, to tell you the truth. Their primary mission is using smoke generators to create smoke for the battlefield for the infantry or armor units. Very exciting stuff. The second thing you do is decontamination. When chemical weapons are deployed, who do you think is coming to clean it up? The Chemical Corps. That was probably the most intense part. You undergo something called live agent training. It was a multimillion-dollar facility built to practice handling real chemical weapons that had been exposed to various pieces of equipment, and you have to go in and clean it up. The alarms are going off, you've got on full protective gear, and you're sweating.

However, I did some fun stuff that I would actually pay to do now. Repelling off of rock quarries and things like that. I wasn't good at it—I hurt myself—but it was still fun. I had never driven a tank; I got to drive a tank. I have a military driver's license. I've never had to use it, of course. I think what was the most fun was one day where we did the so-called "slide for life." You crawl out over a rope between two trees and drop forty feet into a river. Yes, I would definitely pay to do that stuff now.

"That could've been anybody's kid."

Tami Tovar

My most memorable experience in the lab was being left by myself on a Sunday, which seemed like such a quiet wonderful day to be working, and then I got this blood sample from a sixteen-year-old girl whose dad had brought her in with flu symptoms. After checking her blood under the microscope, I'm like, "Something is really wrong here." I went to my shift supervisor, who said it was no big deal. That supervisor had been a lab tech for a lot longer. I did not know at the time that he had no experience in the hematology part, which is what I was doing.

And basically I called the nurse and said, "Look, she has too many of certain types of cells." It was just fate that this nurse was a moonlighting nurse, who happened to be an oncology nurse. And within hours this girl was life-flighted to a children's hospital and getting a bone marrow transplant, because she would have died. She had a rare and acute leukemia that had sudden onset, and she would have died in days. It was so traumatizing that I could not even talk about it for six months without crying, because I was like, "Oh my God, that could've been anybody's kid!" Any one of our kids. We all had kids.

"We were basically out there naked."

Chad Lackovic

I was military police. The border town between Iraq and Kuwait is called Safwan, and it was the main route between Kuwait and Iraq. Our mission was to secure that town and secure the MSR, which is Main Supply Route, and to keep it free. It wasn't a very big town, but the road went right through it, and you couldn't go around it, apparently because of the river, the Euphrates. We would just stretch out along the highway and make sure the roadway was clear and keep all the Iraqi civilians back. Once it started, it got scary because no one wore uniforms anymore. So you didn't know if they were good, bad, or whatever, so it was pretty intense. Such huge crowds gathered around. And nothing bad happened to me or my people in that town, which is a miracle, because the crowds would just gather and keep coming closer, and we had no idea what would happen next. And since we were a reserve company, we did not have armored Humvees. We did not have armor for our flak vests, so we were basically out there naked. We had weapons, but it's a miracle that we didn't get blown up. Crowd control was hard. There were so few of us. I don't know how one little platoon out of a company got tasked with this mission, but the rest of our people went and did another mission and secured an airfield or something. We were attached to the 101st Airborne. It was scary.

There weren't a lot of men. There were tons of females, tons of kids, and they were rolling nonstop vehicles through the town. Some of the truck drivers would throw out water, candy, and crap like that, and plenty of people got squashed in that town. Just stupid. They'd just run out in the road. These idiots would throw stuff out with crowds on the side, and it's like a parade, with people lining the streets. The kids probably never seen a candy bar, and they would run out. It was ugly. The women wore the full burqa, only their eyes showing. We heard rumors that they'd come up with bombs strapped to them. Nothing happened to us, though. Then there were times where we could have gunned civilians down easily and been justified in it, but we didn't. We did that mission for a while, and then we eventually went to convoy escorts. That was pretty dangerous, because there was just three vehicles, with three MPs each, escorting a hundred tanker trucks full of fuel or whatever. It was scary. Some trucks got hit, and it was like an amazing fireball.

The first six months over there was crazy. We were right near where that whole Jessica Lynch thing happened. We were probably a mile from where their unit got attacked and she was taken hostage. After we secured the town and were doing escorts, we took over this base called Nasiriyah. It was an old Iraqi base, and we were there for the majority of the rest of the war.

Our mission was to secure the base and the entire outer perimeter. There was a fence around the entire air base, and a little road around it, and we would ride out in the desert all around the little base. But the Air Force was tasked with securing the inner perimeter, so there was a road around the fence on the inside, and they set up trip flares. And once every twelve hours they had to come out of the gate and do a lap around the road on the outside, and we messed with them so bad. We'd put stuff in the road and we'd make MRE bombs, and for some reason they drove with the back hatch of the Humvees up, so we'd make MRE bombs and throw them in the hatch. They'd be driving, and it takes twenty seconds to go off, and we'd put something in the road and they'd stop and they'd take off and BOOM! That was awesome. We'd have the big water bottles like this, and an MRE has the heater element, and you take it out and put it in there, and then you put water in it and it expands. Sometimes we'd put Tabasco in there, just to add a little flavor. We had fun over there. It wasn't all bad. There's camels everywhere.

"I will always remember that day."

Joe Vera

I got back to the States, and my unit told us that we would be training hard and gearing up for our next deployment to Iraq. We deployed to Iraq in November 2007. A lot of people on my next deployment were about to get out of the Army, but this was around the time of the Stop Loss. I had many friends who were Stop Lossed, and some even made it all the way home and then got called back to my unit for our deployment to Iraq. One of my good friends, Sgt. Austin Pratt, was one of those. He was called back and, like a good soldier, he did not hide or fight it. He simply went back to work. Less than a month into our deployment to Iraq, Sgt. Austin Pratt died from friendly fire. He was an honorable man who always did the right thing. He will always be remembered and never forgotten.

During this deployment I had no idea what was about to happen or how much adversity I would face. I did not know that I would go forty-five days without showering, nor that I would sometimes go without eating either, because I was on patrol for hours on end or food was scarce. My company was charged with patrolling an area that was pretty brutal, relatively close to Sadr City. Sadr City was built during Saddam's era as a ghetto, or so I was told. To me it was not a ghetto city, and in fact it was one of the best-kept neighborhoods in Baghdad, mostly due to a man named Muqtada al-Sadr. This guy was religiously and politically very influential, and it was his militia that we fought daily. We learned quickly that this enemy was not to be overlooked. We experienced numerous firefights, bombings, sniper attacks, IEDs, and EFPs [explosively formed penetrators].

An explosively formed projectile was something new to us: The enemy created a new roadside bomb that penetrated our armor like butter. We came into contact with many EFPs and saw how deadly they could be. It got so bad that primary roads that we used were declared black status, meaning they could not be used because of EFPs on the roads. I remember seeing a convoy on a route that had been deemed black status. The unit was not ours, and it soon learned that it was in the wrong neighborhood. It had about six vehicles, some of them tanks. They got hit with about ten EFPs, one after the other. I saw this from our outpost's rooftop. I felt bad for them.

My next encounter with the enemy came in February 2008. I was sitting on gate guard of our little outpost, along with a gunner manning the machine gun. Sitting in a Humvee, we were the only thing preventing people from driving into our compound. When friendly units arrived, I would move the Humvee. On this day I was sitting in the Humvee and SPC Chantland was manning the machine gun, and I heard him say, "Oh shit, get down, get down." I screamed back at him, "What's going on?" And then, with no options and nowhere to go, I just leaned over with my hands above my head thinking, "Please, God, don't let me die." Then I heard what sounded like a roaring train and felt the bombs hit. The bombs were so powerful that they rocked the six-ton vehicle from side to side with ease. Several bombs had been launched at us from a truck parked about three hundred yards away. They landed in a circle around the Humvee, and not one of them actually hit it.

After everything settled, I got out and looked at the front of the truck. Less than ten feet away was a rocket that had not detonated. In fact, there were two rockets that didn't detonate. Each of them had made a hole in the ground about as wide as a Humvee and about three feet deep. The concussion of those rockets shattered every window in our building and somehow set the building on fire. We were lucky that no one got hurt, but I will always remember that day.

"He was like a fifteen-year-old."

Elyana Ramirez

Being in charge of a division of twelve junior sailors, I learned some ways to manage people: how to work with them, how to lead them, and how to get shit done, because essentially that's the whole purpose. I had this one kid, who was actually not a kid, he was a grown-ass man, he was probably like a year younger than me, but he loved to play video games. He's got a PSP, he's got a Nintendo DS, he's got an Xbox, and he takes all this stuff with him when we deploy. But our maintenance schedule is, like, down to the minute. So you have to ask permission: "Can I take this equipment down, offline, where it doesn't work?" And they're like, "Yes, you have permission, you have three hours to get it done." If you don't do it, then you miss an opportunity, and you just make everybody look like shit. His name was Seaman Johnson. Well, he was probably a petty officer by then. But Johnson needed to get his shit done, and he never did.

He would come down and he would bring his PSP, or he would bring his little mini DVD player, because this was right before the iPad, he'd bring this shit with him, or he'd bring a book, and I'd be like, "Johnson, you can't play that on watch. You've got to take it with you, you've got to keep it in your pocket." And he never would. He would never get his work done, he'd always be tired because he'd stay up all night playing video games. He was like a fucking fifteen-year-old. It was awful. You always had to remind him, like, "Go take a shower, Johnson. Did you change your fucking clothes? Did you remember to get the laundry bag? Did you remember that you have to clean berthing today?" It was like he was a fucking child.

And I was like, "Johnson, how do I get you to do your work?" "Uh, I don't know, just remind me." "Um, I remind you all day long. I'm not going to come find you." It got to the point where I did have to go find him, I did have to go pull him out of his rack, like, "Hey, Johnson, I know you're sleeping." They have little curtains on your rack. I'd rip them and say, "Johnson, what are you doing?!" "What are you doing down here, Ramirez? Uh!!" I'd be like, "Johnson, get out of your rack, go get this shit done, they're waiting for you to get this done, you've only got two hours." "I don't have the materials!" "Well, that's not my problem. Just fucking find a way to get this shit done."

It was constant, and then I'd get shit because something wasn't done. So I was like, "Johnson. I'm not going to yell at you. I need you to tell me how do I get you to get your work done." "Uh, I don't know." I'm like, all right. So I put this boy, this man, actually, this grown-ass man, at parade rest, which is where you stand up with your feet like shoulder width apart and your hands behind your back. You're not allowed to talk when you're at parade rest, and I'm like, "You're going to stand there at parade rest in the hallway, and when you figure out how we can get you to get your work done, you can come tell me." He stood there for like two hours, bawling his eyes out, making sniffling noises and everything, and I'd walk by and I'd be like, "Johnson. What have you got for me?" "I'm suh-suh-suh-sorry!" I'm like, "You shit. I want to know how we're going to un-fuck this." Our chiefs would walk by, everyone just cracking jokes, and he's standing there bawling his eyes out. I don't even know what solution he came to. Basically it's hazing, but I don't care, because I needed him to get it done. It was just a constant battle with him, just like a mom would be with her kid.

"Being an enlisted man is like being a servant."

Jim Lee

I did not love being in the Navy. It was not one of my favorite things. I was at first a seaman recruit, then a seaman apprentice, then a seaman, then a third-class radar man, then a second-class radar man. I was an enlisted man. In the Navy, being an enlisted man is like being a servant somewhere, because the officer class treats you as an inferior. You may be smarter than the officer you're working for. When I began as the head radar man, we would get these young men that came in from the Naval Academy, and they didn't know anything. We would teach them what they needed to know about radar operation. Within a month, they acted like they had always known this and you didn't. I think that's what I disliked most about the Navy.

They wanted me to re-up, as they used to say, to reenlist. If I reenlisted I could pretty soon become a chief petty officer, then after years I could retire with $138 a month. I wasn't about to do any of that. I did not want to be in the Navy. There were moments: I would never have seen Treasure Island in San Francisco Bay, I would never have seen Honolulu, I would never have seen Mount Fuji. But if I had to do it all over again, I wouldn't. I don't know what I'd do.

When I first went aboard that ship, I was a deckhand. They are always chipping the paint off and repainting it, so I did that for a while. Then for a few months I was a radioman striker, but I was never going to be successful at that. You had to know the Morse Code up to about twenty words per minute. I got to about fourteen words per minute, then we got to the Far East and I was no good to them. So we left Pearl Harbor and they put me on mess cooking, which is an extended KP. I was on mess cooking from the time we left Pearl Harbor until sometime after we got to Japan. That was some of the most miserable duty. I was big. My job was to carry the food from the main deck, down two decks to the mess hall. The food came in inserts with handles, and an insert of mashed potatoes would weigh a hundred pounds, an insert of soup you had to be very careful because ships are moving. Out of Honolulu it was smooth, and we got to Midway. When we left Midway we got into a bad typhoon, and I was having to carry this food around. They didn't have mashed potatoes or soup; all they had were sandwiches when we were in the typhoon.

"Major, I think we have a problem."

John Thompson

I love the military. The five years I was in I wouldn't trade for anything. The military is truly the gift that keeps on giving, in life and friends and support.

As the base transportation officer at my first assignment, I got a call one day from a division-level colonel, and he said, "Lieutenant, I want you to bring one of those shipping containers to General Wells's house to put his yard equipment and tools in so he doesn't mess up his garage." And I said, "Sir, I can't do that. Those belong to the Army, and they need them all for shipping material to Vietnam." We went around about it for a little longer, and he was getting angrier as I kept saying no. Finally he said, "Lieutenant, I want you to put that thing on a truck and personally deliver it to the general's house." I was pretty hot myself by now and I blurted, "Fuck you, sir, I can't." My first sergeant was sitting right across from me, and he literally slid out of his seat. I could hear the steam coming out of the colonel and he shouted into the phone, "Get up here, now!"

Realizing I might have just committed a grievous error, I called my boss and said, "Major, I think we have a problem." He was about three months from retirement, so he was not really happy about this. So he calls our boss, the base commander, and tells him what happened. About ten minutes later I got a call from the first colonel, who said to disregard the order. Later, my boss and I were ordered to the base commander's office. We report, and the first thing he says to me is, "What the hell were you thinking?" I said, "Sir, I was not thinking, I was mad. I had just received orders from the Oakland Army terminal to get every container we have on base to them immediately. I told the colonel that, but he just kept pushing it." He said, "Well, lucky for you the colonel and I have been competitors since we were junior officers. We are always trying to make the other look bad. What I told the colonel was, 'You were way out of line for ignoring the chain of command to call one of my officers with this order. I will make sure the general knows about this.'" Then he said to me, "You were way out of line on this, and we can pretty much throw the book at you. If I hadn't enjoyed sticking it to him, I would. For now, don't ever do that again, Lieutenant. Dismissed." I didn't.

"He thought it was a game."

Elyana Ramirez

A lot of women have suffered from sexual trauma and stuff like that. I never was exposed to that. I saw it happen a lot, but I was never a victim in that situation, and I think it's because I always try to carry a more intimidating persona, like I essentially have taken regular things and used them as weapons on people to get my point across.

Like, one dude slapped me when we were at the beginning, when I first got to San Diego. "Ha, ha, ha," he thought it was a game, and he was a big guy, and he just slapped me and thought it was funny. So I shoved my pen into his neck and I was like, "I don't play games." Another kid punched my sandwich. I don't know why he thought that was a good idea, but he punched my sandwich, and I jabbed my fork in his hand. So I kind of gave myself a reputation where I was like, "You know what, I'm not going to mess around." But I know a lot of women have had that issue, and it's a really big issue. It happens way more often than you could possibly imagine. And nobody really gets in trouble for it. They just send them somewhere else, and it happens again.

But I'd do it again in a heartbeat. I miss being at sea. I miss it. I don't miss my hair being in a bun twenty-four hours a day. I don't miss wearing black socks and getting black sock toe jam. I don't miss the shitty food. But I do miss the camaraderie.

"The bullet coming at you, I don't like that sound."

Marty Leewright

After the invasion of Cambodia, there was one night when I thought I was gonna die. I thought I knew what fear was, and I have never known fear like this. And I prayed to God, and said, "God, if you let me live through this night, I promise you I will make something of my life, I will serve people." And that really changed my life, and I got a book. I had a book sent over to me that was *High School Subjects Self-Taught*. It was about a six-hundred-page book. And I kept that with me everywhere I went after that, read that cover to cover, came back and took the GED test or whatever it was, aced that, took some college-level examination program, CLEP tests, CLEPed out of several courses, even physics and stuff. When I started at a community college, a counselor and a psychology professor said, "We're gonna work with you. Your test scores are off the charts."

Now they may have been totally lying to me, but I believed I had ability when they said that, and so they put me in this remedial reading program, and I had to go to the counseling center and they had all this stuff set up and it was like a color-coded thing. You go through level one, green, you get to level two, orange, you get to level three, purple or whatever, and I just zipped through those and caught on and, like I said, really went on to use that GI Bill. I'm like a sponge. I was absorbing everything I possibly could in the training. In basic training I think I graduated second or third in my company, and in advanced individual training I think I was first or second. And when I went to Vietnam, the interesting thing is you learn so quickly in an environment like that. You learn survival skills. And the guys that had been there even three or four months longer, they would help you distinguish between a bullet coming at you—that sound over your head or nearby, it's just zinging by you—and a bullet going behind you, going away from you. There's a very subtle different sound. Now, the bullet coming at you, I don't like that sound at all.

Q: Are you glad you were in Vietnam?

Yes. It's a million-dollar experience I wouldn't give two cents to go through again. It's an education that you can't buy. Being in any kind of war zone, it's just a different world, it's so surreal, and when you come back they say, "Well, he never talked about Vietnam, he never talked about World War II," or whatever. It's 'cause you don't have anything to relate it to. It's like me trying to explain to you what it's like to prepare for and try a big jury trial. If you've never done it, I can explain it to you, but it doesn't really make a whole lot of sense until you do it. You could explain to me what it's like to interview people and write a book, and until I've done it I really can't appreciate that.

And in a world where you're afraid of dying just about every day, and you see people dying and you wash out the back of a truck where there's brain tissue and hair and things like that, pieces of skull where some of your friends have died, or you see dead bodies, you just don't forget that.

Or you're so fearful, like I was that one night that I prayed. There's no way to relate that. I came back, and then you have these war movies and stuff like that. I couldn't watch 'em, 'cause they're so phony.

Q: *When and how did you learn about Kent State?*

Newspapers. We got newspapers over there. It was right after the invasion, within three or four days. But when we were in Cambodia we really weren't getting mail and newspapers. Before we did, and when we came back out we did. I don't think I learned about it when we were there. When I came back out I learned about it. But we knew about demonstrations before we went in.

I wasn't angry at the people that died [at Kent State], certainly not. They have a right. I felt like I was there fighting for Americans' right to free speech and free expression and stuff like that, so I wasn't upset. I thought it was very, very tragic. I was probably a little angry, not at the people that got killed, but at the students. 'Cause I guess we kind of felt like some of those students were cowards. We were there fighting, and some of the students had evaded going in the military and got deferments and things like that. They were—I don't know what the right word is—wusses. And we were over there getting shot at and getting killed and seeing our buddies shot at and killed.

It was just that feeling that we didn't have support. So I didn't understand the whole Kent State thing. I just knew that people were demonstrating, and that they intensified after the invasion. I wanted people to understand: "Hey, we went in there to protect ourselves. We went in there defensively, not offensively. We went in there defensively to disarm and de-supply the enemy." I don't think there was ever an intention of staying in there. I've never really studied the Cambodian invasion. But from my perspective, it was just going in there to clean it out.

I think the students pretty much saw it as an expansion of the war, and I think Nixon had been saying for a while that we weren't gonna go in there, we weren't gonna expand the war, and I think that the military leaders probably convinced him that we needed to clean that area out and get all those supplies out. And like I said, we felt like we'd had our hands tied behind our back. We were getting attacked, they were coming in there and hitting us with rockets and stuff. And they had all kinds of supplies amassed along that border. I'll show you pictures of the stuff, anti-aircraft guns, heavy machine guns, large mortar tubes, bazooka-type launchers. We found American weapons, .45s new in the case, M-16s.

There were trucks. I remember seeing a GMC truck that was captured, some stuff that looked like it was left over from maybe the French or World War II or something. Old, old stuff that they'd keep going, keep using.

I didn't understand the geopolitical issues or military strategy at all. As a young soldier, you don't get any of that. My job as an engineer was very specific and literally earthly. We were digging in the dirt. I can show you pictures of us just filling sandbags, thousands and thousands of sandbags. We'd put these big culverts, anything from maybe something small enough for you to slide down on a cot and slide into, to a culvert that you could stand up in and put your hands up and barely touch it, that maybe eight, ten, twelve guys could sleep in. And we'd put sandbags on top of that, or we would take the front end loader and just dump dirt on top of that, and put barrels in front of the doorways and fill them with dirt to absorb any shrapnel that might hit.

I have pictures of some of the kids where we would share our C-rations and stuff with them. Some of us had cameras, and if you tried to take their picture they'd go like this [puts hands in front of face]. You know why? They didn't want pictures with American soldiers, because somebody else may be coming along and see those pictures, and they'd probably get killed. So they didn't want their picture taken. The villagers were very nervous.

"I'm a male war bride."

Shirley Beck

My husband always told everybody, "I'm a male war bride." He was so kind and sweet and supportive. He would send us care packages. The hospital dietician and I shared a tent, and every day we had a dust storm. We'd leave at six in the morning to go to the hospital, come back about six or seven at night, and we'd have about that much dust on the top of our sleeping bags. "Well," he said, "I've just the thing that you girls need," so here comes in the mail two cardboard chests of drawers that we set up. He said, "Now, that's to put your undies in to keep the dust back."

My neighbors were so wonderful. One of them sent me a card with the ruby slippers from *The Wizard of Oz*! She said, "I'm sending you these slippers so that you can click 'em and come home." When I did come home, the whole neighborhood had a big party. There was a pie, a cake, something on this big table to celebrate every holiday I had missed, and then the kids had crepe paper on their bicycles around the wheels and going up and down the street. They were all there. It was just so, so kind and sweet. The neighbors were helpful to Charles too. To them it was a big deal that I went to war and I came home.

"That food stayed right there good."

Alcee Chriss Sr.

When my mother used to bake, they call it cheesecake cookies. Boy, she was a good cook. And then she would pressure fry chicken. They don't do that much anymore. And do you know that chicken, when I'll get that box from home, guys in my tent know we have a party. We gonna have that party the whole week almost. That food stayed right there good. The weather was good, and I used to go swimming in the ocean, boy. And look down in that ocean, it's so beautiful down there. It was warm. All the time we were there it was warm. And do you know that it had some Japanese prisoners? And talking about going and invading Japan. That would have been some long, long hell. It'd been something if it hadn't been for the bomb. We'd have been fighting eight years I guess, trying to get there.

"He has a hard time with change."

Barbara Wahl

I loved being a military wife. When I got married, my mother and father's friends said, "She's going to become a vagabond, and she's going to be driving around and packing her clothes in paper bags, so watch out. You're losing a daughter to God knows what with the military." Now, most of the men of this group had served in World War II. The wives never went anyplace. They weren't long-term military families. Their separation was generally four or five years, not a year like we had.

But we had a station wagon, and we drove from San Antonio to Cincinnati. I packed all the clothes in paper sacks and put them in the station wagon. You could get only half as much in suitcases. We loved moving. My family loved moving. George is the one that doesn't like moving. He has a hard time with change, but he does it because of his job, and he likes when we get to the new places, and he likes meeting new people and talking. He's very social, but he doesn't like the transition, packing up and unpacking at the other end. I'd have things ready to go one way, and he'd come in and change them. I said, "You take care of the paperwork, I'll take care of all the rest." And it worked out much better. When we moved, the kids would take all the boxes before they were packed and go along with putting blankets over them so you'd have this little house here and you'd go through this little tunnel and find something. The kids learned to move happily, because I was happy.

When we would get to a new community, I'd take the map and say to the children, "Okay, we're going to find every place in this place where we want to go to and what's around." The children would then say, "Oh no, here we go again, we know we're going to get lost." That was before GPS, and it's a wonderful experience. We've been in our current house eleven years. I hate being settled. Every day I wake up and say, "Where can we go? I gotta move." I love it. When we retired it was actually harder on me than it was on him.

"I looked at our life as an adventure."

Shawn Keane

Bradley did not stay in one career field while in the Air Force; each assignment was a different MAJCOM (Major Command) with a unique mission. His first assignment was a missileer (ICBM crew) at Malmstrom AFB in Montana. He later moved to Davis-Monthan Air Force Base in Arizona, where he graduated as a distinguished graduate, Ground Launch Cruise Missiles (GLCM) nuclear combat crew commander. He also worked in the schoolhouse writing war scenarios and teaching airmen before they were deployed to field the GLCM weapon system throughout Europe. Around 1985, he was sent on a remote tour to Belgium to establish the first GLCM base on the European continent where mobile missiles were aimed at Russia. This base contributed to the dismantling of Soviet intermediate-range ICBMs aimed at Western Europe and the collapse of the Soviet Union. Eventually, the Intermediate Range Nuclear Forces (INF) Treaty was signed, which represented the first treaty to abolish an entire class of ICBMs. He returned to Tucson, Arizona in January 1986.

We were married a little over a year after his return, March 12, 1987. In 1988 we had Melanie, our first daughter. Not long after Melanie was born, our family moved to Texas. Bradley took a position as the freshman instructor for Air Force ROTC at TCU.

After our family was settled in Texas, our second daughter Melissa was born in 1990. Melissa's birth coincided with the beginning of the first Gulf War. I shared a hospital room with a woman at C.L. Thompson Strategic Hospital in Fort Worth, Texas. She was alone, without her husband, during the birth of their child. I saw this woman again in the pharmacy several months later. She told me that her husband had been deployed to the Gulf, 82nd Airborne, and had been dropped into Iraq, behind enemy lines, at the beginning of the war to liberate Kuwait. He had yet to see his newborn child.

In 1992, we moved to McChord Air Force Base in Washington state, where Bradley became a Section Commander for Maintenance Squadron. At the time of the move Melanie was four and Melissa was two. We drove up to Washington State via the I-5 corridor during the winter time. Washington was my favorite place to live. We did two tours at McChord AFB in Tacoma, Washington. This experience was like heaven on earth.

While we were in Washington Bradley changed jobs several times. He became the Chief of Public Affairs and later the General's Executive Officer. Our son, Bradley II, was born in 1995 at Madigan Army Hospital. Five weeks after his birth we moved to Omaha, Nebraska, Offutt AFB.

Bradley became a SIOP advisor in the Underground Command Post and aboard the "Looking Glass" Airborne Command Post, where he directly supported presidential execution of our nuclear war plan based on attack assessment and various attack options under Top Secret Single Integrated Operation Plan. He worked in an office three stories underground and read nuclear war scripts. He advised three-star and four-star generals during phone conversations with the president of the United States on what to do and how quickly to react. The job required a significant amount of calm under pressure.

In 1997 we moved back to McChord AFB, where Bradley became the Recruiting Commander for Alaska, Washington, and Oregon. His squadron went from number eighteen in the national ranking to number one in the nation by the time his two-year tour was over. His efforts drew the attention of a three-star general who sent Bradley to Air War College in Alabama in 2000. After a year, he graduated with his second master's degree.

In 2001 we moved to Great Falls, Montana, Malmstrom AFB, where

Bradley took the position of Support Group's Deputy Commander. Two years later our family moved yet again, back to Fort Worth, where Bradley became Commander of Air Force ROTC at TCU.

Throughout his career, I stayed at home to help create a smooth transition and to raise our children. Early in our marriage we decided it was a better plan for me to stay at home and not to go to work because of all the moving that was in our future. My life mainly consisted of ironing uniforms, setting up the new homes, packing, moving, and raising children. When you are a spouse of a military person, you need to be flexible, selfless, and willing to compromise. Often, you must abandon your comfort zone of family, friends, and what you have always known. I always looked at our life as an adventure, but this life is not for everybody. Some people are not able to handle all of the challenges of leaving their family. I have never thought too far in advance, like, "Wow, this is going to be the rest of my life, I'm missing out!" I was more like, "Oh goody, we get to go to Washington, let's pack up. We're going to live in a new house, decorate, and do landscaping."

But there were times I could have used my mom. When we moved to Washington the first time, it was right after the new year. It was very rainy, dark, and gloomy. We were waiting for base housing, so we lived in a one-bedroom duplex for four months. It was okay, but it was old, kind of dirty, not my style, but it was fully furnished. We paid the rent month-to-month because we did not want to sign a lease. We were waiting patiently for base housing. While we were waiting the combination of gloomy weather, sick kids, Bradley learning a new job, and the uncertainty about whether or not Bradley would be promoted created a very stressful time for me. We also did not buy a home when we moved to Washington. This was during the nation's major base realignment and closures, and I was nervous about buying a home in Washington because I thought McChord might be on the list to be closed.

"Instantly that's your family."

Charlotte Cole

I loved being in the Marine Corps [as a spouse]. We always lived on base where we were at, because we were in California most of the time and of course off-base living was out of the question because it was so expensive, so we lived in base housing. When we first moved into base housing, we just thought that was the most amazing thing. We decorated, and all the families would come to our house. When you're in the Marine Corps and you're on a base, no one's families live there, so instantly that's your family. So Thanksgivings, Christmases, they were the best. We'd set up tables in the middle of the street. Everybody came to it that lived on base. That was your family.

So many friends. I still keep in touch with all of them, but when you're younger, of course you have people that are in leadership positions. You look up to them, and you attend all the things. But as you move up the ladder and you've been in there longer, then you become the volunteer, and then you have the younger wives and key volunteers. I was a key volunteer. So when the husbands would be deployed, you were kind of a point of contact in two different directions. When the Marine Corps needed to get anything disseminated, they would let you know and you would tell the younger wives. And then if they needed anything, they'd all come to you. Even if it's the middle of the night, they'd call you crying or whatever, and you'd give them the best guidance you could or direct them to the person they need to speak to. Being a key volunteer was a lot of fun. I even got a certificate of commendation from the general when they came back from deployment, because of being in that leadership position. I loved being in the Marine Corps. I didn't want to get out. At the end of the thirty years I'm like, "Wait, it's already been thirty years?"

I loved living on base. You have something in common with everyone. Even if you don't know your neighbors, you instantly have something in common, because you're in the military. And everyone's there alone. You're all going through deployments alone, and we went through multiple ones. When Jordan was three months old Bruce deployed for six months, and then again when she was four, or three. And Bailey was born, our younger daughter. For the birth of the babies, my family was nowhere around. His family wasn't there either, so I just really enjoyed the friendships you make, and they last forever. Like I said, I still keep in touch with all the Marine wives I met, even though they're not still married to their Marine. We have lots of divorces in the Marine Corps, because if you can't deal with deployments and being the mom, the dad, the construction worker, the engineer, the accountant, the maintenance guy—I mean, I did a lot of things on my own, but I loved it. I absolutely loved it. I put up a fence on my own. I loved being in the military and being on base. The wives that couldn't handle that, during deployments they would go back home and live with their parents, because they couldn't even stay at the base and deal with everyday life, which I didn't see a problem with. I was like, "Oh, okay. Well, I'm going to put up a fence today, because that's what needs to be done."

Now, I went kicking and screaming when he said, "Oh, we're leaving Southern California"—the best place—"and we're going to the little island of Okinawa." I went, "Uh, no, I'm not living there three years." So he said, "Well, we for sure have to stay for two." And then at the end of the two years he goes, "Oh yeah, we're here for three." But by then, we had already been there and we had learned to like it. We made friends over there, Japanese friends, and we would have Christmas at our house and all the Japanese people would come, like thirty of them. They loved the American food. We made a lot of friends, and we still keep in touch with them.

"My dad got to see us pull into San Diego."

Paige McCloud

I was an Interior Communications Electrician. I worked on things like the ship's helm, the alarm and warning systems. I was on the USS *John C. Stennis* based out of Bremerton, Washington, right across the Sound from Seattle. Oh my gosh, I want to go back. It's so pretty. It's so easy to eat clean there and recycle. Everyone recycles. When I first got there, the ship was in the yard. They had contract workers come on and fix things on the ship. So the first six months or so, it was all on land. I'd just go to the ship every day and come home. It was like a normal job, and it was awesome. And then in January 2011, we started going back and forth between San Diego and Bremerton, because Air Wing was based out of San Diego. I love San Diego. The whole West Coast is pretty awesome.

We were supposed to do Fleet Week right before I deployed my second time, but the USS *Nimitz* didn't pass their Sea Trials, so they were pretty much broken down, so we had two or three weeks' notice before we were deployed again. So we ended up missing Fleet Week. And then we were supposed to do Rim Pac, which is three months in and out of Hawaii, and we had to miss that and ended up going back to the Gulf, and the *Nimitz* got to do it. They break down and get to have the fun!

My dad got to see us pull into San Diego when I was coming back from my first deployment. He thinks it's the coolest thing ever. He actually got to take a Tiger Cruise with us, which is like your parents can come on board, and they actually get to ride on the ship for a few days. So he came on in San Diego and rode up to Washington. It was probably the proudest moment of my life, because my dad could come and see what I was doing. It was pretty awesome.

I learned a lot. My job was mostly around being an electrician, but I think what I learned the most was when I was temporarily assigned duty at this place called MSC, maintenance support center. Basically what you do is handle all the prints and the schematics for the ship. Electrical drawings are not like your maps, but I think everything I learned, like looking at the electrical drawings and learning how to follow the lines, really helped me learn how to read maps, because I didn't know how to read a map. So I learned a lot about reading schematics and blueprints and things like that.

"Family trips always have detailed itineraries."

Rachel Ziomek

My dad retired, after twenty-two years as a fighter pilot in the Air Force, just before I started third grade. Growing up in a military family left an imprint on me that remains today.

For starters, I had lived in four locations before entering the first grade. With respect to stability, I'm very glad my dad didn't stay in the Air Force for the rest of my childhood. However, I did enjoy the perks of being in a military family. I remember how fun it was to go on base to shop at the commissary and the BX. It was exciting to see the soldiers at the gate salute my dad, a lieutenant colonel, after checking his ID. When pilots returned from deployment, families were allowed to go right out onto the tarmac to greet them. That was pretty neat, but at the time I didn't appreciate the loud noise of the jets. I also went to a good number of ceremonies and airshows as a kid. Since my dad now works at Lockheed Martin with the F-35 program, our family still has not parted from the world of fighter jets.

To me, it was totally normal for my dad to leave on TDY (temporary duty). I remember feeling annoyed when civilian kids complained when a parent went out of town for a short time. My dad was gone for at least half of every month while we lived in Virginia; he missed a lot of things. Even so, it's hard for me to imagine what it is like for the families who have service members stationed overseas for many months, and in much more imminent danger. I don't have any memories of actually fearing for my dad's safety, although I'm sure my age played a part in that. As I've gotten older, I've realized that my parents went to a number of funerals for squadron mates.

One of the longest times my dad was gone was for three months. I remember how excited we all were for him to return home. We found out the day before he was scheduled to return that the deployment would last another month. That was a bummer, and we all cried. As a pilot, he would also be gone for reasons that probably don't affect other military personnel as much. If there was going to be a major storm or hurricane, they had to "hurravac" (hurricane evacuation) the jets to a safer location. When we lived in North Carolina, my mother, my sister, and I rode out Hurricane Fran in the closet under the stairs and went three days without power, all while my dad was safely in Ohio with the jets. Basically, when anything major happened, he wasn't there.

My dad was already TDY on 9/11, and of course he wasn't returning home any time soon. After school that day, I looked out the front window with my mom and sister as a Humvee, with a soldier perched on top manning the giant machine gun, drove right in front of our house and down our street. It was so surreal, especially since we lived not directly on Langley AFB, but in a separate neighborhood of off-base military housing. Our lives were affected even in small ways. We couldn't get mail or newspapers delivered to our house for a few days, because they wouldn't let civilians into our neighborhood. Not long after, a gatehouse was installed at the front of the neighborhood. After that, whenever we had birthday parties, we would have to give a list of the attendees to the gatehouse guards.

Another impact was growing up with the personality of a military officer. My dad is very "Type A" and concerned with organization and efficiency. (The last two traits definitely rubbed off on me.) Family trips always have detailed itineraries, laid out in military time. These tendencies even show up at things like my Sixth Grade Play Day, where my dad volunteered. It was basically a fun day at the end of the school year, where students play a bunch of games like tug-of-war. I remember coming around the corner of the school with my classmates and seeing my dad there, directing people with a bullhorn. No one had given him the bullhorn; he had just taken it upon himself to "impose order" on Sixth

Grade Play Day. My family has never let him live that one down.

Being a military brat also influenced my vocabulary. The military has an abbreviation for everything. Whether it's asking for the ETA (estimated time of arrival) on a trip, or joking that someone needs more SA (situational awareness) when they miss something going on around them, I still use the terminology regularly. Just the other day, my dad was proud when he caught me saying "O dark thirty" (early enough that it's still dark outside).

I may have been young when we were still an active duty family, but the Air Force definitely had a strong influence on my life. Most of my friends don't come from military families, and I appreciate that I have a different perspective on military life. And, of course, I still proudly sing along whenever the Air Force song plays somewhere: "Off we go into the wild blue yonder, climbing high into the sky . . . "

"Hey, you'd be a good cop."

Brad Murphey

I would have gone into something other than law enforcement. Law enforcement wasn't something I wanted to do. 'Cause I came from a family of cops, and I just didn't want to do that. So when I got into the Air Force and they said, "Hey, you'd be a good cop," I'm going, "Great." If it was today, I would go into computers.

I guess low points would be being away from my family on temporary duty, like when I went to Panama for three months, that was pretty rough. But that's nothing compared to the six months to a year that my boys have done going to war. I have a son who was in the Army, and now he's in the Navy. And I have a stepson who was in the Marine Corps, and I have a boy who's about to join the Air Force. I'm proud of them, and they didn't actually come to me for advice, which I sorta pushed my advice on them. And they ignored it, so that's what kids do, though. They ignore their parents. They come back later and say, "You know what, you were right." It's not for everybody, but it is a good alternative to college.

"I could almost become anyone."

Maria Brown-Spence

"Where are you from?" For most military dependents like myself, that is never an easy question to answer. It could range from where was I born, to where I lived the longest, to what military base was my favorite, to where my parents are from. Moving almost every year would cause anxiety or frustration for most, but not for me. I loved being able to meet people from all over the world, and I considered myself something like a chameleon, learning to adapt and adjust to my new surroundings. I could almost recreate my image and become anyone I wanted to be, because no one really knew me.

As I became older, I started to understand that this could be toxic and mentally draining for some young people, because you didn't have the opportunity to establish lasting relationships or grow your talents or skills, or because you had to be abruptly uprooted, never getting to finish a team sport or grow with a childhood friend. But for me it only grew my resiliency, adaptability, and extroverted spirit. As an adult, those experiences have allowed me to connect with any and everyone I meet, adjust to high-stress situations, and maintain relationships even years later.

"Military kids have the attitude of like, 'Why not?'"

Jordan Cole

Going to high school on Okinawa was normal to me and to everyone else there. I went to high school on the military base, so I think everybody else kind of had that in common. It was more Americanized I guess, being with everyone who speaks English as their first language also. But then you can go off base, and in five minutes you're at the sushi-go-round and doing karaoke, and kind of the best of both worlds in having the American culture still around you, but also being able to go out and experience the Japanese culture.

Most people don't really get to move around the world a lot when they're growing up, but I was just handed the culture and the experiences and getting to go places like that. We would have five to ten people selected from our high school for a certain subject or a certain sport, to go compete with the other Pacific schools. We would usually go to Tokyo and we would do math at a Tokyo university, or we would present science projects. So I got several academic trips to Tokyo that were really fun.

I'm still taking Japanese as my foreign language. And when I go on other trips and experience other cultures, I don't see as much of a barrier, and I'm able to integrate them more.

I think a lot of my confidence came from my friends, especially in Japan. A lot of the military kids would have the attitude of like, "Why not?" So I kind of adopted that by hanging out with a lot of them and being kind of in the military kid culture, where it was always just, "Why not try out this? Why not go to this? Why not just try everything?" So I think I started adopting that there, and it has just grown more in college as well.

I'm incredibly proud of my dad's career, and I think what makes the difference between his upbringing and mine was that he always made it very clear that I had the option of many other things. I don't think it was ever silently expected for me to follow, but it was definitely appreciated and bragged about all throughout my childhood.

"I thought I was going to have a best friend."

Enrique Brown-Spence

During the time that my dad was in the military, I thought it was really cool. When I was young I would look up to him like he was a superhero. Even though my mother, April Brown, was also in the military, I was too young to remember it. My father stayed in the military until I was in seventh or eighth grade. Through those times I thought it was fun moving all over the place, living in new houses. Then when I got older I started to realize that it was not so fun after all. Picking up almost every two years, leaving friends behind that had a special bond and knowing you will never see them again made me sad. I never had a childhood best friend. That friend that grew up with you. A friend that had childhood memories.

I can say that one person that I had memories with was my sister Elaina. She was only a year and some months apart from me. We were in the same school together, and we played together when there was no one else to play with. So, all those times I had to leave schools and leave states, making new friends over and over again, I knew that I still had someone that was with me, and that was my sisters Elaina and Maria.

Every now and then I think about those people I met from schools I went to, and it makes me wish I would have stayed in contact with them.

Marine veteran Richard Spence with son, Enrique Brown-Spence.
Courtesy of Enrique Brown-Spence.

I remember, the only time I was sad about moving to another state was when I was living in New Orleans. I was in second grade and I met a classmate named Harvey at Belle Chase Academy, the first charter school for military dependents located on a base. Harvey and I would hang out and ride bikes all over the base after school and on weekends. We were also in Cub Scouts together. For the first time, I thought I was going to have a best friend. After the school year of my second grade came to an end, the summer was here and we hung out every day until I was about to leave to visit my grandparents in Indiana.

The day I was leaving, Harvey came to see me to say goodbye and to ask my mother when I came back can we ride bikes together. My mother responded that we were moving and we were not coming back. At the time I did not know my dad had just received new orders again, but I knew at that moment that that day was the last day I was going to see Harvey.

"To have an open mind makes life so much easier."

Nathaniel Peoples

In Italy, you had people from not just America and Italy, but from Asia, Russia, all over the place. It was very global. Living in both Italy and Japan helped me be a global citizen and connect with individuals from around the world.

Since it was just my mother and I, I went overseas and stayed with her the whole time. It really changed my perspective on life. It enabled me to connect with people from all walks of life. Whether it be your race, or religion, your sexual orientation—it doesn't matter. I think it was very beneficial to have that global mindset. That's what I'm appreciative of. To have an open mind about everything makes life so much easier, because without that, you aren't going to enjoy where you are, no matter what you do.

To get out there and travel really changes your whole perspective on life. It enriches you, where you just come back as a changed person. Growing up overseas motivates me to travel more. To go see and venture to these unknown territories and really meet new people and get to know them and what they're like. That's what I appreciate the most.

There were challenges, not overseas, but coming to America. It was very different. It was a huge transition, because over there you have people from Africa, America, China, all over the world. It's awesome! People from all walks of life teaching you something. While you go to America, and it's not like that, and they're not as accepting.

When she was in the military she was tough, she was a tough mom. "Do the dishes or else!" "Or else what? "You'll get my boot." It was pretty intense. But it was tough on her. But as she retired, the good things in life started to come back together, and she was more calm and collected and started to enjoy life. It's tough being in the military—that's one thing. She is a woman, and an African American woman. She was in the military for twenty years, and that's a long time. It was very hard for women to move up the ranks in the military, much harder than it is today. That was very challenging for her, to move up and to overcome certain challenges. And she did! She pursued and persevered through the trials and tribulations that came her way, but she had to tough it out and keep pushing through that brick wall—and she made it. That's the tough part, pushing through that brick wall and finding yourself. She appreciated the fact that even though she had a tough time in the military, she remained herself.

She didn't lose herself in the military. And she remained warm.

I had to grow up very fast while she was in the military. I was an only child, house to myself all day until I was about ten. She would go to work at about six o'clock in the morning, come back like four. I was at the teen center all the time, playing video games and hanging out with my friends. But if that wasn't the case, I'd be at home, taking care of the house, making sure it didn't catch on fire. Do the dishes, cleaning up everything. Like, "Hey, I'm leaving the house for you while I go out of town for a day or a weekend." I did that since I was seven years old, so it was very interesting growing up like that.

To dive deeper into it, for Japan, I learned from it, just being in a mercenary culture. I had to understand their definition of hard work. And their hard work beats a lot of other countries' hard work. When it comes to mathematics and science, it's intense. So I was able to develop those habits, and that really changed my perspective on hard work in science and math and all that stuff. Italy, that really gave me a global perspective when it came to family traditions. Getting involved with other people, inviting them to your house, becoming family, and really connecting with people and making them feel like they're not just an individual, but they're part of something bigger—they're part of the family. You want to invite them over all the time. Really family-oriented people. That was the best part, really being involved with the Italian culture, meeting people, and eating awesome food every day.

Italy. The food was amazing. It was the bomb. We lived with a family, and they lived below us, and they had a garden, a huge little mini mansion. A garden on this side with these vegetables, and a garden on the other side with those vegetables. And it was fresh food every day. And they made it for us! It was very awesome, so one of my most cherished memories was walking through the garden and picking out tomatoes and stuff like that. And in Japan, it was definitely going to Tokyo. It's like New York, but a little more packed. It's kind of intense, but it was so advanced that it just blew my mind away. You had stuff that they have there we still don't have here, and that's sad. I really miss the fast-paced environment of Japan. It was so fast, people really loved to get to know you. It's so Americanized in Japan. People wouldn't have any idea. Like, "Oh, I can't go there, they're not gonna speak my language." Yes they do. They speak nine other languages too, it's what they're supposed to do in school, learn four to five languages to be marketable. That's what I miss most about both places.

"My experience in the military was wonderful."

Shawn Keane

Once you get on the base, everybody comes out of the woodwork. My experience as a spouse in the military world was wonderful. I had fun. I think it's all in the attitude that you have, too, and the person you're married to. I have a very good husband. He never made me do anything I didn't want to do. I asked him, "Well, Bradley, maybe I should be in the Officers' Wives Club." He replied, "No, you don't have to do that. I'll make my own career." We always prioritized taking care of the children and family first, and then I could do what I wanted. We made sure that all of our children did well in school. I spent my time volunteering at schools, Officers' Wives or Officer Spouses Clubs, gardening, and enjoying my wonderful neighbors on base. When we were in Alabama for ten months, I joined the Gardening Club and worked with master gardeners to help landscape the Shakespeare Theater. I also spent some of my free time participating in book clubs.

Most people do not understand all of the activities that someone can be involved in just by being a stay-at-home spouse. You can be active in the community through volunteer work: gift wraps, decorating the Officers' Club, fundraisers for scholarships, in the school system. A big priority for me was being there for all of my children, and other people's

Melissa, Shawn, Brad, Bradley, and Melanie Keane.
Courtesy of Shawn Keane.

children too, through volunteering in the school system. I enjoyed the opportunity to be there for my children, and I even was able to teach a children's Bible study when we lived in Montana.

As a stay-at-home spouse, it was also important for me to be there for my husband. His shift work was horrible for me when he was a SIOP adviser at Offutt AFB in Nebraska. He was working twelve-hour shifts. During this time, we had to keep the house quiet on a Saturday because he worked from ten in the evening until six in the morning and had to sleep in the day. This was no easy task with three little kids. The kids and I often went to the zoo or children's museum, because I had season passes. We also went to pumpkin patches, apple orchards, and the library, basically wherever we could go to get out of the house when the weather was good, we did it.

Packing and unpacking from base to base was always a challenge. I got in the habit of setting up the house as quickly as I could whenever we moved. Some people lived out of cardboard boxes their whole career, because it is so much work to unpack. For many people it always seems like you're packing or unpacking. Personally, I wasn't going to wait until twenty years later, or twenty-five years later, or twenty-seven or whatever it was, to finish unpacking. I was always in such a hurry to unpack. I wanted to actually live in my home, so I unpacked everything. The kids were also used to me unpacking everything whenever we moved. When we got to Alabama, the kids wanted me to make cookies, and I was like, "I don't know where the cookie sheet is. I'll try to find it." And they were like, "Gosh, Mom, we really want cookies." I could have just gone to the BX and bought a cookie sheet, but no, we were just not having cookies until I found it. Eventually, I found the cookie sheet with the bedding instead of the kitchen stuff.

"I had no doubt that I would serve."

April Brown

I had no doubt growing up that I would serve in the military. I imagined it would be the Air Force, but my path took me to the United States Marine Corps. I commissioned in the Marine Corps in 1985 as a second lieutenant. In many ways, I followed in both my father's and my mother's footsteps. I served in the military and have a career in higher education like my father. I am a military spouse to Richard Spence, and we have three children. Maria chose to serve in the Army prior to starting her civilian career and continues to support the military community through her nonprofit organization Hearts 2 Heal. Elaina is a graduate of TCU and an MFA student at the University of the Arts. Enrique is a digital media major at Prairie View A&M and a rugby player. All three would experience multiple transitions to new locations during their childhood and youth. They continue to talk about friends they've met and those that they left behind. My spouse and I are both Marines, and although we both understand the sacrifices our children made while we served, we feel it has allowed them to be adaptable and to recognize that everyone has something unique to offer to this world.

Marine veteran April Brown.
Courtesy of April Brown.

While serving in the military, I experienced opportunities that broadened my understanding of the world and of the communities that exist. I met people from diverse locations, domestic and international. I learned different languages and lingo from the people I met while serving. I remember the first time I heard the word "Aggie" while at The Basic School in Quantico, Virginia. At the time, I could not have envisioned that I would someday live in Texas, the home of Texas A&M. I learned how to two-step at country western clubs, as well as the protocol for being a guest in another country. I had the opportunity to train alongside foreign military officers from Haiti, the Philippines, Thailand, and other countries. As a public affairs officer I attended the Defense Information School, then located in Indianapolis, Indiana, with officers from all branches of the military and Department of Defense employees. This background served me well when I was assigned to support joint exercises. I also recognized and appreciate the diversity that exists in the military community.

There were a few challenges while serving in the Corps. Somehow I missed the information about the requirement to swim. My vivid memory of swim qualifications haunts me to this day. Our company of approximately 200 second lieutenants were marched to the swimming pool. We were asked to raise our hands if we were a weak swimmer or a non-swimmer. Of course I raised my hand, thinking that we would be separated out and given additional instruction to prepare us for this task at a later date. The next instruction was, "all weak and non-swimmers, line up by the tower." I was confused. I was certain I had not heard these instructions correctly. With dread, I realized that we were going to be the first group to experience the tower. I took my place in line and, when it was my turn, took the steps to the top of the tower. I looked my platoon commander in the eye and refused to show fear, knowing in my heart that this might be the day I would drown. She looked at me with sympathy, knowing full well that this was not going to be pretty when I hit the water. It was not. There was plenty of thrashing, sinking, probably would have cussed if the water had not been going down my throat. I was finally pulled to the side by the water safety instructor, who informed me that I would get to jump off this tower every day until I learned how to swim. I needed no other encouragement. I learned to swim within a week.

After my initial active duty tour, I stayed in the reserves and began working on my master's degree in Higher Education Administration and Counseling at Indiana University Purdue University at Indianapolis, also known as IUPUI. I was recalled to active duty in support of Operation Desert Shield and Desert Storm. This was one of the most unexpected components of my military service. There had been no major activation of the military since Vietnam. I know my family wondered what this meant, and I'm certain other families who had Marines recalled had similar concerns. This is very different for those serving in this present-day military. Many reservists now experience multiple deployments. Desert Storm gave me a close-up view of the transition that military members experience, but also of how activation impacts the family unit. This topic was one that I would research extensively when I would resume my master's program in Counselor Education at East Carolina University in Greenville, North Carolina.

"I felt that I was distant from my family."

Michael Washington Sr.

I had rest and recuperation leave in September to see my second son be born. I was very proud to see him. But the fear in my head was constant. I felt that I was distant from my family because it was hard telling them everything that had happened. Once we returned from our deployment, it was time to finally take a break and relax. They encouraged us to get some counseling, to integrate you as a soldier back into your family life.

Army veteran Michael Washington Sr.
Courtesy of Michael Washington Sr.

But we had several people that were dealing with a lot of personal things and felt that suicide was the best option. In April of 2012, several soldiers attempted suicide. This caused a ripple effect on the unit. Everyone was under a lot of stress, so now everyone was forced to take extra classes on suicide and family integration. My escape from the stress was to drive from Fort Hood to Dallas, see my sons, relax, and do things outside of the military. I didn't want to do anything, see anything, no military contact. I just wanted to get away.

"Are you sure there was a gorilla?"

Carl Castillo

I'm like, "What do you mean fuckin' something is out there?" He goes, "We heard some rustling." And I'm like, "Could it have been the wind?" He's like, "No." "Where was the rustling at?" He's like, "Just in front of us about twenty meters." I'm like, "I didn't hear anything when I came up here." He's like, "There's rustling out there." Fuck. I don't hear anything now. "Why didn't y'all respond?" "We just heard it a minute ago." I'm like, "Okay. Where's it at?" I said, "Where's your flashlights?" He's like, "We've got 'em." I'm like, "All right. Get your flashlights. We're going to check to see what it is." It might just be a fuckin' monkey or some other shit.

One had the radio on his back, and they both had their rifles and flashlights. We pop up, flash our flashlights over there, and sure as fuckin' shit there was a damn gorilla. The gorilla looked at us, and we looked at it. Then, all of a sudden, fucker just raises his hands like that and then just starts running at us. I'm like, "Fuckin' go! Go!" We haul ass all the way back to the camp. We finally get there, and we were all out of breath and shit like that, because we were trying not to trip and fall in the trees and shit like that and fuck, we had a gorilla, you know, chasing us and shit.

My assistant squad leader was like, "What the fuck is happening?" I'm like, "Wake everybody up! Wake up! We got a fuckin' gorilla behind us!" Everybody wakes up when they hear that shit. Everybody got their rifles. Fuck, they got blanks. I got my pistol. I turn around, and the gorilla's not there anymore. I guess the gorilla gave up. They were like, "Are you sure there was a gorilla?" I'm like, "Yes! Fuckin' gorilla was chasing us. Ask them!" They're like, "There was a gorilla. It was fuckin' huge!" My assistant squad leader, like I said, that's how I knew I wasn't thinking correctly. I was fuckin' tired. I had been up all night. He was like, "Why didn't you shoot it?" "I fuckin' forgot I have my damn pistol." If I knew, I would have shot the damn thing, but if I shot the thing, I would have to fuckin' report it. So, at that point, I call in OP1 and OP3 like, "Hey. Y'all get back in." I'm only gonna push fuckin' ten feet out from the base. I don't want to deal with that gorilla shit again.

We get ready to go back, and we're training and everything like that, and I'm like, "All right, guys, nobody fuckin' talks about the gorilla. We keep that shit to ourselves." I was like, "It just didn't happen." We get back. I don't know how they found out about the gorilla, but by the time I got back, everyone knew about the fuckin' gorilla. I'm just like, "How did y'all find out? We just fuckin' got back." Apparently somebody had radioed it in, and I didn't know.

After that, we got called Gorilla Whisperer. So, I was like, "Fuckin' gorilla." Damn thing just raised its hands and started chasing us. I mean, I don't know when it stopped chasing us, to be honest with you, because I was just fuckin' running. Like I said, that's when I realized I had my fuckin' pistol. I could have shot at the damn thing. But then, like I said, then I would have to file all this paperwork, if I killed the fuckin' gorilla and shit. I'm kinda glad I didn't shoot it. Yeah, got chased by a gorilla. Funny times.

"They'd try to kill themselves."

Stephen Rivera

I did one "deployment." I'm holding up my quotes here if you can't see them, but I went to Guantanamo Bay for seven months. As a medic my job was to provide sick call for detainees on a regular basis. Basically, it looked like a prison would look like, and there's a guy in the center of the prison, and if you needed to get into a cell block you wave him down, he lets you in, the door closes behind you—only one door can be open at one time, very like working a prison. Once a week they'd get a sick call. Basically I'd go in every morning, knock on each of the detainees' door, and like, "How are you feeling today, do you need any medical, are you sick at all?" They would give me their complaints, I would do everybody on that block, then I would go back and dictate it in the medical record, then the doctor would come once a week and take a look at all the medical records and see who needed to be seen, we would bring them into our little medical shack that we had, and the doctor would see them there.

And a lot of the time they'd try to kill themselves. They're obviously big anti-American, so any scars they can get, they want them so when they go to court they're like, "I have this scar, they're testing on me, they're trying to cut me open," stuff like that. So a lot of the time it's kind of just managing them. We had to go into cell blocks a lot when they would try to kill themselves, get them on the ground, all that stuff. We just basically were a medic provider for them in any scenario. I was there for seven months. It wasn't all bad. You're literally in the Caribbean, Cuba, the water's seventy degrees, I worked for two days and I was off for two days. And those two days I was off I could go to the beach and lay out and swim and snorkel and all that stuff, so that's why I used the quotation marks. It wasn't really a deployment like many other people. We could drink too, so for one deployment in the Navy I had to say it wasn't too horrible.

Honestly, leading up to it is more terrifying. You do four weeks of training before you go, obviously make sure all your shots and everything are up to date, because you don't want to get sick out there, and then they do two weeks where they bring actors in, military veterans who volunteer to come be actors, full-on fake prisoners type thing. The guards walk up, they tell the detainee to stand behind a certain line, once you're behind that line they open up the little feeding hole, and they shove this metal thing in there so the detainee can't stick his hand out and grab you, then you put the cup of medicine in there so the detainee is able to come forward, grab the medicine, step back before we close the door. Then we have to do a mouth check, the detainees have to show us that they're not hoarding the pills, that they actually took them, but leading up to it when you're doing the training the actors are gonna make the worst possible scenario. So they're screaming at you, they're trying to spit at you, they're trying to grab you. And I'm nineteen years old, I've never been in a prison, I don't know what that's like, you hear terrorists are crazy, they're all out to kill you, so you're shaking because you're so scared. And then he tries to grab you and you freak out. My first time I dropped the meds, and I was like, "Holy fuck, he just tried to grab me!" He's an actor, obviously he's not gonna hurt me, but you're terrified.

I remember the first time I was stepping on a block, I was like, "Holy crap, these are terrorists, these people, you can read about them, they have profiles on them." One of my detainees was a guy—and it's public record, you can go on Google and google these guys—he was like a 9/11 conspirator-type thing. They'd done all crazy things, some of them were wrong place wrong time, stuff like that, but you read about these guys and you're passing them medication, and you have to come up with fake names. You weren't allowed to use our last names, so all of our uniforms were changed to say like what our fake name was. So they called me Flip because they thought I looked Filipino, so that was on all my name prints. Where it said Rivera, it all said Flip, because we didn't want them to see anything about us. When you're on the block you can't talk about where you're from, you can't have a conversation. I couldn't be like, "Oh yeah, I was drinking this weekend," or "I called my mom in Texas this weekend, yada yada yada," because they're really good at getting word from one cell block to another. I don't know how they do it. So it's scary in that sense, but once you get comfortable with your routine and stuff like that it's not too bad.

You don't want to sympathize for them because you obviously know that they did something bad to get there, but at the same time it's interesting to look at them and be like: "They're humans." I mean, they weren't ever aggressive or mean towards me. I had one guy, I'd be like, "Hey, what's up?" And he'd be like, "Can I tell you a joke?" And he'd tell me a joke every single day, for six months straight. Every time I was on block he'd tell me a joke. Or like one guy was asking me if I could teach him how to play Sudoku. He's like, "It's so boring in here." They have pictures of their families and stuff like that, so it's like you really don't want to sympathize for them, but at the same time it's like we're all human, so it's hard to have that separation where like, "I don't know your story, I don't know what you did to be here, but all I know is you did something wrong and I have to treat you that way." That whole psychological aspect of it was always tough for me to kind of grasp with. I forget what the psychologist's name is, but like the prison dilemma where like once you switch roles you become this asshole.

"You get to go to all these ports."

Paige McCloud

When you deploy with a Navy ship, you get to pull into different ports. And I got to pull into Dubai many times. Dubai is awesome for two or three times but after that, it's very repetitive. I had to go to Bahrain two or three times, Singapore, Thailand, Malaysia, and Kauai. The fun part is that you get to go to all these ports and experience these different cultures and do all these different things. And you're on the ship and you're underway for, like, forty-five days.

I kind of miss my coffin rack. Sometimes I have to cover my face at night and sleep with my face covered, and it has to be completely dark, because I got so used to those little bitty coffin racks. In berthing you have three beds that are stacked on top of each other, but you only have like this much space for you to crawl into. But underneath where your mattress is, you can lift it up. It's like a coffin, and that's where your clothes would be stored. You can shut the curtains and it's dark. It's smaller than a twin-size bed, but I'm pretty small, so it wasn't that big of a deal for me. My chief was a big guy, like six foot two and huge, and he would tell stories about how he wanted to roll over at night, and he would have to get out of his rack and turn around and then crawl back in the other way.

When we were traveling the Straits of Hormuz, Iran was threatening us, and they would have their boats near us, but we were on this big carrier. So we would go into River City, which means we would have no communication off the ship for enlisted people. You have River City one, two, three, and four, and the higher the number gets, the less communications you have. Your satellites and radar and things will shut down, so you can't be detected and stuff. The reason we can't get communications is so we don't say, "Oh, we're traveling the Straits of Hormuz and Iran's here," then reporters get hold of it and it gets blown up a lot bigger than it was. So there were times like that, and we caught pirates on my first trip. Or technically, I guess, the USS *Mobile Bay* did. I like to say it was us because the *Stennis,* which is the carrier, has a brig, so the pirates were moved to the *Stennis* and kept in the brig there. That was pretty cool.

And then, in Bahrain, I guess this isn't really combat but it was kind of scary for me. Me and some of my friends that were in E Division, which is the Electrical Division, went to the mall. This is the first Muslim country that I'd ever been in. This was pretty fresh into my first deployment, and we were told that they do their prayer and they may sing and do all this other stuff, but we didn't quite understand like when it was gonna be and exactly what it looked like. So we're at the mall, and it has an area in the middle where you can see across and you can see all the way down to the different levels of the mall all at the same time, and we started hearing singing, or what we thought was singing, and then people kind of walking around on the different levels. And then all of a sudden it just started getting louder and louder, and for a while we were watching. And then the shops started closing up and so we were like, they're closing and praying.

And then we started realizing that the girls weren't singing, they were like yelling at the men, and then they were taking off their hijabs, and we kind of realized at that point that this isn't singing and praying, something's going on. So we started trying to walk towards this exit. And when we turned to go to the exit, there were riot police that were charging in and we were like, "Oh my goodness," so we took off running the opposite direction, because they were running. It scared us, and we took off running. And then this shopkeeper was like, "Americans, Americans," so he pulled us inside and took us out this service exit, and they put us on the street, and all the Navy personnel from the *Stennis* and the *Mobile Bay* pretty much lined up there and exited from the building. It was kind of scary because we were super exposed, and you could tell we were Americans. Turns out they were protesting the election of the prince, that I guess wasn't really an election. That was probably the scariest moment in my Navy career. Which is nothing compared to what the guys with boots on the ground go through.

"I met with the number five in Korea."

Thaddeus Rix

I was working in the J-2. The J is intelligence. But that doesn't really make sense, because I wasn't doing intel. I was kind of a translator. And I worked as a translator once. I went to Korea and translated for my colonel, which was really awesome. That was the only time I actually translated. After that I was doing more transcription, where I was taking Korean documents and turning them into English documents so my office could read them.

I did a little bit of liaisoning with the Korean government, because I made some relationships when I was on that trip—drinking *soju* with the Korean government. I met with the number five in Korea, which is pretty cool. I poured him *bokbunja* and he poured me *bokbunja*, and we took shots. At first it was a little hard, because I think it had been a year since I had actually used my language. But after a few glasses of *soju*—it's like red wine—I started getting really good. It was weird. We were at this dinner, and they kept pouring me more and more and more. And you drink what they pour you—it's respect. So I was pretty blazed, in service, which never, ever, ever happens. You never get drunk while on duty, but the colonel approved it, so. I was just amazed because, by the end of the night, I had been talking to these three guys for over two hours—full Korean, not a single word English, because they don't know any English at all. And now I was like, I know about them. We have a relationship; I understand their thoughts and their feelings, and they know me. And I didn't say a word of English. It was just an incredible experience. I think it's one of the coolest things I did in the military.

"Now I have a piece of paper."
Rodney Baker

My final tour of duty in the Navy, I took orders to Newport, Rhode Island, to the Surface Warfare Officers School, where I became an instructor for engineering, where I would teach junior officers, future captains, ship engineering principles. I was certified as a master training specialist, made senior chief petty officer. And in late 2003 I put in my request to retire in 2004.

And primarily the reason I retired, when we got to Rhode Island, my son was in third grade. And there was a decommissioned aircraft carrier in the harbor. As we come across the Bay Bridge, he sees that ship. And he says, "Dad, I thought you said you weren't going on any more ships." It was time to let it go. If I had stayed for an additional five to ten years and gone to sea duty again, he'd have been fifteen to sixteen years old. I'd have come back, I wouldn't be able to tell him nothing. I would've missed so much. And so I was there, and he was my little buddy. I got into coaching football, and I actually got a chance to coach for the Naval Academy. They had the Naval Academy prep school there at Rhode Island.

While I was in Rhode Island, I got a college degree from Roger Williams University. Used my military benefits, so it cost me a whopping $300. Got the undergrad in industrial technologies, which is basically what I did in the Navy. So now I have a piece of paper that says I know what I know. I think that's what got me in here.

"Tell your mother-in-law not to call Humphrey."

Dan Southard

Marine OCS was not easy, but I managed to graduate in September 1968. I returned to college to complete my required upper-level course. Then, just as the captain had promised, I was commissioned following graduation in December and received orders to report to TBS (Basic School for Marine officers) in April 1969. My wife and I were married in March, and we left that evening from Mankato, Minnesota, for Quantico, Virginia. We were in Quantico for six months while I attended Marine TBS.

Following Basic School, we moved to Fort Sill, Oklahoma. I had been assigned the MOS (military occupation specialty) of 0802 (artillery officer), and Marine artillery officers are trained at the Army base at Fort Sill. Following four months of artillery training, I was assigned as an FDO (fire direction officer) for a Marine artillery battery at Camp Lejeune, North Carolina. I received orders for Vietnam on May 4, 1970, and left for Vietnam in July 1970. I remember the exact date I received my orders, because May 4 was the same day as the Kent State incident with the National Guard.

In Vietnam I was first assigned forward observer duty and was attached to an infantry company. My primary purpose was to plan artillery support for the infantry, and to seek out targets of opportunity. My infantry company (Gulf Company, 3rd Battalion, 7th Marines) patrolled the Que Son Mountains southwest of Da Nang. We would patrol for two to three weeks and return to home base (LZ Baldy—a hill 30 miles south of Da Nang) for three days rest, then out again. During those three days we could eat hot meals, sleep on a cot, read mail, and write letters home.

During one three-day rest period, I received a call from division headquarters. I should indicate that lowly lieutenants never receive calls directly from division headquarters. I was apprehensive (to say the least) about answering the call. A colonel (the commanding general's assistant) wanted to know why I was not supporting my wife. As it turned out, my wife, who was living in Minnesota with her parents, was not receiving my paychecks as I had instructed. Consequently my mother-in-law, a personal friend of Senator Hubert Humphrey, had called Senator Humphrey to tell him about the issue. Apparently my mother-in-law and wife did not want to "worry me" with the problem. Humphrey proceeded to contact the commanding general for 1st Marine Division (Commander of Marines in Vietnam), and I received the call from the general's assistant. After indicating that there must have been an error at disbursing and I was not neglecting my wife, he arranged for special transportation to division headquarters, where several Marines (one was a major who was the head of division disbursing) were waiting with the appropriate paperwork to send paychecks to my wife. I promptly signed the papers, and I remember the major saying, "Tell your mother-in-law not to call Humphrey for any other Marine-related problems." My wife received all back checks and following monthly checks to the end of my deployment. For years later, my wife and I would laugh at this incident and remind my mother-in-law not to call Hubert Humphrey to solve any of our problems.

"I caught a lot of grief for that."

John Thompson

At my next base in Japan, one of my three assignments was as an air traffic control officer. We monitored flights and approved all departures at two bases, prop planes at one and jets at the other. We served cargo and troop traffic between the States and Vietnam. One of the protocols in place was providing air transportation for parents of fallen troops in Vietnam to accompany their sons' remains back to the US. Our jet base was the first stop for C-135s after leaving Saigon. It was pretty chaotic there, because you had cargo and critical equipment on-loads and off-loads, as well as crew changes. There might be up to twenty planes on the ground at a time.

So one night on grave shift I was the duty officer and launching these flights, when I get a call about 0330 from the tower. The controller says, "Hey captain. Remember flight so-and-so that left at 0200? I think you have a problem. The dad is on the plane, but the remains are here on the apron. We have some critical parts onboard, with a quick turnaround needed. We can have them there on the next outbound leaving in six hours. What do you want to do?" Thinking about the time and grief this dad had experienced with this, and what he would go through when he got to California with the rest of the family waiting, I told the controller to turn them around. I caught a lot of grief for that. You know, wasting fuel, impacting flight schedules all over the theater, critical parts for missions, holding up the war effort, blah blah blah.

Army veteran George Wahl.
Courtesy of George Wahl.

"Is this really happening?"

George Wahl

When you're in combat in the Army on the front lines, the Graves Registration troops are normally co-located or very, very close to the brigade medical company, and if a soldier expires in the medical unit or he—I say he because these were all males in 1967 and 1968—is killed in action, he's always brought back to the Graves Registration area. When I could get out, I would jump on a Huey and go out on air evacuation missions to help get the soldiers evacuated out of the field when they were hit. And one time, I went out to recover body bags. It was during Hill 875 at Dak To. That was a very serious battle of November 1967. And something that was just very disturbing was that when you get the body bags back to Graves Registration, of course the soldiers would have to unzip them to identify and do what they do, and see the seventeen- or eighteen-year-old kid. Rough, very rough.

One time, I was going down to Dak To. There was a dirt airstrip. I was going down to the end of the airstrip to get something, I guess a supply item or a pallet, and as I was rounding the airstrip, there just happened to be four C-130s sitting on the pad in the parking area. And all of a sudden a mortar attack started on the C-130s, maybe a hundred meters away. And mortar rounds you can see walking, so the NVA, the bad guys, the guys who wore the black pajamas, knew just what they were doing. Of course, Dak To was surrounded by highlands. I started walking toward the aircraft. I saw most of the crew members running toward their aircraft, and the shrapnel perforated both wings of one of the C-130s, and the fuel cells are in the wings that extend from the fuselage, twenty or twenty-five feet back from the fuselage, the JP4 was running out of—not dripping, but running—out of the wing tanks. They cranked that bird up, I guess to get back to Pleiku. One of the birds was damaged enough that they couldn't crank it up. It didn't catch fire, but it was pretty well perforated. The others got away. One apparently hadn't been hit, or I couldn't see the damage. And I'm sitting in my jeep, and I thought, "Wow, is this really happening, or is there a movie going on?"

That would have been October or November 1967. I was still at Dak To. And the real big battle of Dak To was right around Thanksgiving. We lost hundreds, hundreds, hundreds of paratroopers.

I was aware of [antiwar protests and political turmoil in the US], and it was not bothering me that much, because I had my hands full. I was aware from reading, because we would get the weekly Pacific edition of the *Stars and Stripes*. The political upheaval and the antiwar protests were kind of a gnat on my worry back, compared with the elephant of being in combat and trying to keep American soldiers alive. What bothered me the most, and it still sticks in my craw, is Jane Fonda, Hanoi Jane. In spite of all the wonderful things she has done, I will never forgive her for flying to Hanoi and saying the anti-American things vehemently, saying how bad the United States was and the baby-killers and the rotten, nasty American military and the crap that they're doing. I'll never, ever forgive her for that.

When you were in a twelve-month combat zone back in those days, you were given a one-week R&R. I had a choice of three or four countries to go to, and I thought that Bangkok, Thailand, sounded like a place that I would never go on my own. There was an R&R hotel that the military had contracted and it was very, very nice. Not luxury, but nice. And there were all kinds of things that you could do, and of course I did all the touristy things, like the boat through the floating market.

And my wife's going to kill me for telling the story, but I'll tell it anyway: I got hooked up with a real nice guy, and of course he wanted to practice his English, and he spoke English perfectly, and he said that his friend's uncle owned a jewelry store. I wanted to get something nice for Barbara. And I had been looking at sapphires. I went to all the touristy stores, and they were a little more than I wanted to pay. In fact, they were much more than I wanted to pay. I found one at his uncle's jewelry store and it looked as nice, if not nicer than the ones I saw, and I ended up with what I thought was a reasonable price. It was a couple hundred dollars, and that was one of the things I brought home, and my wife had it made into a ring. And it's been appraised and, yes, it's real. Just like in Saigon, prostitution was rampant in Bangkok, and I'm proud to say that I'm sure I talked to prostitutes, but that's as far as I went. I mentioned to Chris [his grandson, then TCU Army ROTC cadet Chris Lamoureux] the other day that in my thirty years in the Army and post-Army, that's one thing I didn't do. And I never smoked marijuana. It was just enjoyable to get away from the combat.

So when the Tet Offensive hit I was on my way back to Vietnam from Bangkok, Thailand. I was flying to Cam Ranh Bay. Then we got buttoned up there in Cam Ranh. I couldn't get back to my unit because my unit was in An Khe in the Central Highlands, so I was buttoned up there for two or three days. It was a very big deal. I think it caught the American military leadership off guard. I don't think we thought the NVA was capable of executing a mission like that. And it wasn't just here or there, it was from the Delta all the way up to Saigon, Nha Trang, Pleiku, and we were maybe a hundred kilometers from Pleiku. That was the next-biggest city in the Central Highlands, and we were north of that location. I think it changed the thinking and the tenor of the ebb and flow of battle. I really think it caught us off guard. We didn't think they could ever have done that, and it caused a lot of damage. There were a lot of KIAs. I think it helped strengthen the antiwar movement, and I think it gave Johnson the second thoughts that he had: "Well, maybe we need to figure a way to get out of this Vietnam mess." Which they eventually did.

Combat is not safe for women, children, or living things. It's just not, and it doesn't always accomplish what the national leadership thought it was supposed to accomplish. I remember going into Vietnam. We were invincible. We're the American military, for goodness' sakes. Here's a little pipsqueak. It's just like saying ISIS is the JV team. I would never underrate an opponent. I'm sure there were political handcuffs put on military leadership in country, and that's another whole issue: whether or not we could cross into Cambodia. We know now that we did, because

I provided support for our forces that went into Cambodia and weren't supposed to, as early as 1967.

I'm not sure we should have ever entered Vietnam. I'm really not sure. Part of me says we should have, part of me says we shouldn't. But I would hope, from a historical perspective, as lessons learned, we would never enter a major combat zone, theatre, operation, without the intent of winning and doing whatever it takes to win.

"Not everyone was supportive of troops."

Dan Southard

Following five months as a forward observer, I was assigned as the battalion's assistant S3 officer (operations officer). My new duty was to clear all artillery missions in the battalion's operational sector and calculate firing data for battalion artillery batteries (three batteries of 105mm and three batteries of 155mm howitzers). This duty required that I work from a bunker at the top of LZ Baldy. The days were long, but the bunker did have advantages (hot meals and a bunk out of the elements). Following two months as the assistant operations officer, my next assignment was to command an artillery battery. I remained a battery commander until my discharge from the Marines.

The battalion left Vietnam and sailed home on an LST (landing ship transport, USS *Cayuga*, LST 1186). Prior to leaving Vietnam, we met with the ARVN (South Vietnamese army) and offered to give them all the battalion's equipment rather than pack it on the ship. We were amazed and disappointed that the ARVN rejected our offer because the equipment was not new. Therefore, we loaded all our gear (jeeps, trucks, artillery, weapons, etc.) in the hull of the ship and sailed for San Diego. Three weeks later, including stops at Subic Bay in the Philippines and Hawaii, we arrived in San Diego. We offloaded the gear and began a forty-mile drive to the Marine base at Camp Pendleton, California.

It was on Interstate 5 that I discovered that not everyone was particularly excited about our return from Vietnam. I was the junior Marine officer and the only battery commander returning by ship. Consequently, I was in charge of the convoy to Pendleton. I was located in the lead jeep, with all other vehicles behind me. Halfway to Pendleton, the California Highway Patrol pulled my jeep over to the side of the road. There were twenty-some vehicles pulling howitzers, loaded with troops and weapons that followed. The officer got out of his patrol car and walked towards my jeep. My first thought was that he would provide us an escort to Pendleton. I was wrong: He wrote a citation for each vehicle because it did not have a pollution control device. I explained that we had just returned from Vietnam. He didn't say a word but dropped each citation in my lap and walked away. I remember yelling to him, "Thanks for the welcome home!" or words to that effect. When we arrived at Pendleton I explained the situation to my commanding officer, and he promptly tore up all the citations. I never heard any more about the issue, but realized that not everyone was supportive of troops returning from Vietnam.

There were other indications that not everyone supported troops in Vietnam. Before members of the battery could go on leave, it was mandatory that they attend a lecture on how to react to civilian protestors they might encounter. They were instructed to protect themselves if necessary, but to ignore anyone who yelled profanity or spat on their uniform. A couple of weeks later, a member of the battery returning from leave was concerned that he was in trouble with civilian police. He explained that an individual had spat on him at the San Diego airport, he had broken the person's nose, and security had grabbed him and taken his name and military address. He was concerned about possible civilian jail time. I told him not to worry and that I would likely have done the same. Other incidents ranged from general disrespect to physical intimidation. I should add that there were also a number of broken noses at the San Diego airport! Thankfully there were no repercussions from such incidents, but it was once again clear that not everyone was enthusiastic about our return from Vietnam. The general attitude of the public towards military seemed very different in 1971 than it is now!

It was later in June that I was able to go on leave. I was expecting trouble in the San Diego airport, but I boarded the flight to Minneapolis without incident. It was then that I had an "uplifting" (no pun intended) experience on the flight home. I was wearing my uniform—a requirement when flying military passage—and was the only military person in uniform on the flight. During the flight, a number of anonymous passengers bought me drinks (rum and Coke as I remember). After receiving the first two I asked the stewardess to thank individuals but to decline additional drinks. Instead, the drinks just kept coming and piled up on my tray. At the end of the flight, all the people ahead of me waited while I exited the aircraft. The experience renewed my faith in the public, and

I took this as an example of the "silent" majority.

Following my release from active duty I attended graduate school at the University of Iowa, graduated with a PhD, and accepted a position as assistant professor of kinesiology at TCU in 1980. The rest is TCU history.

"We loved the young men and women under our command."

William Dwiggins

One of the most difficult tasks a leader never wants to do is to write a letter to a mother, father, sister, brother, wife, husband, and loved ones, telling them that their son or daughter has lost their life while serving in uniform. This is a most difficult assignment that is deeply personal and impactful.

Being a commanding officer is a position of responsibility, which allows you to lead and command men and women in uniform. A lesson learned only through firsthand experience is the burden that command carries with it.

We loved the young men and women under our command. If even one of our members in the command was to get hurt, injured or lost, this hurts. It is a memory that is never lost as part of the burden of command. So I pray. I have not really shared with anyone for years that I would pray. Probably more than I realize when in command, and particularly while in combat. Having to write a letter to a family, prayers are needed more than ever.

The letter cannot be a long one. In most situations, the family has already been notified of the loss of their loved one. So before a leader sits down to write a condolence letter, which is not a long letter, detailing that loss, the family is aware of the loss and wants closure about what happened, when, where, and how. This letter is not the one that deep detail is written into. You do work diligently to explain what you can, and how valued the servicemember was to the unit and among their companions. This is when a leader gets personally close and involved with their feelings and shares our personal side about how deeply we care for those men and women in uniform under our command. We talk about the person, what they were like, and how we pray no harm is ever done or inflicted upon them.

We want the family to know that we understand that it's not easy for them to accept that they lost someone that's precious to them and to our nation. We search for just the right words to express the sincerity of how important this one letter is, and how much each word will mean to the family. I truly believe that there's no greater love a man can show or give, than to give his life for his fellow man.

I have struggled with how to say, in a page or more, what the family already knows. I still struggle with the face of that young man I lost early in my career, which is imprinted in my mind forever, as I'm sure it is in those families' hearts. We live in a great nation, and we humbly thank these families for the opportunity to have been with such a great American.

As leaders, you write that all-important letter thirty or forty times before you get to a decent heartfelt letter. After you have written that letter, you always wonder, "Did I say the message correctly and clearly?" At the end of the day it's just, "I'm sorry for your loss, but this nation is so thankful to you."

And you can't say, "Wishing for the best," or anything like that, because you know that's not possible. As a leader you are humbled, and you are thankful. And that's about as deep as you can really get.

As leaders, we write that unthinkable letter on behalf of the United States of America. I was going to say the military, but really, it is on behalf of this great nation.

Leading the Way

The Story of Robert MacIvor

Virginia MacIvor Meyn

Originally titled "Waiting for My Dad to Come Home." Drawn from an audiotaped memoir (1995), archived letters, and interviews. Virginia MacIvor Meyn is the mother of TCU Professor Till MacIvor Meyn.

I was four years old when my father, Robert Jewell MacIvor (Bob), joined the Army. On March 29, 1942, he boarded a bus with a group of other young recruits at the Oakland Hotel in downtown Marysville, a village in central Ohio. I keenly remember going with Mother to take him down to the bus station. He headed out with bold dreams, "innocent and simple as I was," of serving his country as a combat infantryman. He was twenty-eight years old, owner of an insurance business in its infancy, and married to the woman of his dreams, Virginia Cox. It would fall on her shoulders to learn the business and make it thrive until Captain Robert MacIvor returned on February 2, 1946 . . . and to find help to care for me, as well as the little brick cottage we shared at the end of town at 804 West Seventh Street.

Why would a striving young businessman, husband, and father nearing thirty years old choose to enlist, against the odds that faced him? He recoiled at the thought of leaving the warmth and safety of home, and he was by nature a sensitive man for whom combat experience would be predictably traumatic (he described it in his memoir, recorded in 1995, as "soul-searing"). He had a little girl who needed him. His wife had no training or experience in the business world, let alone insurance, and his wife's parents and three sisters all vehemently opposed my father's decision to enlist. In addition, when he volunteered, the draft board tried to talk him out of it because of his family commitments. "But," he said in his recorded memoir, "I knew I could never live with myself if I didn't go through with this thing."

Enter Bob's father, Angus MacIvor, respected physician and church elder pronounced "saintly" by all who knew him, including us. (I spent a great deal of time with Grandmother and Grandfather, who lived only a few minutes from us.) There are few words to describe Bob's devotion to his father and the impact his father had.

Born on Cape Breton Island in Nova Scotia to Highland Scots, stern in essence and Calvinistic by tradition, Angus felt at his core a profound need to be of service, not only in his medical practice but to the community and country at large. This was displayed by his proud service in World War I as regimental surgeon of the 166th Infantry in France for eighteen months, and beyond that, on General MacArthur's staff as division sanitary inspector of the 42nd Rainbow Division. He continued after the war to work in the US Public Health Service, until he entered into private medical practice in 1922. He, too, left a four-year-old child, "Bobbie," behind. In the years following the war, that child became enthralled with war stories his father told at the dinner table night after night. He saw the glamorous side and used to dress up in little Army uniforms in which he was photographed proudly waving the American flag. "I wanted to live up to what my father was," he said in his memoirs. In the months before he died, my father told me this: "I never should have gone, but I wanted to honor my father."

Of course that meant also honoring and embodying the *values* of his father. The numerous letters my grandfather wrote my father during World War II reflect those values again and again. "Keep up your courage and remember that the US Army and Navy and Air Corps are the greatest institutions in the world, because our very lives depend upon the protection they afford us." "I know the life of the soldier. He must have courage to combat all the extraneous influences about him, and he must have the strength to master himself that he may be the best that it is possible for him to be, and no man is the best soldier possible, unless he lives such a life that he is unafraid to die." And on and on, letter after letter. He also wrote, "I have always felt you could take it, Bob."

And *take it* my father did.

Perhaps because he was able to have a perspective on the war as something of a panorama he could view from above as well as from within—another reason he enlisted, as well as how he was able to survive—my father could from time to time stand back and take stock of the bigger picture instead of drowning in the "nightmare of reality" he experienced on the ground. His main field of interest happened to be history, and he was well read and well informed.

A typical pursuit from September 1, 1939 on, when Germany invaded Poland (the "bombshell of destiny," he called it), was to avidly listen to a little Philco short-wave radio to which he had attached a long aerial set up in our backyard. He "wanted to learn all he could." His radio was able to bring in British and German broadcasts very clearly. "The lights are going out all over Europe," exclaimed one British commentator. In came Hitler's "ranting and raving" and the "animal roar" of applause that followed. In came the dramatic battle details from Edward R. Murrow reporting from overseas. In came the new Prime Minister Winston Churchill's eloquent speeches so empowering that in his memoir my father was reciting passages from them verbatim with a hint of emotion in his voice. It becomes clear to us that the call to arms was not only a duty to honor those who fought before or even alone to vanquish an evil dictator, it was an inspiration in one's very soul to serve the highest cause.

The 1939–1940 period that followed the invasion of Poland, called the "Phoney War," deceived many Americans into believing that perhaps the threat of war would fizzle out. My father feared otherwise. He saw how powerful the German Panzer division was. In 1940 the "unstoppable" Germans broke through the Maginot line into France, the French surrendered, and the English retreated back to the sea. Then came the miraculous rescue at Dunkirk and the boost to the British morale. America still held out until the "terrible shock" of Pearl Harbor on December 7, 1941.

My father was lying on the couch in the living room, listening to an opera broadcast, when a sudden announcement broke in that Japan had just bombed Pearl Harbor. That's when "I knew we were in for a long hard time of it," he said. And that's when he felt that he could not escape a calling to serve in the "queen of battles," as he put it, the infantry. He applied to enter Officer Candidate School.

Fate was to have it otherwise. He was sent to Jefferson Barracks in

St. Louis, an Army Air Corps post, for six months, impatiently chafing under the confusion with the paperwork he'd submitted. (I wonder how often this kind of thing happened.) Letters from his father remind him not to complain but to "keep up your courage and remember many others have perplexing and aggravating problems."

Finally, in October of 1942, he was assigned to infantry school at Fort Benning, Georgia, graduating January 6, 1943, as a second lieutenant. At the back of the graduation program is printed a long poem my father wrote commemorating the event (see Postscript). He has still retained his buoyancy, but not without a streak of irony that was to pervade all his memories of the war years.

He was subsequently sent to Camp Wheeler, an infantry replacement training center, for thirteen months, where he was promoted to first lieutenant, then to Fort Jackson for three months, where he was assigned to a service company as commanding officer, a role usually reserved for the rank of captain. My grandfather writes: "I am convinced that you will be happy in the responsibility which calls for personal leadership. The Army is efficient only as each officer and man places special value upon the role he is called upon to play, and applies all the intelligent effort he possesses to the fulfillment of every task." He also exclaims in a letter a few days later that he has little patience with men in the service who are overly emotional or psychologically burdened.

Ah, what a burden those words might have been to my father's ears, and then again perhaps they were uplifting. We'll never know, but can only imagine. We only know my father requested, and was granted, reassignment overseas in May of 1944. After landing in Liverpool (the destination was unknown to them until they were underway), he spent two months in Southampton on alert, waiting and watching the skies.

> We woke up one morning and the sky was full of planes
> from horizon to horizon on their way southeast to France.
> We knew then that the [Normandy] invasion was underway.
> . . . The date was, of course, June 6, 1944, an exciting
> time that certainly made us feel we were a part of history,
> although not as much a part as those who landed at
> Omaha Beach; certainly no one would wish for that
> dreadful experience.

"In July we got our orders and headed across a very rough North Sea to the French coast. Then we headed for Omaha Beach." Nineteen Forty-four was an exceptionally stormy summer, so the seas were too rough for landing. "I would stand on deck at night, watching lightning flashes of artillery and the boom of heavy guns . . . like a huge thunderstorm lighting up the horizon." When they were finally able to land, they headed inland. "One or two of us went down to look at the beach . . . which was strewn with all kinds of armaments, ammunition, helmets . . . almost everything German and American you could imagine."

So far my father has been an observer, taking stock, watching and waiting and, from what it would seem, wandering and wondering. He notes that he and his outfit move up and down the beach with no direct assignment. He reminds us that they were still just a replacement outfit of lieutenants "with very little authority or power and no one to look out for us. . . . It became a way of life." The fact that he had no chance to train in the States with an outfit and go overseas with men he knew was, he said, the most difficult issue he faced in the Army.

As my father's outfit follows the troops across France, his memoir offers us blow-by-blow experiences, some he calls weird, some tragic, some exhilarating, terrifying, boring. In intervals between battles we encounter train wrecks, a bunch of drunken soldiers who fail to make the train carrying their outfit (my father has to retrieve them and also misses the train), and so it goes. Of the battles he reports, "We went from engagement to engagement, some trivial, some black with despair." Many descriptions take us inside the moment, inside the landscape, the trench or the hill or the march on and on.

Encamped on a hill all day, for example, he watches deep combat in the valley below "as if it were a panorama laid out for our entertainment": the unreality of it all—a dead GI lying in the middle distance, a wounded German soldier crawling up the road, other walking wounded, a hospital, a German Red Cross truck unloading the wounded. That night, two or three mortar rounds shook the windows violently and landed in front of the farmhouse where my father and his outfit were encamped. "We started down the road to the 'valley of death,'" he said, to the battleground they'd been observing. Reality swiftly set in—my father's first real taste of close combat.

The emotional toll of combat is not lost on us as we hear him describe a time when, during the night, his troop opened machine gun fire upon having discovered a German patrol near their position. This was followed by yelling and screaming, and then a deadly quiet pierced by the explosion of a German grenade near his post, and more screaming. "Next morning," he said, "we found four men out there, two dead and two wounded who had been crying and screaming the whole night through." In an understatement he adds, "It wasn't exactly a night for sleep."

The following tragic episode is another example of the kind of experience that marked the life of a combat infantryman:

> We were supposed to take a French village by the name of Achen. We went in one morning, met heavy artillery fire above the town, and then we proceeded down into the town, actually walked into a cul de sac, an ambush. At the time I was commanding the weapons platoon, which consisted of three 60 millimeter mortars and two light machine guns, so I was not with the first platoon but was behind them directing the machine gun fire to give them cover. They met terrible resistance in this pocket, and the next morning, after a whole afternoon of rather desperate fighting, we discovered that almost the whole first platoon had been killed. That was perhaps the saddest day of my war years. It seemed so useless and so fruitless, and yet that's the way the war was, and the way it went on.

His responsibilities as a commanding officer and as a compassionate fellow being weighed heavily on him. When his boys were about to loot a house they were occupying, he insisted the German family and their belongings be protected and in fact requested that my mother send them blankets and food—care packages—both during and after the war. We are close friends with this family still.

With the exception of an incident at the end of December 1944, when his face and hands were severely burned by boiling water as he stumbled in the dark hall of a house his troops were occupying, my father did not receive a scratch (a piece of shrapnel pierced his legging with a terrible whack but never penetrated the skin!). After the burn he was evacuated to England and spent several weeks in medical care. When he arrived back in Cherbourg, he slowly followed his division back across

France and Germany up to the banks of the Elbe just south of Berlin. To his surprise he found an entirely different war. "We, for a change," he said, "were occupying the buildings."

The war would soon be over, but my father reports he had no inkling of this. When VE Day finally arrived on May 8, his memoirs tell us that he still continued to move from place to place, trying to maintain order without any purpose whatsoever.

The summer dragged on. And then the dramatic and definitive end of the war came, when the atomic bomb was dropped on Japan in early August, and VJ Day was announced August 14. But the boys? There followed some confusion about who was going home when. Delay after delay occurred, and then at last my father was honorably discharged from the armed services on February 2, 1946: Captain Robert J. MacIvor, 134th Infantry, 35th Division. He returned home to welcoming arms.

What is one to make of his experience? It must have been like many others'. And yet something tells me his unique perspective gives us perhaps greater insight into the breadth and depth of a soldier's experience and of the profound contradictions: both the fruitlessness and the necessity of war, the rigid order and the formlessness, the convergences and the chaos. The irony was not lost on him. He once told me he regretted not having the makings of a hero, which he defined essentially as a man who is able to act without thinking. The fact that a man conquers his own demons to serve a greater cause is hero enough for me.

How did we, his family, manage without him, and then with him on his return? During the war this little girl had nightmares of being bombed, nightmares that pursued her into the light of day. News reports blasted from my grandfather's radio day by day because he'd lost his hearing as the result of a shell explosion. Terrifying pictures were projected on Pathe News in the movie theater. With this kind of exposure I often felt, very simply, terrorized. My mother was working every day in the insurance office my father left behind, and I was watched by a woman from the local Women's Reformatory (prison) when I wasn't with my dear grandmother.

I cannot speak for my mother. She worked steadily at the office but also saw to my care. I remember helping her and my grandmother pack care packages both for the German family and for my father, whom I was instructed to address as "Dear Bobbie" in my letters. I envied him the Hershey bars they carefully included in the package.

The impact hit when dear Bobbie returned. He was a stranger to me, not the "daddy" I had dreamed about and longed for. I knew from my mother that he was having terrifying nightmares of the battlefield night after night, but I didn't understand why I couldn't invite my friends over to play and why I had to be so quiet. He was, and he continued through my teen years at home, to be emotionally unreliable, up and down. In later years, we became good and loving friends who shared a common interest in ideas. By then I had come to terms, and so to a large extent had he.

The burden was on my mother, who became in many ways his care-giver, first of the emotions, and then later of a body increasingly wracked with the pain of rheumatoid arthritis. They made a good life together until their early nineties, and they loved each other devotedly. But I don't think the man she married came home. After my father died in 2003 and we brought Mother to live near us in a retirement home in North Carolina, the only picture of my father she kept was the one of him as a soldier in uniform before he went overseas; she placed it over her desk. I guess she was still waiting. She died the following year.

Postscript

No matter where I go from here
No matter what I do
Oh land of pine and sand and clay
I'm not forgetting you.
For it's fall out here and fall out there
Until the day is done
It's fall out, Corporal! Fall out, Coach!
And fall out number one.
It's hold that base stake! Line that plate!
And line it true and right!
Deflection zero! Give your range!
One round of H. E. Light!
Some days the sweat runs in your eyes
Smeared in with grimy hands
On some you freeze your very heart
And shudder in the stands

But it will end as all things must
  In a life of wounds and scars
When someone says in a loud clear voice,
  "Fall out and get those bars!"
For then you feel that victory's yours
  You're one of those most blest.
You're pretty good. You've won your spurs
  You've passed your graded test.
But ah my boy, the test to come
  Is not of gun nor map
For though it's fall out, Corporal, here,
  O'er there it's fall out—Jap.
For over there they play for keeps
  And if you prove a dud
The test that you may fail to pass
  Is marked in someone's blood.
So learn your lines and lessons well
  To that day which must come
When someone says "Fall out, my boy"
  Your job is finally done.
You've fought the good fight, stood the test
  You knew the gunner's rule
You fired a steady burst of six
  And kept your barrel cool.
And as for me, when life is done
  And age has dimmed my sight,
I hope they'll mount an "81"
  On some stern rocky height.
And there they'll fire one round for me
  A round of H. E. Light.

R. J. MacIvor, January 6, 1943
Officer Candidate Graduation
Fort Benning, Georgia

The Journey Continues

"What he left behind was special."

David and Teresa Schmidt

Teresa Schmidt: Benjamin loved sports. He excelled in competition. And if he lost in anything, he was not a sore sport or anything. As far as he knew, if he lost, he still won. He just kept going. It never slowed him down. I think the military was along the same lines. It kept him pushing forward. I know that was the disciplinary part of him. He would come home on leave from the military, and just was a little quieter. Of course he had matured too, but his reactions—it's hard to explain it, but his reactions to things, you could just tell he saw things differently.

David Schmidt: You could tell that he did not enjoy the thought of killing people.

My own personal thought is that, because we have an all-voluntary military, people just don't get it, which is very, very frustrating. We've been at war for longer than we've ever been in our country's entire history. Vietnam vets were spit on, despised, because it was a bad war. But I think, generally speaking, Americans are proud of our vets that have been in Iraq and Afghanistan. But the normal American citizen does not understand that we are at war. They just don't get it, because the enemy is not your kind of normal enemy. It's not like a whole bunch of guys are going out and marching against a whole bunch of other guys. Instead, guys are blowing shit up, blowing people up, suicide bombers, you know, both here and abroad. They don't get war. They don't understand war. And I think, at least for the military guys I've talked to, that's what's frustrating. Certainly it is for me as well.

The other thing is, it does not appear that we go to wars to win. We didn't win Korea, we didn't win Vietnam, we didn't win in Afghanistan, we didn't win in Iraq. If you go to war, you've got to kill the bad guys and win. When you lose your son in a country that still is a shithole, it's kind of frustrating.

We are still exceedingly proud of him. Even more proud of him for what he left behind. There's not many kids that have the impact even after his death that he did. He's had an impact on TCU that will last forever. Certainly we don't feel like he lost his life in vain. Obviously you don't like that you lose your son, but what he did, what he left behind, is really pretty special.

"If there's a benefit package, you use the benefits."

Rodney Baker

I can honestly say, Mr. Casey, everything I've ever wanted to accomplish in my fifty-one years on this earth, I've actually done. I can honestly say, and you can quote me on this, I have made and spent a million dollars. So I've already been a millionaire. I've got nothing else material that I just gotta have. I can come to work and go home at night, sleep in a comfortable bed. I have a nice car; I have a separate car to drive on Sunday when I go to church. My wife has gotten her education, which, through my hard work, we were able to pay for from the benefits here at TCU. My son is in college. I learned in the Navy that you're not always going to get paid what you think you're worth. But if there's a benefit package, you use the benefits. So that's what I do. That's how I see life.

Q: Have you stayed in touch with any of the young people that you recruited?

Yes. Interesting story, young man, I won't give his name. We had to take the ASVAB score, which is an aptitude test to see if you're qualified to get into the Navy. He was what they considered a category four, the lowest possible score, the cutoff line to qualify. Matter of fact, he was below the cutoff line. We got down to the end of the month, and the recruiting district was not going to make its goal, so they gave us X number of billets of category fours, which is a lower standard. And this young man said, "Officer Baker, I wanna join. I wanna join." So I said, "As soon as I can get a job for you, I'm going to get you in." So at the end of the month, we got him in. He excelled. The only job he could qualify for was the boatswain mate. Boatswain mates paint, chip paint, tie the ship up, sweep, swab, a lot of manual labor, and maintain the boats. But during the course of this time, he qualified as a small boat coxswain, so he drives a small boat. He got qualified as a ship's bridge operator, so he could drive the whole ship. He could manage the steering gears; he could operate cranes and booms. He learned all this, supposedly no aptitude to do this. And over the years, he continued to grow and be successful in the Navy. Right now, he is a US Navy Command Master Chief in Hawaii. And this is a kid that they said he couldn't do it. I believed in him, we worked with him. We talk maybe once every six months.

The very first kid I ever put in the Navy as a recruiter in Columbus, Georgia, Brad, is a senior chief in San Antonio right now, getting ready to retire. And I know his family, we talk all the time. I know these kids by name. One, Cordell, is here. He only served four years, but he went in as a master-at-arms and now he's an intake parole officer over in Plano, Texas. So there are people all over that I've put in, and we stay in touch. I have guys that I served with, we talk all the time, and we go see each other. It's just an extended family. And they'll send me an email: "Hey, do you know anybody that needs this?" Or "Hey, I got a guy that wanted to go to school." And I'm going to say, "Well, look at Southern New Hampshire University. They have a great online veterans' program." And he got into the school, and we showed him how to use his benefits.

"There was a breakdown in the system."

Charles Lamb

My time in Vietnam was really hard on my father. My father had been in the Marine Corps during World War II, and he had a sense for what was going on in Vietnam. I was there during the worst part of the war. My mother said that my father sat in his chair every night and watched the evening news. It was all about Vietnam, and all of the news was bad news. He knew in his heart that I wasn't coming home.

My parents were not notified when I contracted malaria. But the first time I was wounded, the Department of Defense followed a standard procedure of sending a telegram notifying next of kin of a soldier's injuries. This was sent to a place that accepted telegrams close to where the next of kin lived. And we had lived in the same small town for many, many years. The telegram went to the pharmacy, and everybody at the pharmacy knew my parents, and they knew who I was. The telegram sounded like I was hurt worse than I really was, and nobody wanted to tell my parents. Finally someone called them, and they took the telegram over to my parents.

The second time I was wounded, I called my parents from Japan. It was probably two weeks after I'd been wounded. We had pay phones, and I called collect, and it seems to me it was in the middle of the night at home. I told them I was in Japan and I was okay—well, I thought I was going to be okay. They hadn't been contacted, so there was a breakdown in the system of notifying them the second time. It was probably better, as it turned out. If the telegram had said, "Your son has a broken leg, he was shot twice, he has a fractured tibia, we're not certain if he'll have to have it amputated or not," that wouldn't have been received very well. But to talk to me and for me to tell them the story was better. I think they were more relieved than anything else that I was out. I was not going back to Vietnam.

I don't know what the numbers were, but the daily and weekly American casualties in Vietnam were astounding. It's hard on everyone in that kind of a situation. Even though you don't know many of your comrades well, you know them well, you've been around them and you've talked to them. You usually knew a little bit about everybody.

Q: Looking back on all of it, would you have made the same decision to just wait and be drafted?

No.

Q: What would you have done?

I would have enlisted in a less dangerous branch of the military, maybe the Coast Guard. My life was on the line every day that I was out there, as was everybody else's. I would've never taken that risk. If I had to give up two more years, I would've given them up. It was a bad decision on my part. It was a bad calculation. It was the wrong one. It's good for some, but it wasn't for me.

I'm proud that I served my country. I guess that is the most important thing. I just wish it hadn't been so damned hard!

"If you really mean that, don't give me a platitude."

Marty Leewright

I see the big picture now, and the way I feel about it now is, why in the hell was I there? Why in the hell did I risk my life? Why in the hell did my friends have to die? Why did my friend, Don Huey, who had ten days before he was gonna go home, why did he have to die there? He's on the Wall. Donald R. Huey. H-U-E-Y. He died in 1970, I think in September. But it's like, "Why did all these men have to die?" I think our casualties in Cambodia were like 370 dead and maybe 1,500 or 2,000 wounded. And we left Saigon with our tail between our legs. So the perspective I have now is, "Why? Why were we asked to do that?" And the country wasn't behind us. Such a waste. It was years and years before anybody said to me, "Thank you for your service." In the last decade it's become sort of fashionable to say, "Thank you for your service." You hear people say that, you see it on Facebook all the time. For nearly thirty years, no one ever said that to me.

But it makes me angry, because it seems a platitude. It seems like a result and a reaction to guilt that we felt about the way soldiers were treated when they came back from Vietnam and that finally coalesced in this collective, I guess, repentance of saying, "Thank you for your service," for the last two or three conflicts that we've been in. I want to say to people, "If you really want to thank me for my service, do something about the VA. If you really want to thank Vietnam veterans, do something about Agent Orange. Don't let this dysfunctional VA continue for another thirty, forty, fifty years." I can show you articles from 1970 in *Life* magazine about the dysfunction at the VA and the treatment of veterans.

And my own treatment by the VA, or mistreatment, I guess you could say, with my issues with Agent Orange, the denial of disability claims and the delay, and I was supposed to have an appointment with a neurologist at the VA, and they said, "Oh, it's gonna take fifty days, so we're gonna put you in this new Veterans Choice Program and expedite this new bill, you'll go to a private doctor." And they said, "Be sure to call in three days." I did. I called and they said, "We don't have the information from the VA yet, so could you call back after ten days?" I said, "Sure." I called back after ten days. "But we still don't have the information from the VA." I called the VA, and you call the VA and getting lost in their phone system is like getting lost in a labyrinth somewhere, where you finally get a live person and they'll go, "Oh, yeah. We'll call you back. We'll look into that, call you back." And you never get a call back, and so you wait. You wait and wait.

And it's not fifty days. A hundred and nine days later, they set an appointment for me with a doctor, not in Fort Worth, 'cause they couldn't find a single doctor who would take the VA Choice Program here. He was a doctor in Arlington, a different city. And by that time, my wife had insisted I already go to a private neurologist. So I'd gone to a private doctor at my own expense. That's the kind of treatment that we get. It's like Agent Orange was an insult, and the United States government was probably the most deadly enemy that we faced in Vietnam and Cambodia. I think if you do your research, you'll find that not only did fifty-eight or sixty thousand soldiers die there, but probably over 300,000 have died from the effects of Agent Orange, millions of gallons of the stuff that was sprayed all over Vietnam. That was Monsanto and the other big chemical companies that were making millions of dollars on that stuff. They were putting it in used oil from electrical transformers, because when you spray Agent Orange, if you just spray it on the leaves, it rained a lot over there, it will just wash off. But if you put it in oil, it's stickier. Droplets of oil will stay on leaves longer and defoliate better, but it'll also be on the surface of the water you were drinking and bathing in and so forth. Those companies were making millions and millions of dollars off the implements of war and chemicals of war. The most heavily sprayed area was the III Corps where I was, my entire time, other than the six weeks in Cambodia, which was just outside of III Corps, and Cambodia was sprayed too. That whole border was sprayed. That was the first insult. That's an insult that'll last a lifetime.

So what I want to say to people when they say, "Thank you for your service," this would be impolite, and I'd never say this, but I want to say, "Go to hell." If you really mean that, don't give me a platitude. You and our politicians and our government and every American citizen need to do something about the VA and the way they treat veterans, not just from Vietnam, but from all the conflicts, because we send them off to war and we spend all this money, but when we damage these soldiers and the damaged goods come back, there's no money in taking care of them. No money to be made. It pisses me off, and I don't want to hear it. I'm not impolite. I don't say things to my friends and stuff. I'll just nod and acknowledge that they've said something like that, but it's an empty thing to me.

"I use my veteran status as my identity."

Israel Sanchez

Texas has not really been kind to me. Being a gay male, being here has been a complete culture shock. People are not used to somebody like me. Coming from California, I'm very outspoken. I'm not going to bite my tongue. If I see something that's not right I'm going to speak up about it, because I'm just as guilty if I don't speak up about it. So that's what I've been dealing with while I've been here.

That's why I use my veteran status as my identity, because that automatically pushes away the stigma of the LGBT community. But then once I break through that first barrier, now I have to peel everything back like an onion. So now I'm like, "Oh yeah, by the way, I'm homosexual and I am proud, and I'm going to speak up for my community." I think that's where I've become a big advocate for the LGBT community, because we're a minority population that is completely overlooked in medicine.

Here in Texas, being a veteran tells people—well, they're just honored to have you do what you did in the military. I'll give you an example. Yesterday I was in clinical, and I had a patient that I followed throughout the entire rotation, from admitting him to going through surgery. I saw his total knee replacement, and I followed him to the PACU, which is the recovery unit, and then I got to take him upstairs. We were talking about religion, and he brought up that he was a Southern Baptist, and I told him I grew up United Pentecostal. And then he's like, "So you were in the military," and I said, "I was," and he's like, "How was your experience?" I knew what he was referring to. He was referring to the fact that I was a homosexual and he was curious, and he didn't know how to ask me. That was okay.

I'm professional, as I always am, and I wanted to break that barrier with him. But after I told him my story, after I told him who I was, after I told him what I'm planning on doing, he then told me that he had stopped talking to his son for eight years, because his son was a homosexual. And he said, "You have given me a complete eye-opener. Religion has completely ruined my family." We were talking about that, and I said, "Well, it's all in the belief system. But I've read biblical scripture, and I always tell people that sometimes you've just got to go with the true message of why you're considered a Christian." And he was like, "What's that?" I said, "Unconditional love."

"I credit the Marine Corps with saving my life."

Richard Spence

The Marine Corps is what made me the man I am today. Completing twenty-eight years, living in different places and developing different types of programs and writing operational manuals, has been one of those highlights that I've had in the Marine Corps. One of the proudest things I can say is that, in my twenty-eight years, I have never lost a Marine. I also credit the Marine Corps with saving my life and giving me life by meeting my beautiful wife, a Marine, as well and giving me three precious children.

"It shaped me to the person that I am."

Michael Blackert

I learned more about myself. I learned more about how our government operates. I learned more about things that I would have never even thought to think of or learn if I wouldn't have served. Even when I was on the ground, there were a lot of things I didn't believe in, like even some of the missions we were doing. I didn't think they were right. Some of the people that we would detain. I'm taking your dad away at two o'clock in the morning, and your kids are screaming, and the ten-year-old sees all this, and what have I just done to him? I didn't think about it then.

As I kept going over there more and more every year, and I was in some of the same areas, I would see some of the same kids that I had seen three years prior. And they wanted to come up to us then, and now they don't want to come up to us. You start to see both sides. The whole revenge mentality I had going in deteriorated really quickly after that first deployment. After the first few months, it wasn't even that for me. It was like, man, if these people were my age and younger, then that's all they've ever seen. They were born in the nineties or even the eighties. The Iraq-Iran war has been going since the seventies. So all these people have seen is war. There's no such thing as PTSD in Third World countries. That's normal to them. It's not a term that they use. Sure, they may now, because we use it so freely in our country, but to them it's every day. Guns fired, things going off, shady people, whatever.

It shaped me to the person that I am; I appreciate a lot nowadays. I'm a glass-half-full kind of guy, even if it's been a crappy day or whatever. Sure, I have my bad days too, don't get me wrong. But I think ultimately

Army veteran Michael Blackert with fellow soldiers.
Courtesy of Michael Blackert.

and as a whole, I see things a lot differently now. There are certain things that I can't turn off. Like when I'm driving, I'm still scanning when I drive. It's one of those things. I still think, "If we were attacked right here, this is my exit point. I could use this as a concealment area." It's crazy, but that's still the way I think when I drive. I can't turn that part off, at all.

"The military made me a better man."

John Garcia

[Separation from the military] was forced on me. I was hurt. So I was medically retired so, yeah, it was very difficult. I think I had five and some change years until I could actually retire, so yeah, it was difficult for me to transition. I took it pretty hard. I've been diagnosed with PTSD, I've also been diagnosed with clinical depression. I think that, because my PTSD and my depression was just enhanced at the time, it was very hard for me. I shut everybody out, I secluded myself, I didn't want to speak to people, I self-medicated with alcohol. I felt it was unfair with how things went. You ask, "Why me?" and stuff like that. Because I was in great shape at one point in my life, and to just be injured and to feel pain pretty much every day and your career is taken from you—it just sucks, plain and simple.

I can say, knowing what I know now, I would not change a thing. I had no future if I had stayed here. I mean, I was ready to get into trouble, so it was just a matter of time whether I was dead or in prison, and that's the blunt truth about it. Now I'm married, I have three beautiful children and two on the way, we wanted one more, but now we have twins coming. I'd have been the worst of the worst if I had stayed. The military made me a better man, it made me a man. It gave me options, it showed me different cultures, different ways of thinking, so many different ways of living. It embodied who I am today, everything that I am, and it was probably the greatest thing that I could ever do so far as to change my life.

"I was a lost puppy until I was given that responsibility."

Leo Munson

I came out of the service very positive. I have no traumatic events that have negatively affected me. Never had to shoot anything, but it was more than once that I drew a gun. I don't have the stories that so many of these guys have, not at all. If I have low points, it's a conundrum I have had then, and I think I still have now, with society. I arrested a lot of guys, and the guys that I arrested were essentially eighteen-, nineteen-, twenty-year-olds that were away from home for the first time. They wanted to fit in. Most of the stuff back then was marijuana. Today I still believe it's a dangerous drug. I do. Back then it was really taboo, now not so much. But the judicial system would take what appeared to me to be almost identical situations and come up with completely unidentical outcomes. One would be kicked out of the service, one would be sent to the brig, one would be given an A15, which was a slap on the wrist. That bothers me. The inequity of similar situations. I think that still exists today.

I can't stress enough how much my service in the military has taken me to where I am today. Sounds trite, but in my case it is not. I was a lost puppy until I was given that responsibility.

"It was an honor to serve."

Shirley Beck

It's my experience, and it's patriotism. I felt like it was an honor to serve. It was something that doesn't happen all the time, and I didn't just do it to get a little bit of money. One of the things in my mind was retirement, of course; you know you think about that. But some people go into the reserves because they need some extra money, and I understand that, as long as they do their job and serve appropriately. But I think some people think the reserves are not quite as good as the regular Army, and probably we weren't. But people don't realize that it's not the officers that make the Army work, it's the enlisted people. Oh, the command sergeant major was—if you wanted something or needed help with something, that was the man to go to. I had a couple of enlisted people that wrote me some lovely letters about support and looking out for them, and just that kind of thing that you never expected to get, because it was your job to do that stuff.

Army veteran Shirley Beck.
Courtesy of Shirley Beck.

"I didn't know there was something wrong."

Chad Lackovic

My grandpa passed when I was in fourth or fifth grade, but I knew him. He was in World War II, and he was there on D-Day plus two or three, something like that, relatively near the beginning. My dad used to tell me that my grandpa was jacked up. And my whole life, my dad was crazy. My dad is a Vietnam veteran. I don't want to make him out to be a dirtbag, but he would like rage. We could never wake him up from a nap. He didn't sleep much, and he had nightmares. My brother and I would hear him flopping around with nightmares and screaming and stuff, and we knew something was wrong, and I guess they really didn't have a name for it then. But when I came back in 2004, for a long time I didn't know that there was something wrong. I just thought that I wasn't able to re-adjust to civilian life, and on top of that, I was a newlywed with a six-month-old kid. And I thought, "Well, maybe this is normal."

But as time went on, I didn't sleep. I'd have horrible nightmares. I was always angry. I couldn't concentrate. I couldn't remember anything, and all this stuff was wrong. It took me about two years, and then I went to the VA and I'm like, "I need help. Something ain't right." I went back to work at the jail after a while. I actually ended up quitting but yeah, it was crazy. I'm glad I finally got help, because a lot of guys kill themselves, which is really sad. Guys that I've known have killed themselves that never got the help, so I'm glad I did go get help. Twenty-two vets a day. In the beginning, I went through so many different medications. I've been on the same stuff now for about two years and it's working, mostly. I still have nightmares and have a hard time sleeping, but the sleeping stuff they give me either gives me bad nightmares like Ambien, or they give me stuff like Trazidone which is like a damn horse tranquilizer and when I wake up, I can't function.

So it's been hard. I can't study for an exam more than a day before, or I won't remember it. So I'll stay up late the night before an exam and wake up early and cram in the morning, just so I can retain my material.

"You might meet some of my grandchildren."

Alcee Chriss Sr.

Now I was a tailor, had studied tailoring before I went to serve. And I tell you what it did for me, going in the service. We were always sociable. My mother came from the country, rural area, went to New Orleans. But she was social. Everybody leaving the country is gonna see her. Then she'd help them to get jobs. It's always been like that. We had the big charity hospital down there.

When we were getting out, when you have enough points of how long you're serving in that service and how long you're serving overseas, they count up to be so much. When they got near my points, I started watching and see a few more days and gone. But I wrote a letter for my lady friend. She was attending Dillard, and I was attending Southern in

Baton Rouge. Every time I come home, it'd be a dance then and I was her dancing partner, see, and she was mine too that May. When we got to this point, I wrote her a note and said, "Well, you seem to make a pretty good prospect for marriage." *[chuckle]* Then when I got discharged, that was a beautiful Golden Gate. It sure looked good to me, at San Francisco, when I had the points to get out. My brother was living in Los Angeles, so I had to go from Treasure Island in San Francisco to Camp Pendleton in Oceanside.

And I got hooked up with my brother and he was running with a lady, she was from New Orleans also, but he wouldn't eat there. She wasn't feeding him, but sometimes she would fix breakfast. But when I hooked up with my brother, the first Sunday he carried me to a Methodist church. I was a Methodist member, and the pastor got up and said, "Now y'all take to your servicemen and carry them home and feed them!" And when I got up and he had us to stand up and a young lady came back there and said, "Do you . . . " Looking good to me. All of them gonna look good to me now. But she said, "Do you remember me?" I said, "No, I don't remember you, but I can learn you in a second." But she was a classmate. She and her sisters, we graduated high school together. She brought her mother back there to me and introduced her to my brother. And we did go home with them, and she did fix some good meal! She fixed it so good that my brother and I made a deal to eat that very evening. Shit, that almost kept me from wanting to go to Chicago and get married. But then one day I'm walking on Central Avenue and somebody go, "Hey! Chriss!" "What?" I'm walking down, tending to my own business. And that was my old Marine buddy, and we started going out every night.

Then here come my wife, who sent me a note. Said, "If you don't hurry, you might meet some of my grandchildren." I had to run to Chicago after I got that note. We was married for over fifty-seven years. My wife was in Chicago. They had moved to Chicago, because they had one other sister was living there. And they had better jobs up there, working in the steel work. Chicago or Gary, Indiana. They would travel that far to go to work, see? Because it was worth it. In the cold and all of that, those men would work, and sometimes the women don't even get out, except maybe on Sunday, go to church. They don't get out the house. That wind is cold, and there's snow on the ground and all that. But I started working at a clothing store. Five dollars, it cost on every suit. You'd come in, you'd like that big size, we'd cut it down for you. We'd tighten it all up and get it to fit you. See, now with all that time we took to fit that one guy, we didn't do anything much to this other guy and the five or six other guys, see. So the cost of five dollars pays off, when you don't have to do it for everybody. So I worked there a while.

But what struck me, though, when I first got out, to apply for loading dock jobs, warehouse jobs, I said, "Man, I had charge of . . . " "We don't care what you did in the service. It don't matter here." That was in New Orleans. I went home first, then got to Chicago. But tell you what, they would bet on us. Some of the people would serve us, and different companies will give benefit, even for transportation. You'll travel. You a veteran, and a lot of people give you 10 percent off. They did that good. They did good. In fact, they did better than they did for Vietnam people.

"My goal is to get two spots for vets to go on this trip every year."
Richard Puett

Richard Puett participated in the 2017 Biodiversity and Human Development in South Africa student trip, led by Professor Michael Slattery of TCU's Environmental Science department, to work with veterinarian Dr. William Fowlds at Amakhala Game Reserve.

Chris, he was in the military too. Me and him bonded a lot over the entire trip. He's South African. He was one of our guides. He's actually now at Kariega, one of the other reserves nearby. He's their lead ecologist now. He's got really good friends in Botswana who are mounted safari guides. Apparently, it's a two- or three-year process just to get your license. You have to get a certain number of hours and miles and things like that before you can actually be a guide in it. You've got to train your horses to be near elephants and lions and stuff.

The gentleman that trains a lot of the anti-poaching units in that area is a Marine, and the guys that worked there found out that me and Matt were Marines. One of the things that he taught our TCU student group was that you keep your magazine in. After you're done firing, you keep it in until you're ready to reload. That way, the poachers think that you still have ammunition. That one thing right there just blew everybody's mind, but that's just something that every military member in the past few years knows.

I asked Dr. Fowlds, "How restricted is that [anti-poaching training] guy coming through?"

He's like, "Well, he's limited to how often he can come through."

I'm like, "You have Marines and military members at TCU that can do exactly what he does, that would just love the opportunity to go out there and just spend a couple of months training your guys." They have two slots slated specifically for Vietnamese students to go on this trip every year. My goal is to get two spots for vets to go on this trip every year.

South Africa is currently in a really bad drought, and a lot of reserves in the area are relocating a lot of their wildlife to reserves that aren't facing issues with the drought. One morning, we got up real early and went to this reserve to do a procedure on some waterbuck. It was in a really remote area near Amakhala. We get down to this valley, the sun was coming up, and it was just so beautiful and unique. You can tell it's an ancient land.

There was five juveniles and one adult male waterbuck. The adults can get up to like six hundred pounds. Dr. Fowlds had to make teams of students to handle injections, blood draws, checking the blood oxidation level of the animal, monitoring the pulse and heart rate, and monitoring the breathing. Because it was just Dr. Fowlds and one other vet tech and one of the guides, and our group of TCU students. We're having to deal with six animals, and Dr. Fowlds doesn't have the manpower to do it. He splits all the students into three groups, and he's like, "All right, who wants to be leader of a group?"

Me and Matt, the other veteran, are like, "We'll do this. We got it." I'd never done anything like this, Matt had never done anything like this. The first thing we do after we get our students, is we go up to the vet tech and we're like, "Okay, what do we do? What do we do in this case? What do we do in this case? How do we draw the medicine? How do we do the injections? How do we check the blood, pulse, temperature?"

We were just reading everything, making sure that we were asking the questions so we would be successful. When the animal is tranquilized, you really have to monitor its heart rate and breathing, especially if it's malnourished or young. We don't want this animal to die on us. Me and Matt spent twenty to thirty minutes just grilling the vet tech on everything that we needed to do. Whereas the other group leader was just like, whatever, shooting the breeze with his friends. We go and Matt and me are there, we're ready, and Dr. Fowlds starts darting them all. As soon as they're all down he's like, "All right, go."

We go and we just do everything. We flip it over on its stomach and make sure it's upright so its breathing pathway is open, so it can breathe nice and easily. We monitor its heart and everything like that. Dr. Fowlds is calling out draws and everything. I was lucky, because I had individuals in my group that were really motivated. I didn't really do much of anything except monitor or write down everything, and just help them with the draws or any questions that they had. Afterwards my group did two, three of the yearlings ourselves because we were so fast, and our group was so good. We did three of them, and the other groups only got to do one.

Then we relocated the male, which sweet Jesus, the thing was just so heavy. Oh my God. We had to walk 150 yards just to get to the trailer. Me and Matt are the biggest people on the entire trip. Everybody else is real tiny, and Dr. Slattery's just a string bean. It just fell on me and Matt to do most of the heavy lifting. Afterwards Dr. Fowlds was talking to us, and he was like, "Man, I really like having you veterans around. You came up and asked questions and made sure you had all the information you needed. You make life a lot easier for us."

"It's my duty to take care of people."

Israel Sanchez

I got a text from one of my chiefs I served, and he said, "You were one of the best damn corpsmen I've ever had in my entire career." And the man had retired after twenty-five years. That tells me that somebody else wasn't out there to take care of their people. That's my whole life and purpose. I'm a caregiver, and a lot of people don't have it in them, and although I question my purpose every single day, I just know that it's my duty to take care of people.

I appreciate you taking an interest in hearing me out, because not a lot of people do, because they don't understand what we've been through. In that sense, and I can go on and on about growing up in complete poverty, and doing all that stuff when I was a kid. It's been a rough life. Single parent. Growing up that way the struggle is real, but I guess my education has always been important to me. I don't care about the status of the education, or being called doctor at the end of the day. It is to prove to society that there are educated individuals out there that can do the job just as well as anybody else can.

My mother didn't know exactly what I did in the military. I didn't really involve my family a lot, because they weren't involved in my military career. They didn't take an interest in it. They saw it as a way of me rebelling from the church and stuff, so they didn't take an interest in it, so I was always alone every time I would come home from deployments.

People were getting care packages, and I was like, "Whatever. I'm just going to buy my own care packages and send them onboard the ship." So they didn't take an interest in that, and I knew growing up in poverty that my mom can't afford any of that stuff. So yeah, she is proud of me. I still take care of her.

"They don't tell you all those obstacles."

Michelle Johnson

I retired from the Army in August 2013. And it took about three months, maybe four, for my Army retirement pay to kick in. And it took about another two to three months more for my VA retirement to kick in. I ended up becoming homeless. And I was blessed to be able to find lodging through an organization based out of San Antonio where all they do is help with soldiers and veterans. They have places set up for people like me. Transition—that word sounds so smooth, don't it? Like all you do is just slide across there, and you're here. They don't tell you that there's a hole in the middle of the thing and you gotta go around it with a rope and a ladder. They don't tell you all those obstacles and things. I ended up having to do that. I stayed in this shelter for female veterans and women who were in recovery. It was a twelve-bed house. Six of those beds were for veterans, and the other six beds were for these other women who were in the process of returning to society sober.

I would wake up every night at least three times. Once I went downstairs and stood in the dining room, surveying the area like an NCO. I said, "Why are y'all moving around so slow? It's already 0700. Somebody needs to be doing something." One of my housemates said, "It's all right, Michelle, go eat breakfast." I was like, "Oh, was I doing it, again? The NCO thing? Okay, let me go find myself something to do."

I was enrolled in classes at San Antonio College. There's this thing we soldiers call the fobbit syndrome. It's like the hobbits, where you just kinda stay holed up in this little cocoon, with everything within arm's reach, just like you were still in the barracks or in the field. It's a comfort zone, a safe place from civilians. For me it was YouTube, my cell phone, my portable DVD player, and my stack of DVDs. I tried to not stay in that zone for too long 'cause it's just not good. Isolation can set in. Every day, I found something to do outside the four walls.

While staying at the shelter, I'd applied to buy a house through the American GI Forum. The process took longer than expected; closing and move-in dates kept changing. One of my battle buddies let me stay at his home with his nieces while I waited for my house to come through. He was going through the retirement process also. I stayed at his house for several months. Then, one night at around ten o'clock, I remember sitting up and saying, "It's time to go home." My family had been going through some challenges. I felt I needed to go home and deal with that.

So I drove from San Antonio, and I think I got to Fort Worth around maybe 2:15 in the morning. It took me about four hours to get here. And I get here and still don't have a place to stay. My service dog and I stayed at the Arlington Life Shelter for one night. Then I stayed in hotels until I found an affordable place. I eventually found a furnished studio apartment and got settled in. The whole time I kept saying, "I'm just gonna be here for a little while." Southern people have a saying. They say, "I'm just gon' go down there right quick." Or "I'm gon' do this and that, right quick. I just need to go check on that, right quick." "Right quick" is always longer than expected. It was over a year since I had said I needed to check on family "right quick." A lot had changed since I'd been gone. I realized that time didn't stop for people back home either. You know?

"'Grim' is a really good descriptor."

Marty Leewright

Q: *With all the perspective that you have, a lifetime's perspective now, everything that you've lived since, your marriage, your career, your experience with the VA over all the years, your involvement in American society since you came back—that's now going on fifty years. What can you say to the situation that our country's in now, with the wars that we've had since 9/11?*

It's like we don't fucking learn. You know? I mean, from my understanding of Iraq, we went in there under false pretenses. I don't care who's in power, Democrats or Republicans, or whatever. But my understanding is that there was false information, and we went in and invaded a sovereign country based on false information that they had weapons of mass destruction, and we raised havoc. We just basically destroyed that country and then we left. And so we spawned things like ISIS, you know? And nurtured hatred for Americans in that part of the world. And then Afghanistan's still going on. And what did we accomplish?

Q: Are you a happy person?
Basically, yeah.

Q: What's the basis of your happiness?
On Friday mornings I go to Moore Elementary School, which is on the north side of Fort Worth, and I help at-risk first graders. It's a Hispanic school, primarily. I help at-risk first graders learn to read and write. And when I go in there and see those little kids and they come out and they're hugging on me, and we're doing our writing and reading and stuff like that, it's better than teaching university students. It's better than teaching law students. It's better than teaching lawyers or judges, which I do all those things too. I get paid for none of that, other than just the wonderful feeling that I get and the funny things that they say.

And I'm always playing tricks on my wife or my daughter, and they'll play tricks on me. We love to travel, and I love to garden and things like that. I see humor in things. My wife thinks that I have a great sense of humor, 'cause I'll see humor in something and I'll just start laughing. So I think I'm a pretty happy person. I may not sound like it when I'm talking about war and Vietnam and the VA, but don't characterize me as an unhappy person.

Q: I ask partly because you don't seem bitter in a general way, but the stuff we're talking about is grim stuff. You're very candid about the grimness of it.
"Grim" is a really good descriptor. Grim. It was grim. It's still grim in my memory. It's still grim in my heart. Vietnam was grim. It was pivotal. It was a catalyst for me. It changed my life. Having survived it, I'm really glad I survived it, and I came back. And also, Ethan, I feel like I owed something to my buddies that didn't come back, like Don Huey. I felt like I owed it to them to come back and do something with my life, to serve others like I promised God I would do. They didn't get a chance to do that. And if I would've come back and I would've been in my fatigues, living under a bridge, on the street, being a homeless person and feeling sorry for myself and being a drug addict or an alcoholic, that would not have honored them.

"I had always gotten through tough times before."

Cristina Mungilla

My forty-minute morning commute to my corporate job was made on this day on the phone and in tears.

It was two years since I had left the Army, and I was struggling in ways I never had before: losing jobs, overspending, severely depressed, angry.

Really angry. The screaming until I lost my voice kind of angry. The throwing and kicking things kind of angry. Blind, often unpredictable rage.

"No pain, no gain." I knew I was struggling, but I had always gotten through tough times before. Hell, I was in the Army! Army strong!

I was late that morning, again. And I still had to drop my daughter Karina off with my grandmother, who would take her to school later. We were both dressed, and all we had to do was brush her hair before we could leave.

Rush, rush, rush. Brush, brush, brush. Karina kept saying, "Ow!" I was terribly annoyed by her complaints.

"We've got to hurry! I'm late!" I said to her, and kept brushing through the tangles in her hair.

"OW!" Karina cried, and she began to sob.

No fucking way. I didn't have time for this shit. I impulsively pushed her to the ground.

Instantly I was in turmoil, regretting, self-loathing, and shocked that I was capable of doing that to my six-year-old daughter.

I immediately picked her up and held her, and we cried together. Never again, I told myself. I am not this person.

After calming Karina, I followed through with the morning. I dropped her off with my grandmother, making no mention of what had happened, and began my morning commute.

I had already been grappling with the idea of seeking help for mental health. I was spiraling out of control, and I knew it. But this I could not live with a moment longer.

Enough.

I called my boyfriend, explaining everything through my tears. It was during the call that I decided to call in to work, saying I was sick and needed to see a doctor right away.

Then I called my mom, still crying, and told her. Knowing she would be concerned, I assured her I was seeking help immediately. I was so ashamed and hurt.

The therapist wrote a note for thirty days FMLA (Family and Medical Leave Act), and thus began my journey toward recovery.

"I lucked out with my mental health provider."
William Howe Jr.

I was coming back in from a patrol, looking out through my back window, and all of a sudden I saw what looked like fireworks and heard the explosions, and they just kept getting closer and closer. Finally we're yelling out to our driver and he swerves us over, and the rocket lands right where we were. I dislocated my shoulder, and because I was the medic and only had two months left, I'm just going to pop it back in and keep going. So that's what I did. But I didn't get it all the way in, and it formed a lot of scar tissue, so when I got back I had problems. I have a pinched nerve; my right hand doesn't work. I can't put my arm above my head or behind my back and stuff. That was pretty much it, and then the concussion syndrome. They determined that I had multiple TBIs [traumatic brain injuries] and concussions.

I lucked out with my mental health provider. I get to see him once every six months, and he's worked really hard to finally get me on the medications that I need to take to be able to function. But it took about three years for that to happen, and it also took me about a year and a half before I got to him. Before that, they were just kicking me around because they didn't know where to send me. They would give me one doctor with this medication, and then another doctor with that medication, and they wouldn't listen to what I had to say. They still won't give me pain pills because they don't believe I'm in pain, even though I am every day. They think all veterans are just searching for pain medicine. Every time I'd try to get an appointment to get my shoulder looked at, it's a month or two for X-ray, six to eight months for an MRI, and if you do get those, then they're like, "Well, we really don't know what to do, if we should do surgery or just wait and see if it gets better." I'm like, "It's been four or five years now and it's not getting any better," but they keep saying, "Let's wait, wait, wait." And the Army wouldn't do anything when I was in, because I didn't have enough time left on my contract to justify the rehabilitation. They were just, "Well, the VA will take care of you when you get out." My upper back and spine, and my whole right shoulder and right arm, are pretty much shredded, but they won't really do anything because they just don't have the resources.

To get approved for Wounded Warriors, I think, took me three months to get in. Even these nonprofit groups that are trying to help us out, it takes a while to get plugged in. That's the thing: coming back and trying to find your role in society. You still want to be that warrior. I carried my go bags for probably two or three years when I came back. I would always carry my medic bag, even though half the stuff in it's expired. I would carry it just in case something happened at TCU, somebody went down, I'd have my go bag with me. But that's somebody else's job now. I saw a car crash. I'd been back about a year and, of course, I grabbed my medic bag and ran to the car crash. And then the firefighters show up and say, "What've we got?" and I'm rattling off everything, and I just remember that my EMT license has expired. I probably shouldn't be doing all this, but it's just natural to me: this is the situation I need to fix. And that, of course, was the adrenaline rush. And then I tried to go to nursing school when I first came here, and I didn't fit in there. They were, "Oh, you're going to have all these rules," and I said, "You don't understand. I just came back from Iraq, where if I needed to cut somebody open or I needed to stitch somebody up or whatever I needed to do to save somebody's life, I could do it." And now they're telling me I gotta ask a doctor to give somebody Tylenol.

"They're still taking care of me."

Jason Mendoza

My transition out of the military was actually very good. I was medically retired. I got injured when I was in, when I was down-range, and the out process was pretty seamless. They take care of you on the way out. But it did take a little bit, over a year and a half, to fully process me out of the military. I officially got retired November 11, 2014. And they're still taking care of me. I'm here at school, getting a full ride. They basically pay for my school, and then they pay me to go to school, so it's just such a great benefit. I didn't know how good it was. But I honestly didn't go in for that.

"I just bawled."

Marty Leewright

I thought about whether I would like to go back [to Vietnam]. I think I would. I think there'll be some areas it would be hard for me to visit, where friends died. They had a mobile Vietnam Wall that was going around the country, and it was in Arlington [Texas]. I went over there, and I walked up to the Wall, and it was actually Don Huey. And I walked up and I thought, "I want to see this." They had displays there, some weapons and things like that. And I didn't think it was gonna hit me like this, but I walked up and put my hand up on the Wall, on Don Huey's name, and it just felt like somebody punched me in the gut. It just was visceral, and I dropped to my knees and just started bawling. There were two people to either side of me. One looked like a military uniform, I think the other one was in like a law enforcement uniform. And they each grabbed an arm, and they helped me up and stood with me for a while, and I just bawled. It just hit that the advantages that I've had in education and marriage and a beautiful daughter and all these things, Don didn't get. And again, that feeling that it was just a wasted, wasted thing.

"I was not prepared for the reaction."

John Thompson

After five years of pretty hefty managerial experience in a lot of jobs, I was not prepared for the reaction I got to my resume on the job search. Employers just kind of "Ehhh" about military experience. One even asked, "What kind of real managerial experience have you had?" I asked him what he meant by that. He said, "Well, in the military, they have to do what you tell them. Nothing supervisory about that."

"Well, no, they don't," I replied. "They can sit down, they can move slowly, they can take breaks. They can be disobedient without being insubordinate. They can be your normal civilian employee. If you're telling me that my military supervisory experience is not good enough to be a supervisor in your company, then something's wrong with your company."

Almost every ex-military guy I've talked to, officer or enlisted, has told me the same thing: Civilians don't look at military jobs as being "real jobs." If you talk to our veterans on campus and ask, "What's the biggest surprise about transitioning into civilian life and civilian jobs?" it's "All my military experience doesn't really count for much." So team-work, leadership, discipline, and communication aren't transferable skills? What about taking guys from New Jersey, California, Utah, Al-abama, with educational and intelligence levels all over the place, and making them work together? And you think that this isn't equivalent to some civilian job?

"Letting go is the hardest part."

David Grantham

After returning from Iraq in December 2008, I felt I was transitioning back into civilian life rather smoothly. Then I found myself playing in a softball game with my local church. I had just returned home, and a friend mentioned that the team needed a replacement for a game. I jumped at the chance.

During the second inning, I was in left field when I heard and saw a loud explosion in the sky off to my right. I immediately went tense, and my pulse began to race: My body was ramping up for conflict. I quickly realized that it was simply fireworks and turned my attention back to the game. My best friend was in left-center field, and after the third out we jogged to the dugout together. Annoyed that my nerves had been frayed, I turned to him and said, "Who the *heck* shoots off fireworks in the mid-dle of December?!?" He looked over at me and shrugged nonchalantly. Back in the dugout I told him, in a very tough-guy, joking kind of way, that the fireworks had startled me a bit. We laughed.

Not long after that, I found myself driving back to my office in North Arlington from a meeting in Fort Worth, when a massive dump truck pulled parallel with me. I was driving my car in the fast lane nearest the Interstate median, so I was stuck there momentarily. Suddenly we hit a dip in the road and the truck's back end jumped, causing a loud, intense boom. The dump truck apparently was empty, so the dip in the road caused the whole back end to lurch violently. Between the tremendous thud and the shrieking of metal, it sounded like a miniature car bomb. I jerked the wheel and floored the gas pedal to, as we say, get off the X. My training had kicked in. It took only three or four seconds for me to regain my composure, but the incident reminded me that I still had a long recovery ahead.

Air Force veteran David Grantham.
Courtesy of David Grantham.

I was not expecting to hear sounds of war stateside, or at least to react to them as I did. The dump truck incident was particularly jarring, because one of the most dangerous places in Iraq was in a vehicle driving along a road. Roadside bombs were so prevalent that a quarter of our pre-deployment training was dedicated to driving tactics for identifying and avoiding IEDs. And in my job, we drove all over the place. Therefore, the minute you got behind the wheel, your blood pressure spiked. That instinctive, bodily reaction apparently did not go away as quickly as I thought it would.

I would add that warfighters are trained. We are schooled in how to prepare and react. But there is a context to all of it. In a deployed environment we carry guns, have heavy protective gear, and are mentally prepared for attacks. Part of returning stateside is recognizing that you don't necessarily have to keep yourself in a state of readiness. That—letting go—is probably the hardest part. When something does happen and training kicks in, we lack the wartime context and we find ourselves, if just for a second, in a confused state of mind.

This was the case during a visit with my family in Florida, a week or so after I returned from deployment. Friends of my father welcomed me home with free tickets to a Tampa Bay Buccaneers football game. The seats were incredible, a couple rows up from the field and right in front of the pirate ship. The ship is a popular part of the stadium, since fans can enjoy the game from its platform and it fires off cannon sounds every time the Bucs score. I forgot about this last point. As my dad and I cheered for the Bucs after they scored a touchdown, the cannons exploded behind me.

The sound would probably have scared any unsuspecting person, but it stunned me. I froze for a second, thinking I had brought the war home with me. I grabbed the chair in front of me and squeezed, not wanting anyone to know that my heart had jumped into my throat. For a second I felt helpless. I was in a familiar, relaxed environment, and the sound confused my context. I was ready to react to war but, knowing I was not in war, I froze.

It took a minute or two before my heart stopped racing. I calmly turned to my father, who was oblivious to my plight, and laughed. "Dad," I said, "that cannon nearly made me soil myself." He laughed, then a quiet sympathy came over his face. He slapped me on the back and said, "I'm just glad you're home."

"I dreamed that I got called back into the Navy."

Jim Lee

For many years I dreamed that I got called back into the Navy, and I was the age I was in my dream, like forty or fifty, and they were all eighteen, and it was miserable. I don't have that dream anymore. Now I'm always dreaming that I've been teaching a class all semester, but I haven't been to it, and I don't even know where it is. It turns final exams, and I have to go and find the classroom where I'm supposed to be teaching. That's my recurring dream now.

"Every day was basically the same."

Ed Adcock

Part of what I missed was that on the submarine there was routine. Every day was basically the same as every other day. Coming back to civilian life, you had all sorts of things going on.

Navy veteran Ed Adcock with Veterans Services Task Force quilt.
Courtesy of April Brown.

"I had a lot of bad nights."

Jon Lippens

That war lasted too long, but I didn't enjoy the results of it, because I still had a conscience, and I was telling myself, "How many of those Germans have I killed? How are we going to deal with God and all that? Who was right? Am I ever going to go to heaven, or am I just going to be going to hell?" I didn't have a good pastor or anything. In my days most of the Catholic mass was in Latin, and you had to know Latin to understand.

I had a lot of bad nights. I saw myself killing Germans, being in battle. That is why at the time I was drinking and smoking. It kinda gets you away from things. It was hard. And then I found out, when I got out, how many people we lost. But those people were really guided by Satan. Hitler's thinking was, "I want to conquer the world just like Satan will conquer the world, and I want the whole world to know that we are gonna take all of it."

We were really sick of the Germans. We really hated them. Germany for five years lived off of the people's food. And they fed their own army and their own people and let the people fend for their own food. The Red Cross made some kind of concoction with vegetables and we don't know what kind of meat it was. We might have had a good fat rat in there. Or a dead cat or whatever. But we had to have food. Every day they served the same thing. If you were stealing the food the Germans requested from the farmer, then the farmer was in trouble. If a farmer was caught giving food to the civilians, they killed the owners. Took all the cattle out and lit the farm on fire. That is how bad the Germans were. Awful people.

"I can still smell gunpowder to this day."

Marty Leewright

There was silence. There was like a gap in the tape, okay? People just didn't talk about it. I came back from being in the military for three years

Army veteran Marty Leewright.
Courtesy of Marty Leewright.

and, other than a couple of really close buddies, nobody said, "Hey, what was it like? Where you been? What happened?" People just didn't seem like they talked about it. Life went on. I came back and I remember I freaked out. A clap of thunder would put me on the floor, or maybe the gravel road had been disturbed or there was a new patch in the pavement or something like that, and I'd freak out and have to remind myself, "That's not a booby trap, you're in the United States." If I heard two or three helicopters flying together, I would have a nightmare that night. One helicopter could fly over, didn't have any effect on me. But three or four helicopters, which is rare in civilian life, because that's usually what I heard in Vietnam, it would trigger a nightmare. I had nightmares for the first two or three years. I had a persistent rash all over my chest, looked like I had jungle rot or something. It finally grew out. It was probably from the Agent Orange, sleeping in mud all the time or just being dirty all the time.

And then I have a tape of a whole bunch of weapons firing. When I'd listen to that I could smell gun smoke, because the air would just be full of spent gun smoke, gunpowder, sulfur. You breathe that in and it's just like fire in your lungs, and it would choke you. You couldn't breathe, it'd burn your eyes and everything. And the weirdest thing is I would listen to that recording and for probably eight or ten years, I could actually smell. It's funny how you hear things like the helicopter and it will trigger things, and when you smell things when you're in a real intense environment like that, and how that comes back. I could smell gunpowder, and I can still to this day. I can hear all the different weapons firing. Fifty-caliber machine gun, M16s, occasional tank or grenade launcher, we had all kinds of weapons. We had .45 service revolvers, service handguns, M14s, AK-47s, Thompson submachine guns. We had .50 caliber, .60 calibers, of course M16s were everywhere. We had incredible firepower in Vietnam, and if it would've been like a head-on clash, we would have just overwhelmed 'em.

But it wasn't a head-on clash. They were everywhere, and it was hit and run and guerrilla, as you know. You never knew where it was coming from. Sitting on top of a grader or a scraper or a 'dozer or front-end loader, you constantly thought about a bullet coming through your head. And you just had to keep working. You couldn't stop, you couldn't hide, you just kept sitting up there like a sitting duck.

"Getting out was what was abnormal."

Brad Murphey

I went in at seventeen, so I didn't know what the real world was about. I mean, I worked a part-time job in high school, but I didn't know what life was really about; all I knew was military life. So it was normal to me. Getting out was what was abnormal. It was way hard, because you don't have the structure in the real world that you do in the military. The first time I heard somebody back-talking their supervisor it sorta—you can't do that. You're not allowed to do that. You're going to get in trouble. So it took me a while to even realize that I was allowed to call in sick if I needed to, because in the military you can't call in sick, you have to go to sick call and then you had a doctor determine if you were sick enough to go to work or not. So those aspects were hard. It was a weird transition.

I didn't want to, actually. It seems like the military, after the end of every war, they try to get rid of people. They always say, "Well, we have no more enemies," and of course this was really before Islamic terrorism was a thing. This was '92, and we'd just finished the Cold War. The Soviet Union fell apart, and we'd just pushed Saddam Hussein back into Iraq from Kuwait. So they said, "We need to get rid of folks." Well, I didn't want to go, 'cause I was happy where I was at. And I was unfortunately in a career field, being the dog handler, where there was no place to promote. I was pretty much at the highest rank I could get. For instance, when we tested for a new stripe we'd test against everybody who was eligible, Air Force-wide, so there might be four hundred people testing for two positions, so you had to score astronomically on the test, and I just couldn't get my test scores up. So they were eventually gonna push me out for failure to promote. I asked to retrain to something else, and they wouldn't let me do that. And what they ended up getting me on, they revamped the weight management program and I didn't meet the guidelines. Which I'm a big guy now, I wasn't then. I was probably 150 pounds lighter, but they still deemed me overweight. So I had an involuntary discharge, but it was an honorable discharge.

I actually went to the Tarrant County Sheriff's office after getting out of the military. Worked there for about eight years, and then I moved to Mississippi where I had family, and worked in a small town out there. Life events brought me back to Texas, and I was working at the Fort Worth Marshall's office, and I had a friend there, another deputy, that came from the TCU police department, and he said, "Hey, they've got an opening there if you want to." And I'm thinking I've got kids getting ready for school, and TCU offers free tuition for their employees for them or their children or spouse. So that's why I came to TCU.

"I never really stepped away from it."

Bruce and Charlotte Cole

Bruce Cole: The only place left for me to work was at the Pentagon, in what they call a purple billet. So, I could have been working for an Army general or an Air Force general or a Navy admiral. And I had kids in school. Charlotte and I would talk: "You know, Jordan graduates high school in two and a half years."

And that played hugely into our decision to finally have a place to settle down. In a way, I would be envious of civilian friends that I made. I went to school while I was in the Marine Corps and got my degree in business, but civilians in my classes would have other friends that they had known since kindergarten. I was a little envious of people who had lifelong friends who weren't just Christmas card friends, but knew each other's business kind of friends, from way back. I have no one like that. But I wanted Jordan to have those deep roots, and Bailey, with their friends. I knew the military was not in their future.

But I never really stepped away from it. I still wear a uniform every day. I teach ROTC at Allen High School. I still report to the Marine Corps. I have bosses all the way up to a one-star general at Camp Lejeune.

Charlotte Cole: We still have all the military gear and clothes at our house. I still miss the Marine Corps, and I find myself, every car that goes by that has a Marine Corps tag or a sticker, I see it. It's like I'm looking for that eagle, globe, and anchor. I'll see them pull into a gas station and I want to pull in behind them and say, "Where were you stationed?" Because you feel that connection. You know that they've been there, and you kind of just feel like you know them. Yeah, I still miss it. But I mean, I do fine because I think that I adjust to change well, or I wouldn't have been able to be in the Marine Corps like that.

"For me it was just coming home."
Joddy Murray

I won't say the transition to civilian life was easy, because I know that this is a big topic right now. For me, it was just coming home, trying to return to normal civilian life. And they did try to provide some transition training: how to write a resumé, how to go out and think about what career you want to have. Some stuff like that before you leave, which they didn't have for a lot of the generations before me. They did try to help with that.

I had a master's degree and I thought, "Oh, I'm just going to walk into a job, because I have this degree, it's for this area and . . . " Ugh, it took me, probably, and this doesn't sound like a lot now, but at the time, it felt like a lot, six months to get into a job, at a much lower salary than

I thought I was going to get. So that period was a bit dicey. But luckily I was helped by my now wife, and we were able to spend that time a little more together. After a long-distance relationship, we needed that time.

"It was moving to be welcomed back."

Tim Cole

What I wasn't prepared for was that everything in Iraq is brown. A hot day there is like 120. Literally, we would wash our uniforms out in a little bucket, and you would hang it up, and they would be dry in less than an hour. Everything brown and it's 120 degrees, and word comes that it's time for me to come back to the States. So you come from Iraq to Kuwait on a flight, spend the night, get up the next day and get on an airplane, and you're in Germany and it's green and sixty-eight degrees at night.

And then we landed in the United States. And I had no idea. We landed in Bangor, Maine, at three in the morning, so the airport is mostly dark. But they had to get fuel, and they were going to let us off the plane, really just a chance to use the restroom, and there were some guys who wanted to get a smoke. We walk into this terminal, it's dark, we come around a corner, and there are about twenty-five people, men and women, mostly Vietnam vets, but it was led by a World War II vet, welcoming us home. I'll get choked up telling this. I wasn't prepared for that. They were handing us cell phones so we could call our families. They hand me a cell phone, but I literally can't talk because the lump in my throat was so big. It was emotionally moving to be welcomed back to our nation. When I think about our Vietnam vets who were not welcomed back, I just think about the regret that as a nation we didn't welcome them home. Man, what a moving and powerful experience.

I eventually got here to Texas, and I remember going to my first high school football game. This is September, and we're having our Texas high school football, and they start playing the national anthem. And I can't hold it together. And I'll just tell you, tears are streaming down my face, I can't control it. Hearing the national anthem, all that just conjures up.

And the other piece of that is absence. You haven't seen family in a long time. And so, just as you've been through six, seven, eight months of growth and change and you've seen things that they haven't seen, they also have had six or seven months of change. You come home, and my wife Mary Anne used that time with me away to train to run a marathon.

She ran her first marathon, she looked great. And she and a friend had refinished a table. With the kids, I hadn't seen them in a long time, I was amazed at how they'd grown. And especially for high school girls, a year's difference is a big difference. The maturity level and the confidence that had occurred. For me, that was pretty tame. I think for other families it's very, very significant. When I was in theater, many times I was helping younger Marines talk about family issues that were going on back at home. Sometimes spouses aren't prepared to handle the full responsibility. Sometimes our men and women come back to a family that somehow has done well without them, and now it's like, "Okay, I'm back here, so now what do I do? Where's my role of fitting back in?"

I remember getting packages. Mary Anne was a schoolteacher—we've got a lot of schoolteachers in our family—so I would get packages from school kids, you know, "Thank you for your service." Those are just moving and touching, and the fun part of that was when you come back. When they started the next school year, I would try to go visit those classes and tell them thanks and let them know that I really appreciated it. I really mean it when I say that. When you're in this place that's so foreign, and like I said everything is brown, there's no color, and you get these colorful pictures and these words of encouragement from people you don't know. But the fact that they came from this school district which is home for you, or this school, or from this class that you know, or they're in class with your kids, it really does mean a lot. I feel like these words are not effective to really convey that. It's a big deal, to know that what you're doing is valued.

"I still feel like I am transitioning."
Steven Gonzalez

I was fortunate enough to be here at home when I separated. I was stationed at the joint reserve base here in Fort Worth, and it came time to where I had a promotion to become an officer. I had to go back to Quantico, Virginia, to complete the school for that. So I had a great opportunity, and I ended up getting a divorce from my wife, and my daughter was here, and I didn't want to just leave her. I've seen a lot of guys who I've helped who are at the base whose daughter or son is in their original hometown or wherever. It takes a toll, and when I sat down to think about it, what I did was take out a piece of paper and write out my pros and cons of staying in and getting out. And I had more cons than pros, so I was like, "All right, I guess I should just get out." And you know, it's been tough. In some ways, I still feel like I am transitioning. It was just a major part of my identity. You don't normally hear of people doing twelve years and getting out just to get out. You get out at twelve years because you are hurt or medically retired or something or another. I got out just simply because I was tired of moving, and I wanted to be here at home with my family. Everyone who knew me, knew me as, "Oh you know, that Steve, yeah, he's a Marine." And now it's just like, you know, it's tough. I'm just a full-time student, so it sucks at times.

Marine veteran Steven Gonzalez and his dog Lola.
Courtesy of Steven Gonzalez.

I was diagnosed with the PTSD in 2012, and it was what they called a delayed onset, because I felt good coming back, but I started getting nightmares and visions and all kinds of stuff. It was easy when I was on active duty to go to therapy and get the help, because everything was there on base. Now that I'm out, the VA, they have been a little help. But when I have absolutely needed them, or needed help in a crisis situation or whatnot, it's been hard. And it sucks not being with your friends. That's what I think I miss the most, is the people that I served with and the close relationships that we built. I have friends all across the country and all over the world. It's really cool to share that bond. I probably have a friend in every major city, and I can just call them up: "Hey man, I'm coming into town." "Hey, if you need a place to stay!" So it's pretty cool.

My wife has been very supportive. If it wasn't for her I probably wouldn't be in school. I would be like a cop right now. I preached this to all the Marines I talked to, several thousand Marines I helped guide. I had to come up with a plan for myself, which was the hardest thing. So, I can honestly sit here and say that every goal I set out for myself I've reached so far. So yeah, I hopefully can continue to reach those goals and ultimately become successful, and I think for the rest of my life I'll always be an advocate for veterans.

"Finding myself unprepared was shocking to me."

Carl Castillo

Separating from the military was kind of like the boot camp experience again, but on a much grander scale. The things that I did in the Marine Corps, I did not necessarily want to do in the civilian world, and/or I guess some of them did not transition into the civilian world very well. So, realizing that I came out unprepared personally was rather a kick in the face. Because I thought I had all the answers and was prepared for most everything that I ever did while in the Marine Corps. Finding myself unprepared leaving the Marine Corps was rather shocking to me. I tried to alleviate that as quickly as possible, but even then, I was two steps back. Playing the catch-up game was something I never liked to do and never wanted to do. It was rather difficult because then you're looking at, "Where am I at in my life, as compared to others?" I never looked at it in that way until that point in time, and it pissed me off. And I hate being pissed off. Well no, actually, I don't hate being pissed off. I hate being pissed off at myself, because I feel like I failed. And, like I said, my motivating factor was always to beat someone else. I have always been competitive, and coming out finding your friends were at a point in the civilian world where you felt behind pissed me off. Not that I begrudge them or that I hold anything against them, but it pissed me off, because I did all this, and now I have to start back at square one, and it's not a feeling I enjoy.

When I left, one of the biggest things that was always in the back of my mind was what my friends and family were doing. How is it going to be changed, you know, being away for three months, six months, a year?

The sad thing about it was that coming home each time, nothing fucking changed. My friends were still doing the same stupid shit they were doing. Maybe they got older, maybe they got fatter, maybe they had more kids. It was always the same fucking thing. I was fucking glad that I got out of here. The city changes, the area changes, things come up, things go down, renovations here and there. For the most part, it's like it froze in time every time I came back. I never had homesickness, because I knew as soon as I came back, it was like I never left, it was like yesterday basically. I thrive on change, variety. I like new experiences and new things. I was kinda glad I left.

The inevitable question does come up, so I'll let you ask it whenever you want to ask. *[Long pause]* If y'all don't ask, I'm fine with it. I'm surprised y'all haven't asked it, to be honest with you. I'm kind of glad, but if you do, I'm not disappointed either. If you ask it unknowingly later, I'll tell you that's the question.

Q: *I think I get what you're getting at, but the question is a bit hard to ask.*

Just voice it out if you think you know it. If you think you know it, just ask it. If not, I can talk about something else. You can ask it later on.

Q: *Okay. Have you ever had to neutralize anybody?*

You know what, that's actually a much better way of saying it than most people usually ask, and that is the question. Yes. I have been in combat. *[Starts to cry]* You do what you got to do in combat. My mindset has always been, I'm going to protect the person to the right and left of me. And in doing that, you do what you got to do. So, yes.

"Getting out is a very scary thing."

Felicia Lawson

It was difficult, even though I was married to a service member, so I still had some tie to it. It was awkward because things you say don't make sense to anybody else in the civilian world. The jargon, the terminology on this stuff. You don't know when you should or shouldn't talk about your military service. Getting out is a very scary thing. You're worried about the transition, you're worried about if you're going to get a job when you get out. You're worried about how your resumé is going to look. There's a whole website dedicated to changing what you did in the military and then making it civilian-speak because, like, I can't put on my resume "IMRL Petty Officer, saved the command $2 million based on accuracy." They'd be like, "What is an IMRL Petty Officer?" It's someone who's in charge of all your equipment and it's a big deal, but you have to be able to translate that. So translating your resumé is difficult, and just you're overall fearful of what's next.

The biggest problem I had was finding what to wear every day. In the Navy you know you have to wear this uniform every day, and if it's a special occasion you put on your dress whites or your dress blues. If I'm not in flight deck gear, I'm in my blue digi camis. It was just scary not knowing what to do next, and the military has been your identity for however long you've been in. For me it was over eight years. That's a long time, especially for someone who joined at nineteen. My identity turned into a Navy spouse, and I didn't really like that, because I had been in the military prior.

"It's been a pretty long, hard road."

Jake Melton

I'm proud of my personal actions. I think I performed in an above-average manner. And I might not have been the best soldier in the world back in the rear, but in combat I was good. I was real good. You could count on me, and I'm proud of that. However, I've come to realize that possibly the intentions of the war were not 100 percent pure. But I know it was a good thing. I wanted to do something my kids could be proud of: they could look up to me and be proud of their dad. And I think I've done that.

But the lasting effects of the TBI—I'm fairly well recovered from that but, man, I just didn't think it would linger on this long. It's been pretty bad. I had to get two or three hours a day therapy for some years. Now I do maybe thirty minutes a day, four days a week, but it's simple things like crosswords and Sudoku and these brain academy and brain edge games for the Wii. You'd be amazed at how much that stuff helps. But I went to the brain center in Dallas. They had a thing that teaches you how to think again and how to make decisions and whatnot, and it's strange that you would actually have to retrain yourself for that. It's been a pretty long, hard road, but I think we're almost there.

"Truman was a tough little man."

Alcee Chriss Sr.

April Brown: *What area in New Orleans were you living in?*
Pontchartrain Park. It's a nice area.

AB: *And that's where you joined the Montford Point Marine Association. It was the New Orleans chapter.*
It was New Orleans chapter, Chapter Seven, yeah. And boy, they was good too. We had a good relationship with the chapter in Atlanta, because they had the same football league, Atlanta and the Saints. And when we had the same game, we'd have somebody entertain the people from Atlanta at Montford Point, kept the whole relationship going. Did I tell you about receiving the congressional medal this summer?

Ethan Casey: *No, tell me please.*
They had been working on it with this lady in Georgia. I can't recall her name right now, but she worked and helped get this award, because it went through. When she got it, she said it was a vote unanimously. That's after sixty-seven years now. And she got this vote, and so they arranged to have us. They had someone in the government, in charge of helping the Montford Point Marines to organize how they were gonna do it. So they said I could bring one relative with me and myself, and they paid all the plane fare and hotel. Oh, let me go back, tell you about Truman. Truman was a bad little man. A little haberdasher. MacArthur, he ruled the Pacific. But he was a good general. But Truman had to knock him down. He said, "The buck stop with me." So Truman did this again. He desegregated the Montford Point. See, the only place the black Marine would go to recruit, go to Montford Point. See, but he cut that down, said, "No, you could go any place, any recruiting place." That's why I say he was tough, when he bust down MacArthur. See, he was tough. I say, he was a tough little man. He did that in 1949. And that's when they closed down Montford Point.

AB: *What was it like to see the statue unveiled this summer [2016] when you went to the reunion?*
Oh, yeah. I did that. But I didn't even tell you about the congressional medal. My son and I went, and he announced on the airplane, and the whole plane had to salute me, and I said, "Whoa! What's this?" And we got to Washington, DC, and they had horses giving us a greeting, and that evening we had another little party, and dancing and whatnot, and

drinking. And they outlined what was gonna happen the next day and the next day. The next day we went for the congressmen to greet us, and each one of them were talking about their favorite son who was in the Montford . . . Are you a Republican?

EC: No.

Okay, all right. Okay. Even those Republicans were congratulating and betting on their folks from their home states. Who was the leader of the Republican Party?

EC: John Boehner?

Yeah, Boehner. Yeah, Boehner got up there and said some good word about his guy. Yeah, all of 'em did. They had Republican and Democrat in the Congress. And they all came up and spoke about their guy. We had almost four hundred of us out there. That's good to have left over four hundred.

EC: Were you disappointed that you didn't see combat?

Was I disappointed? No. You know what? I didn't go overseas to fight, but I went overseas to help people to fight. Help my brothers to fight, help the Marines fight. See, no matter what kind of job you take or how small it is, it can be valuable to somebody or for some purpose. See, if you didn't have that job, job might not be done, and some of them are gonna be missing out on some of that. No, I'm not [disappointed], because I know I have saved some lives out there with sending them signal lights and all of that kind of stuff and battery. That's what I'm talking about in the warehouse. Because they might think that was a small job, I mean, these guys out there fighting say we need some more guns, some more powders, some more lights, we need some battery to start whatever. Now, if they don't get that, then they can't do all that. No, no, no.

EC: Did you enjoy your time on Guam and Saipan?

Oh yeah. I tell you, my mother sent those boxes of cookies every now and then. I enjoyed them. It's a funny thing. I don't remember none of these guys' names. I don't even remember the captain's name now. The first sergeant was from California, and he was a good swimmer. I can remember their face, but I can't recall their name. Yeah, I enjoyed it. I wasn't mad with nobody.

AB: Mr. Chriss received a community service award this summer, for his work in the community at ninety-five years old. Just turned ninety-six.

Ninety-six, yeah. I've received a plaque from the judge. I went to the judge last week and he celebrate every year some of these service brothers. I've been getting quite a few awards, working in community. And I worked in Boy Scouts for about forty-four years. I was a Scout. Then when I was on the ship, coming back home, and I say, "What can I do to give some service to the community?" Then it hit me about being a Boy Scout, and I started a Boy Scout troop at my church. When I left there, I moved out into Pontchartrain Park, started a church in my house. The Bethesda United Methodist Church started in my house. Then I started a Boy Scout troop in the Pontchartrain Park community. And I

Montford Point Marine Alcee Chriss Sr. and Marine veteran William Dwiggins.
Courtesy of Dora Aguilera.

stayed with that, my own son was in that. And went to Chicago and helped with the scoutmaster there. We had a good troop there and my buddy, scoutmaster, he was the bus driver. He worked at night.

And in the daytime I can get all the kids out to church and get my wife to a school where she was teaching. And I even fixed breakfast. Because I used to cook anyway for my family, because my wife came up where they had beautician. The mama and aunt fix hair. And they don't cook, they fix hair. And she didn't learn how to cook, so I had to teach my wife to cook. My mother had four boys, and we all knew how to cook. You know, we red bean eaters down there. Ate red beans and rice. But we'll cook. So we'd be out there playing, one of us who'd be responsible for cooking that day, watching that pot, out there playing. "Hey, I smell something!" "Boy, you better go and get those beans straightened up!"

Do your job, that's it. You learn your job, you do your job. That's important.

"She wanted me to be safe."
Stesha Colby

It's not that I didn't enjoy my time in the Marine Corps, I just wanted to go back to college. So when push came to shove, I made the decision to leave active duty and stay in Fort Worth, and not move back to Memphis. I had fallen in love with Fort Worth. My cousin was dating a girl that had graduated from TCU, and I went with them to a football game. I think that was the deciding factor, that football game.

I would rather have been deployed. I joined the Marine Corps in time of war and Marines, if anything, are not cowards. Anybody during my generation could join the service. I would not call us cowards. We join knowing full well that we are at war in two different countries. There's conflict all over the world. It's not an easy time to be in the service, but we join anyway. So I would like to have been deployed. On the other hand, though, looking back now, maybe that was a good thing. I lost friends. My parents were anticipating that I would get deployed, and they were fearing that deployment. I was all for it, and my parents were like, "This is my oldest child, this is my baby." My mom and I grew up together, she always says, because she was seventeen when she had me. We grew up together, and she didn't want me to not be a Marine, but she wanted me to be safe. And what parent doesn't want their child to be safe?

"I couldn't handle civilians at all."
William Howe Jr.

I couldn't go out and enjoy anything, and I just couldn't be around people. There's a meme that goes around military guys that comes from that movie *Elf,* with Will Ferrell, and he's sitting in elf school and all the little elves are sitting around him. The first year using my GI bill, that's pretty much how we all felt. Not that we're superior to people in classrooms with us, but we have an experience and a worldview that they don't have. And they're talking about petty things like, "Oh, TCU doesn't have enough parking." Or in grad school even people were complaining about, "Oh, I can't get all this grading done. I had to stay up, I only got five hours of sleep last night." And I'm like, I've gone three days without sleep before. But civilians are civilians, and they haven't had those experiences, so that's something that I've tried to reconcile. And I've gotten better at it, but the first three years coming back, I couldn't handle civilians at all. I couldn't stand them, if they hadn't been military. That's the thing with the VA, with the vet center they would send me to. The civilians working there had never had the experiences, and I'm like, "How are you supposed to counsel me on how to cope with this, if you've never done it yourself?"

So I lost my family, lost my wife, lost my daughter, lost my house, my car, like a country song, just lost everything coming back. It just jaded me so bad. And then with my injuries not being taken care of, I felt like I couldn't function. I tried to go back to work, but the anxiety just got so bad with work deadlines. I was working as a mortgage loan officer, and I just couldn't function. I'd get red, I'd get flushed, I'd get hypervigilant. I couldn't sit in an office with my back to people. It's so hard to transition back. Part of it was that in the military there's this culture of "Don't talk about your experiences," and a lot of it comes from the guys from Vietnam: If you really went through tough shit, then you shouldn't talk about it. There are stolen valor guys, and that casts a bad shadow on the true veterans that have actually done things.

Because I feel that talking about it is the only thing that's helped me: talking to my therapist every week about what I did and what I experienced. That's the only thing that's helped me. But if we're putting those people down and it's, "Oh, you talked about your experiences so therefore you're just bragging," or "You're a warmonger" or whatever, then it's like we're casting them aside and not giving them the help they need to be able to recover mentally. You volunteered to go, but we wouldn't say to a rape victim, "You shouldn't talk about your rape," but we say all the time to military guys: "You shouldn't talk about your experience. You need to keep it bottled up, you need to keep it inside." And that's not healthy for anybody. That's why, when we got back, we just wanted to fight. The first six months I was back, I would go to bars and find guys in a fighting mood and just pick fights with them, because we wanted to feel that rush again, and there was nothing to simulate that anymore. And I found other ways, through gaming and through debate, that I've been able to experience the adrenaline rush of what it feels like, but many of us can't fulfill that. That's why most of the guys I know that I went with that actually saw shit are on either drugs or alcohol, or they've committed suicide by now.

I was Doc, which is a title earned in the Army. You don't come into a unit and, "Oh, you're Doc." You have to earn it, and I didn't earn it until about six months in, when I'd gotten my save. So they know me as Doc, and they know that they can trust me. I had guys coming back with all kinds of problems, like "I have this rash" or "It burns when I pee" or whatever, and they knew I kept it all secret and I guarded it, because I'm a medic and my first responsibility is to protect my patient's right to privacy. So I guarded it all there, and so now they carried it over to here. But it almost gets to be too much of a burden to me sometimes, when I have the same guys call me five times in the last year, and guys call me to bail them out of jail.

They just say they can't take any more. Most of them, their wives cheated, they're divorced now. They can't find a good job. Some of them got kicked out for marijuana use or drug use, and most of them have family issues, like me. I got divorced, and I haven't had a meaningful relationship since. I can't find a girl that understands me and who I am. Because we're changed, we're different, we see the world differently, and it's hard to find girls that understand that. So they talk about their frustration, and that they're tired of being alone, and they just want to end it all and be done with it. I have to reassure them that, "Hey, there's guys like me out there that still care about you. There are still people that want to help you, and there are some programs that I've found helpful to me." They trust me. They don't really trust the military. It comes down to us taking care of our guys, because they don't trust the government, because we know what we did, and we know what the government had us do in some cases that may have crossed the line, so we don't necessarily trust what the government has to say about a lot of stuff.

And I have a couple of friends that are still homeless. It's weird, because a lot of people you hear are people who never actually went and saw shit and did shit but they just stayed on base. And there's nothing wrong with that. We need support personnel just as much as we need combat troops. But most of my guys there served as combat troops, and they have problems with PTSD, and a lot of them will not even admit it. I believe, as a medic, that everybody that was in a combat role in Iraq or Afghanistan has PTSD. That's my personal opinion. It may be small, it may be large, but they have some degree of PTSD. But before we deployed, our commander told us that there's no such thing as PTSD. He said it's just a made-up disease, like ADHD, and that if you say you have it, you don't. It's a fictitious thing. That was the mindset of a lot of the military guys: I just can't say that I have PTSD. It's a weakness. I won't be able to get a gun. I won't be able to get hired by the police department. So they hide it and, by hiding it, they end up making their symptoms worse. Because they have no place to talk about it.

"I guess I'm kind of learning."

Chad Lackovic

I'm studying criminal justice. I've been an MP and in corrections for so long that all I really know is the law enforcement kind of stuff. After college, I honestly don't know what I'm going to do. I don't really want to be a cop because all the time I was military police, I got to do SWAT team, detective. I was Protective Services, like bodyguard type of stuff, and I got to do all the cool cop stuff that I've ever wanted to do, so I don't want to do that. And besides, a lot of the places won't hire me because of the age cutoff of thirty-seven, and I'm long past that.

Honestly, I don't know what I'm going to do. I applied to grad school, and hopefully I'll get that. And I'm working now at a place helping people coming out of prison get reconnected with their kids, which is okay for now. They don't pay very much, so it's definitely a temporary thing. I'm helping people, and that's pretty cool. I never thought I'd do anything along the social work lines, because it's really hard looking at people from this side of the table when I'm used to looking at them as bad guys or criminals. Now I know they're criminals, but I'm having to help them. I guess I'm kind of learning.

"They've seen buddies maimed, blown up, and killed."

Bob Doran

I've had the opportunity to teach former military students at TCU who have served in Afghanistan, Iraq, and elsewhere. Many of them have been through so much; they've seen buddies maimed, blown up, and killed. They've been through all kinds of issues involving trauma and stress. I deeply appreciate their amazing service to the country and am honored to teach them. I also realize that I was fortunate not to have had to risk my life in actual combat as they have.

When first asked to contribute to this project I thought my statement and experience wasn't worthy of it, especially in comparison to the sacrifices of those I have just mentioned. Then I thought, well, if I had been called to serve in combat, I would have gone and risked my life just as others have done. So, I decided to go ahead with the project.

"There is no greater honor."

April Brown

There are many stories. I believe my journey prepared me for my passion and purpose. I currently work at Texas Christian University, as the director of Veterans Services in Student Affairs. I assist our military connected students, both veterans and military family members, in their transition to university life. For many, this is also the beginning of a transition back to civilian life and to finding their home in our communities and in our nation. There is no greater honor than continuing to serve our veterans and their families.

"We have to support our service members."

Maria Brown-Spence

Even though my time with the Army National Guard came to an abrupt halt in 2015, I knew that my dedication to serve military members and their families would not end there. I knew all too well the struggles with mental health, physical health, racism, adversity, and challenges in general, and that I could not put this experience behind me.

In May 2018, I would become the founder and CEO of a 501(c)(3) nonprofit called Hearts 2 Heal, to assist military members and their families with mental health challenges or bereavement experiences through peer support, education, and advocacy. I hope to create programming that will educate on the importance of mental health and suicide awareness, and reduce the stigma around these issues. We

Army veteran Maria Brown-Spence.
Courtesy of Maria Brown-Spence.

have to support our service members and their families, on and off the battlefield.

"Your first semester here is going to suck."

Richard Puett

I work in the registrar's office for the VA, and I make it very clear to new students when they come in, I go, "Your first semester here is going to suck. You're going to hate it. You're going to hate it. You are. You're going to hate it. You need to take it easy your first semester. Don't go doing any crazy courses. Go get settled in. Reach out to your professors, talk to your professors. Don't just blow off some of these other, younger students. Keep an open mind."

I wish I would've had that same advice when I came here. I was looking at transferring after my first semester, because I absolutely hated it here. The one thing I noticed here is that you have no additional support. You're just a one-man army up here. Whereas I have some friends that are going to school and they're like, "Our veterans' affairs department here has twelve people." I was like, "We have one, and she just gets assistance from other people in the department to help out." I have a friend that's going to Baylor and he's like, "Yeah, man. Baylor's got it going on. We have our own massive space that we can study in."

TCU's mission statement is: world travelers or global citizens. But the thing is, how can a student be global if they just go on a European trip study abroad? Whereas you actually have veterans who've served missions around the world, things like that, you have people that have done rescue missions, they've served in combat. Going on that South Africa trip was a life-changing experience for me. It opened my eyes to a lot of things and made me realize that this is something that I do love and want to pursue.

My whole purpose here is to go to school, but at the same time I see that there's a very big gap between what vets know and can do, and what they should do. A lot of them come out of the military bitter and scared, so they lash out and they don't know what to do, and so they start to crack, because they don't have that support now that they're out. For me, what I finally realized and accepted was: pursue something that makes you happy, knowing that you have a goal that you can pursue, and pursue it. Focus on that. That's how I was able to deal with being out of the military. You want global citizens. There's no one more global than a military veteran that's deployed. They've seen the dark side. They've seen the good stuff, and they've seen the really bad side of the world.

"It's a completely different world."

Nick Sellman

The transition out of the Marine Corps is harder than the transition into the Marine Corps. I retired and started coming to school here, I think it was two months after retirement. Going from being on deployments when you spend twenty-four hours a day with these guys, and then being in class with eighteen-year-olds that are just fresh out of their house—some were barely being born when I enlisted—is a lot different. It's a completely different world having to deal with this stuff, but at the same time it also gives you a better perspective on getting back into civilian life. I guess it kind of puts me back in a category with people who are trying to figure it out themselves, too.

Walking around with a Marine shirt, and I'm obviously older than a lot of students here, no one makes eye contact with you. I walk around and smile at people, and they look away. There's been a lot of stuff in the news, like veterans with conditions and stuff, and obviously war is not fun or anything, but they're not all crazy people. You can say hi to them. I did a program right when I got out whose big thing is about helping military people get back into the community, and the president of the organization's biggest thing was that the military is starting to get a reputation. People think we're all broken now. I'm sure everyone who's gone to war has his or her issues and stuff, but we're not all completely helpless or broken. People should be accepting of them and bring them into society. Don't be afraid to talk to them.

I don't know if I can tell all the stories. I wish everyone could be as blessed as I have been to do all the things I've gotten to see and do. I got lucky. In my last deployment we were based out of Spain, and it was a Quick Reaction Force to help out any of the embassies in Africa. We took full advantage of it. We got to do some training in Germany, saw the pope in Italy. Got to go to the Sistine Chapel. It's crazy to think you get paid to do that. My wife hates it because she wants to see these things, and I'm like, "Eh, I've been there."

There's been some stuff, like guys I've known that have been killed by car or motorcycle accidents or stuff like that. I guess it's easier to cope with if you go to war and your buddy is killed. You're like, "Okay, I understand that." But one of my former bosses did three or four combat tours and was good, then came back home and died of a motorcycle accident. It's kind of like you go through all that and then come home and die for something that doesn't mean anything. It makes it kind of hard.

"I have to redo everything I've learned."

Israel Sanchez

I just want to make a difference. The good thing about us veterans is that we actually can see everything in a global perspective, and we can see things that differentiate what needs to be changed, because that's always been the mindset for us: human factors and human errors. We're constantly looking at what needs to be improved, how we improve on it, and then, how do we make a big impact?

The nursing program at Harris College of Nursing, they didn't understand. For example, me being a Navy corpsman, they didn't understand my medical knowledge and my capabilities, so we already have an issue with that. I am a male in a female-dominated environment, so they're going to find me intimidating, and I don't go in there acting like I know everything. I'm always like, "Show me. Teach me your ways, because obviously I've got combat experience and shipboard experience, and I've done certain things that maybe they haven't, but that's where we learn from each other." I think a lot of my faculty ended up getting very intimidated. They didn't know how to handle me. I have PTSD, and they didn't know how to handle that. When I got anxious, or when I told them I needed help, a lot of times they would brush it off.

I have written letters to Kay Granger, the congresswoman of my district, explaining to her that the conversation started with, "Why do we spend so much money on the Montgomery GI Bill?" Remember, they were trying to get rid of the Montgomery GI Bill. So I wrote to them and I said it's ridiculous if you get rid of the GI Bill, but if you really want to save money on the GI Bill, you should probably have us all credentialed, so that we don't have to start all over from scratch. That would be the smartest way to save money. We already have a truck driver in Iraq that knows how to drive through bombs, and next thing you know he comes here and he has to take another course to be able to do that. The man knows what he's doing. As a corpsman, I've already gone through basic corps school, combat casualty care school, independent duty corpsman, which is similar to a physician's assistant or a nurse practitioner. It's a year of intense schooling, but now I have to redo everything that I've already learned how to do, because of the fact that nothing crosses over. You're only going to get credits for like physical education and military credits, which don't even equate to anything. There's a program in Corpus Christi. They're the first ones in the nation to develop it, where they take military experience and count it towards a degree. It's a year or two years, and it's an online program. Then you just go to clinicals, because you already know what you're doing, so you do everything online. I wish I would have taken advantage of that, but then I'd have to be in the local area of Corpus, and I had no idea that was being offered.

"This campus is like 60 percent female."
Felicia Lawson

I love TCU's campus and it's beautiful, but having worked in such a diverse place, TCU was a shock. I don't think I really researched that. I wasn't looking at the demographics. I was like, "It's in Fort Worth, that's Texas, it's in DFW, so multicultural." And I got here and I was like, "What happened?" Even Frog Camp, it was so mixed, I was like, "What happened, people?" But it's so weird coming from the military, where there is everything, everybody. Oh my goodness, I had friends from the Dominican Republic, Ecuador, friends from the United Arab Emirates, people from the Philippines, everything, all walks of life, all different colors. And I was just like, "What happened?" It is such a shock, because you don't think about diversity until you're not around it anymore.

Veterans, though, like structure. A lot of them have really good leadership skills. So they get in a classroom, and people are mulling over decisions, and I don't know what the group's going to do, and they kinda just jump in and take charge. You want the normal college experience, but you can't just sit back and watch things unfold. So it's awkward.

The one thing that I will say about this campus is it is totally polar opposite of the military in the female count. Because this campus is like 60 percent female. In the Navy you're outnumbered, thirty-five to one on an aircraft carrier—so five thousand people, every thirty-sixth person is a woman, and then seventy-five to one in the Navy. That was one of the good shocks. I was like, "Okay, I've never been to a predominantly female area, ever. This is awesome."

I think in the military and the military spouse life, you see so much and you do so many different things, and then you don't know how to sit still. It's like always time for a change, but eventually that won't be the case. I'm going to have to settle in one spot after school. It's so weird, but I think in the Navy especially, and I don't know if other branches are like this, the travel was the best thing ever, 'cause I would have never seen the amount of countries that I saw without it. It was awesome.

"For them it's a milestone."

Michelle Johnson

Since I was back home, I thought, "Well, Lord, what did I do before I left the military? I mean, before I joined, what was I doing?" I remembered that I once majored in music (voice) at TCU. So I went to Ed Landreth Hall at TCU and started communicating with the music department again, to see about auditioning times and requirements. I kept all my music and had been studying my repertoire. I never got rid of anything. Steve Brock signed me up for the audition and told me to show up on such and such day. I showed up early, with my church dress on. I looked cute, like a girl! I waited near the auditorium and kept wondering, "Did I miss the time? Maybe they changed the venue." I went and asked the music department secretary. She told me that my audition was "yesterday" and that the jury (music faculty) had already left for sabbatical in Europe; they go every year. So then I was like, "What now, Lord?! What else did I like to do before I ever joined the military?" I remembered that I really enjoyed art. I mean, I had my church dress on and looked cute. I couldn't let it go to waste. So I walked across the street and talked to Sally Packard. She was my Design I teacher at UNT back in '98. She helped me start the process of returning to TCU. So now I'm an art major, pursuing my BFA in Printmaking.

I decided to come back to TCU to finish what I started before I joined the military. I always really liked TCU. It seemed so prestigious. When I was growing up, when I was younger than y'all are, a black person didn't come to this side of town unless they were cleaning, cutting grass, or doing something else over here. My grandmother always warned me to not be over on this side of town after 5:00 p.m. Jim Crow had a lot to do with her words to me. But I always wanted to go here; I thought TCU was such a wonderful school. And it is. It still has its PWC [predominantly white campus] issues. I thought, yeah, I wanna go here. When Thanksgiving and Christmas rolled around and Aunt Virginia asked me what's been happening since she last saw me, I told her that I'm going to TCU. She said, "Ohhhhh, TCU! You go, girl!" For them it's a milestone. It is for me, too.

"You need to be a good learner."

Tim Cole

If I were talking to a young man or woman that was struggling getting back into civilian life, I think I'd start with a little edification and encouragement and honoring: "Listen, what you've done is a great thing. You've put service before self. You've done this great thing. But, for whatever reason, you've chosen not to continue that. So, just like at the beginning of your military career, it was uncomfortable and out of place, and it was unusual the way these drill sergeants were talking to you, and it was a real stretch and change. The same thing has to occur now. You need to figure out what this next phase of your life is." And that's the blessing sometimes of an academic institution: It's a fairly neutral ground, before you're actually into that work world. I would say, "You need to be a good learner, show up with a good attitude, but also take on that information."

"The key word is discipline."

Jim Lee

The key word is discipline in the military service. Discipline all the time. When I used to assign students to write an explication of a poem, I would say they had to write three pages. A page has twenty-six lines, every line has sixty characters and spaces. When you've accomplished 60x26x3, you've completed the paper. Two or three lines short, and you haven't. Two or three lines over, and I ain't gonna read it. That makes me like the people from boot camp who were pushing me, but it was good for the student to do that. I've written a lot of stuff in my day, and one of the things that made my writing better was that for several years I wrote a thriller column for the *Houston Post*. I reviewed thrillers, mystery novels. Four books in three typed pages. You can't wander around when you're doing that, and I think that improved my writing.

"It's different in a civilian world."

Jim Hille

I don't have a huge staff here, but you do management type of principles or leadership type of principles, engagements we have with all the people we work with. When I was at Texas Teachers, I had about seventy-five that reported to me, and some people might get intimidated by that, but it was normal for me. You just learn how it's different in a civilian world, right? It's very different. And that's one of the adjustments that career officers have to adjust to. You can't bark orders at people and expect people to do anything. And the good leaders in the military don't resort to barking orders, either. That's one thing that we were trained in at the Naval Academy quite a bit. If you ever had to bark an order,

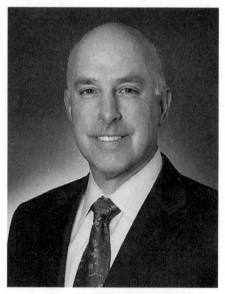

Marine veteran Jim Hille.
Courtesy of Jim Hille.

then you may be in trouble. You lead by example. You lead by other methods. You lead quietly.

"Fail a little, and learn from the fail."

Joddy Murray

Most of the leadership that I learned at the Academy has stuck with me. I've found myself being attracted to leadership positions, in part because of my experience at the Academy. That's why I encourage students to get as much leadership experience as they can, even if it's just to run a small book club or gather students for advocacy, or whatever. Do whatever you can to exercise those skills. Fail a little, and learn from the fail. You find yourself going, "Oh wow, I have to figure this out." And it's like, "Oops, that was a mistake. I am going to learn from this mistake." I have a little bit more of a sense that I can put my mind to something and maybe not do it well at first, but at least give it a good go.

"You have to have that mindset,
or you just go bananas."

Steve Weis

You have to listen to the student carefully. If they're running from something and running to the military for the answer, that's the wrong reason. If it's a desire to serve, and truly serve, then I usually say "Go." But you have to have that mindset, or you just go bananas. Because there's a lot of nonsense in the military as well.

"It gives me something to focus on."

William Howe Jr.

I'm working on communications studies now. I work with our debate team, and I help tutor the student athletes. I want to get my PhD in either communications studies or rhetoric. For my master's thesis I'm actually looking at indoctrination into the military and comparing that to indoctrination into the fundamentalist Baptist churches' seminaries, and seeing what the correlations are between those two situations, and how they use words to change somebody's identity into what they want it to be.

I don't know what the answer is, but I do know that there needs to be more social support for our military. Like I said, I go home at night and it's just me. I go home to a two-story house, and I just sit there and try to find something. With my college readings, it helps. That's the only reason I'm in college; it gives me something to focus on.

I'll try to watch some TV, but there's no way for me to connect with people that really understand the schema that I have and what I've been through, and I can't go to regular single events. They're just talking about such mundane, trivial things that to me it's just boring. I want to be stimulated intellectually, and I want people to have a bigger worldview than just "My parents believe in Fox News so I only watch Fox News," and "We're the opposite with MSNBC." People are so steeped in those, but if you can't tell me why you believe in something, then why are you telling me you believe in it? And then the price for my family: I think my family had no idea what it was going to be like coming back, and they had no idea how to respond to it, and that led to me estranging myself from them basically for about two to three years, where I didn't even talk to them. My dad and my mom live in Arlington, and my two sisters live in Arlington, and my one sister I still pretty much don't talk to, because she thinks I'm just mooching off the government and I don't have any injuries and all this stuff and just trivializes everything. My other sister is just jealous of the fact that my parents have a high regard for what I did in Iraq.

And my parents, they tried this whole thing of "Well, you're only saved because we were praying for you." My dad's a pastor. "God was looking out for you" and stuff like that. Well, why would God look out for me and not look out for my friends? Just because they didn't have people praying for them, they died? That doesn't seem fair to me. I would get into those arguments so much that finally I was like, "When you guys want to talk like a family about normal family stuff, I can come back and talk. But I'm tired of talking about Iraq and what I did and those experiences there, because you're just going on and on about how it was God that saved me, and maybe it was and maybe it wasn't, but you have no proof." And that just makes me feel like God didn't love the guys that died over there, or that have died from suicide since I came back. I mean, suicide is still killing more people than Iraq or Afghanistan ever did, and it's because we're not giving it the right attention that it needs, and I don't know what the answer to that is. And if they're not committing suicide, they're living on the streets. They're living in drugs and alcohol. All I did the first three years after I came back was drink. I never did drugs, but I did drink a lot, and pretty much every night I would drink until I passed out, because the VA wouldn't give me any sleeping meds.

I've tried to go back to church for social reasons. Maybe it's real, but it just seems too fake to me when I go in there and I see these families that look perfect. I feel really guilty at the same time, so maybe it's my problem. But I'll go to church and there'll be a couple there with their kids and they just look all happy. And I'm like, that should be me and my wife and my daughter, but because I decided to join the Army, I lost all that. Now maybe that's not true; maybe me and my wife would have ended without that. But I feel like in my mind, it's my decision. I screwed up by joining the Army and, although I did a lot of good, that's why I feel like I sacrificed a lot for the Army and the "All gave some, some gave all" thing. And I feel like a lot of guys gave their families for the military, and a lot of guys cannot have a healthy relationship with people, because of the way their brain is programmed from the military. We're so "Get to the point, let me know what you want, let me do this," and most girls just don't get that.

I tell my sisters never to date a military guy, because 99 percent of them are jackasses and they're going to cheat on you, because it's just cyclical. A lot of guys came back and found out their wives had been cheating, and now they're like, "Well, if my wife's going to cheat on me, I'm just going to sleep around with everybody." So then at Fort Hood when people are deployed, they start sleeping with the wives of other guys who are deployed to Iraq. It's a cycle: then those guys come back and it's like, "Oh, you cheated on me while I was gone, so now I'm going to cheat on you with these other wives." And it's just a bad cycle that happens, and it cheapens relationships in our minds, and it makes it hard to connect.

"I feel like I came here from another country."

Jarrod McClendon

I want to say that the Army will bring certain things out in you. There are certain things that I've done in my time in the military. Like I never thought I'd jump out of a plane. I never thought I would go through SERE School and go five days without sleeping, seven days without food. You don't know that you can do these things, and the Army has this cool way of nudging you in a direction. It might be peer-induced but, for the most part, you can do way more than you believe. You don't know these things until you test it, and no one's going to put up their hand and volunteer to be tested. So you have to kind of light the fire underneath them, and that's kind of what happened to me with a lot of things in life.

I finally had this revelation recently: that my graduation from here was really a means to an end. I didn't want to graduate from college; I wanted to be an Army officer. So I'm thinking the only way to be an Army officer is to graduate from college. And of course TCU, this is where I grew up, in a neighborhood that said I wasn't supposed to be here. So to come back to Fort Worth was like, not only do you check off something that you've had a problem with since you were a child, but you can also be what you wanted to be in the Army. It's a pretty cool ride so far.

I grew up in the neighborhood called Stop Six. It's maybe ten miles east of here, and that neighborhood is poverty stricken. I remember a long time ago a teacher asking, maybe in elementary school, "What do you want to do? How do you want to become the man that you want to be one day?" And I said, "I want to go to TCU." The purple and white is everywhere in Fort Worth. If you live in Fort Worth you know about TCU, and it's a dream. This is the beacon of light; this is Oz. So I was eight or nine years old, and the teacher said, "Does your family have money? Do you come from means?" And I'm looking around. I know we don't.

So she says, "Well, you're good at sports." I was probably sixty pounds then, and I knew for a fact I wasn't going to play sports. I wasn't propelled in that direction. I was a book reader. So she was like, "Hey, there might be a shot for you, but I want you to just go ahead and prepare not to go there."

This is a heartbreaker that I'm being told to deal with. A white teacher, in a

Jarrod McClendon, US Army.
Courtesy of Jarrod McClendon.

black neighborhood. It's a double-sided coin. There's a positive to it, because she placed something inside of me that eventually would cook and burn and propel me to do more. On the other side, why tell a child something like that? Not everybody will recover the same way. I got lucky. I really do feel like somewhere there's something divine saying, "Hey, come this direction."

In the [ROTC] cadet lounge right now, there's a form signed by the colonel that says, "You cannot go to Stop Six." It actually says "daytime robbery and theft." The irony. I was told, when I was a kid, "Don't come up this way, because the police might not like you driving around here." And I'm here now, and I'm bridging a gap, and now they're telling me I can't go back because it's off limits. But no one lives there now. They've all been shuffled out of Stop Six. My mother lives in the same apartment complex that I do over off of 30 and Brentwood Stair Road, and a lot of my immediate family live in the Forest Hill area. No one is in Stop Six anymore anyway. But I was there at one point, and now I can't go back. Well, I'm not supposed to go back.

If it were not for certain people, I would feel like a complete outsider at TCU. I'm talking white, black, or otherwise. There are some people here who are very supportive of me being here, and that's awesome to me, and that's really all I've needed. But for the most part, I do feel like I don't belong here a lot. I feel like I came here from another country, and it was to get a degree, and then I gotta go back. It feels weird. I feel foreign here. And there's a certain experience, just the fact that I've seen the sun come up a few more times. After a while you get a little bit thicker skin, and there's a lot of stuff that other cadets are not used to yet. But I think the military will give them what they gave me. They're going to rub them raw, but they'll grow a callus.

I value the fact that the military can take somebody like me and actually make them something. I feel indebted to the Army. I feel like it gave me the opportunity to become a man. It showed me certain things about the world, and it showed me certain things about myself that I didn't know existed, and I think that it can do that for anybody. Colonel Randall, the professor of military science here at TCU, said training is preparing you for the known, and that's what the Army did. A lot of time, "Hey, look, do this, over and over and over again, because if you get into a situation like this, you prepare for it." Training is preparation for the known. Education is preparation for the unknown, and that rings very loud to me. But I would not be the man that I am now without that training. You have to have both, and I believe the Army offered me training, and this education is offering me the opportunity to understand the unknown.

"How many children did we collaterally kill?"

Christa Banet

Growing up, I was just a brat. I was selfish, and I didn't care about anyone else or what anyone thought. I was just my own person, and sometimes it's difficult to overcome that. I've been gone for so long, but they still think of me as the teenager that was a selfish brat. It is who I was, but I'm not that person. I go home and I'm really quiet, and I like to observe things. I know I'm talking a lot right now, but I like to observe things whenever I go home. And I've missed out on so much stuff. I've had so many family members be born and die, so I like to just sit back and watch and see how people have changed, and see where I can step in to help, or if there's anything I can do. I think that kind of caught some of my family off guard. They expect me to come home and be this raging brat and expect everything on the spot, because that's how I was. I'm not the same person that I was before.

I would definitely do it again. Don't get me wrong, there's stuff that we're not going to talk about in the interview that happened during military service that is awful, and you don't ever want to go through stuff like that. But that was one part of the experience. It's like you have a bag of apples and you've got one bad apple. You're probably not going to throw the whole bag away, you're just going to throw that one apple away.

Even though I never directly shot anyone, I know people who have, and I've never been directly shot at, but we were still fixing aircraft parts that were going to Iraq to fix the planes that were flying out and dropping bombs on civilian populations. Our commanding officer came back. Wendy Smith, I'll never forget her. She's this little short four-foot-eleven lieutenant colonel commanding officer. She was just so tiny and frail-looking, but she got up to speak and you felt her presence. She's just tiny, but this big person. And she commended the entire unit, even everyone that was back in Yuma, because we had dropped one million pounds of ordnance on Baghdad. I thought about that: one million pounds of explosives on a city. How many children, how many people who weren't opposed or fighting in a war, did we collaterally kill? And that's one thing that you have to take into consideration. I had a really hard time. I have not directly killed anyone, but I have aided in the deaths of thousands. I don't think millions, I hope not millions. But that's kind of a hard pill to swallow. That's why I've prayed a lot. I've forgiven a lot. A lot of the bad stuff that's happened to me, I have learned how to forgive.

I'm thankful for the experience at TCU because I think it's like 70 percent women on campus, right? In the Marine Corps it was 7 percent women, so this is like a hundred times better. It's kind of brought me back down to earth. Instead of being rough and tumble with the boys, having to constantly be on guard and trying to prove myself, I don't have to do that here. I can lay back and relax and be calm. And I don't do well in aggressive situations now. I've dealt with that enough with the guys. Being around girls, it's calmed me down a lot and brought me back down to earth.

I like having a classroom full of women, and hearing the voices of women speak. It's empowering in a way that the military wasn't. I got confidence and individuality and independence and empathy and appreciation out of the military, but I had to go through a lot of really crappy stuff. I love sitting in class and listening to the thoughts and opinions of your generation, young women speaking about what the world is like for you, because what I have come up with hasn't been that great. But I know that the preceding generation—like April Brown's generation, she was a major in the Marine Corps. How much crap did April have to put up with? But all that crap that April went through and put up with, and not even put up with, but stood up against, she opened doors for me. So I know that everything I went through, I've opened doors for younger women.

And it sucks to know that I had to go through all this crap, but it was worth it, because now it gives your generation a whole new window of opportunity, a whole new door to walk through. I interact a lot, I talk a lot in class, because I love school. Sometimes I'll play devil's advocate just to get people thinking, and sometimes I frustrate people, but I like to challenge the mindset. Like, "Okay, I see you're thinking like this, but how would the real world come at this? Right now we're in a college setting, so how would the real world come at this thought that this young woman or this young man has just expressed?" And I will poke the hornet's nest to get them to respond, or to get them to think.

"I love being a TCU student."

John Garcia

When I was living with my mom and she was sick, we lived in shelters off Lancaster. We lived in a car. And I remember, I don't know what we came here for, we were at TCU, maybe we were just walking around or something and I—and I put it on a pedestal. I loved TCU, but I never thought in a million years that I could be able to attend it. And so it was very special that that chance came up for me. I love being a TCU student. I did not anticipate the workload that y'all do. I came from Texas Central College, and I didn't even have to open some of my books there and I still got an A. I came here thinking I'd be able to do the same thing. That was not the case, so it kind of kicked my butt, and it still kicks my butt, but I know I'm better doing what I'm doing now. I love TCU.

What I would always tell my oldest son Alex is, "Go to college. If you go to college, you can be better than what I am already. You can be smarter, faster, stronger, whatever, just go to college and learn." I always told him that, every time I see him: "Go to college, go to college." And one time he asked me, "Dad, where'd you graduate from?" And I was dumbfounded. I didn't. And because he said that, it sparked me and I started taking classes, and I was into it, and I started learning stuff, and I was enjoying it. And one day I can tell my kids, "Look, I'm thirty-seven now and hopefully when I graduate I'll be thirty-nine." I can say, "I did it. I was thirty-nine, but I still did it. There's no reason why y'all can't."

I know why my first wife left me, and one of those reasons was our anniversary. I had just got back from being in the field where you're away from your family and you're living in the woods pretty much, and you do everything out there, you train out there. We were out there for quite some time, I remember that. And I came home and I was just agitated and frustrated, and I was just ready to be home and relax. I grabbed a beer out of the refrigerator and went to sit on the couch, and she was already upset at me for something, I don't know what it was. And she said, "You know what today is?" And I said, "Just another effing day," and I drank my beer. That's pretty much probably the straw that crushed her back. It was rough, because I was always gone. We were both young, and I couldn't give her that time. My first marriage was my fault, I'll take that. I've been married three times. This is my third one. That should tell you about military life; it's very rough. Not everybody's like me, but there's quite a few of us that are multiple times married. I won't blame it on the military. You know it's hard. Yes, it makes it harder, but at the same time I think I could have put in more effort.

I loved everything I did. I wouldn't want my children to do it. That's crazy for me to say because I'm very pro-military, but I just want my kids to not have to go through what I went through to make a better life. I sacrificed a lot for them to not live the way I did, and I wanted to give them opportunities. And they have opportunities now. If they want to do it to serve their country, the patriotic part, I will support them a hundred percent. But if it's an economic or a pressured kind of thing, no.

"One of my coping strategies was working out."

Aaron Tombleson

When we got back, we were running right into Christmas and the New Year. We went through our post-deployment therapy or assessment. It was just really quick. Even looking back on it now, I just graduated nursing school, and I'm starting my new job, and definitely a lot of that stuff was way too quick and not done right. But at that point they were just trying to get the Marines to be with their families and get them to get some kind of joy for coming back. But then I was only there for about a month before I started turning in all my stuff, then I was pretty much gone. I moved to Arkansas with my little brother. He had a pretty nice big old house over in Arkansas where him and his wife were making pretty good money, and they were both in the military. So I moved in with him for about a year. And the whole adjustment was pretty intense for me. It was kind of my own way of doing things. I didn't really use anyone else.

So I got lucky in a sense that my coping skills and my techniques worked, because if they didn't I probably would not have been here right now. You just kind of get a hit or miss. So that's why they really try to help you when you come out. And they are really proactive about that now, because a lot of people's coping skills or their support isn't strong, so they get into complications. They start spiraling down, and then suicides start happening, and I'm sure you guys have heard a lot about that. That is probably the whole point of you guys doing this interview and the book.

I was so young when I went in. Even now usually nobody would even guess that I am thirty. People are like, "Oh, you're twenty-four, twenty-five." My face is starting to show it, but nursing school kind of makes you tired. When I went in, I was still kind of young and hadn't really gone anywhere. Or seen too many things. I was very arrogant and hardheaded and driven at what I wanted to do. The Marine Corps gave me a focus for a little bit, and it organized me and gave me the methods that I needed to steer myself towards where I wanted to go. And just really grind. I'm a grinder. I just stick at something and do it day in, day out. I can eat salad for lunch months on end. And everyone is like, "Man, how can you keep having salad?" and I'm just, "I like eating salad." It doesn't really bother me. So it kind of gave me a way to maneuver that to where it worked toward my advantage. That is something the Marine Corps did for me.

One of my coping strategies was working out. I worked out a lot, and I used to throw, and in high school I threw shot disc for the track team. So I decided to just start doing it again, even though I had hurt myself. When I got out, working out was a way for me to kind of grind and just focus on one thing, and I got my personal training license as a personal trainer, group exercise instructor, all sorts of things that would keep me busy throughout the day. But then I started throwing again, and started getting good, and my PR started climbing up on the boards, and then TCU was looking at me, and they made it where I could come throw with them. So that was pretty cool, and they said, "Hey, we'll get you into the nursing program if you're here." I don't think they do that anymore, because being in the nursing program and trying to throw just doesn't work. You can't be good at both.

No hate towards you guys or anything like that, but when you go into class people from different experiences, or maybe a little bit younger, would say things that might not be appropriate. Now I would see it from another point of view: They might be young, they might not really think about what they're saying before they blurt something out. But back then it was a little harder to adjust to something like that, because your history would come into play and you would get angry really easy at what somebody would say, so you kinda kept to yourself.

"I'm starting to learn how to steer."

Jake Melton

You kinda look back on your life and say, "If I'd have had a little more forethought to guide myself to the experiences that would have been most beneficial, the most exciting or something, instead of kinda just letting life take you where it will." And that's kinda where I'm at now. I'm starting to come at it more with a eyes-wide-open type deal. Just so I can get to the life-altering events that seem more appealing.

It's like when you're in a dream and you wake up and you vaguely remember it and you think, "It would be really cool if I could kind of steer the course of action while I'm in the dream. That would be a really neat experience." I'm learning how to do that now in real life, instead of just kinda going down the path and then letting life take me where it will. I'm starting to learn how to steer that a little bit.

"These vets lose their close group of friends."

Gabe Merigian

Something very important to me is a push for better mentorship and mental health treatment for those while they're still in. They may have had some traumatic experiences in the theater downrange and aren't getting the help they need, and then get out and are in a bad place. Large amounts of veterans are getting out now. These vets lose their close group of friends and become isolated, lonely, and depressed. I think there needs to be a focus on getting them in a good head space and involved with a community where they're moving before they get out. Twenty-two veterans commit suicide a day. That's a very real number to all veterans, because we're losing our friends. I lost my friend Jon Gee to suicide two months after I got out. Jon was experiencing mental health issues and took his own life in his barracks room, largely because of the toxic environment that existed there at the time. There were two other suicides in that barracks while I was living there. It just felt like you couldn't rely on the higher-ups to care about your well-being.

"I was one of his patients."

William Howe Jr.

That was a crazy time. I had just gotten back from Iraq. It was a DSRP building, which is the building that you go into when you're about to deploy and when you're coming back from deployment, and they do your PTSD evaluations there and all that stuff that's easy to fake or pass, whichever you want to do. So that building is the one he [Army psychiatrist Major Nidal Hasan] chose to attack [at Fort Hood, Texas, on November 5, 2009]. I felt vulnerable because I didn't have a weapon. If I'd had a weapon, I would have been fine. In Iraq, when I was in a firefight, even if I was bandaging somebody, I always had my M-16, so I always knew that if somebody did come up on me, I could defend myself. In this case, I had nothing. I had the police officers, but if they went down . . .

And I had actually talked to him before. He did actually counsel me when I came back. I was one of his patients. I saw him once, for about thirty minutes. I filled out the PTSD thing, so I had to talk to him for thirty minutes about my thoughts on PTSD. I remember him being kind of aloof. I guess that would be the right word. I've heard this so many times before, which I guess is part of his defense: that we were saying the same things about his countrymen or his fellow believers and stuff. But that's how I felt. And the guy that helped me capture the top-five guy in Iraq was Palestinian and a Muslim, and he and I were great friends. I had nothing against the Muslim people, and that's one thing that helped me realize that all Islamic people were not that way. My best friend in the Army, that was helping me fight against them, he's from Palestine and he's Muslim. But a lot of guys didn't have that, I guess, so when they came back they would just classify all Muslims as extremists. So I guess he heard that too much.

I wasn't there when he came in and he shot. I was supposed to be, but I wasn't. I remember feeling like, "If I only had my M-16, where's my M-16, where's my gun, where's my weapon?" I didn't even have a knife, I didn't have anything with me, because of the restrictions they have in the Army. It's like my first year at TCU, walking around, I felt so naked because I didn't have a weapon with me. It was the same way when I was at Fort Hood. I felt like I'm here on a military base, and I have no weapon to defend myself from this guy that's attacking and killing us. Mass shootings are one thing, think of Columbine or Sandy Hook or these things where people die and you look at the numbers and it's sad, and these are kids that they're killing, and it's horrible. But when you think of Fort Hood, these were for the most part trained military guys and girls that he killed, and they had military training. They could have fought back, but they had no weapons. They couldn't defend themselves.

"I was never in harm's way."

Jeff Coffer

Unlike many military veterans, I was never in harm's way. So in retrospect, while I did serve in the US Army, I certainly have an even greater respect and appreciation for those women and men who did serve during times of conflict and continue to do so today.

"It helped me become who I am."

Michael Blackert

I think what helped me was I didn't take a lot of time between getting out and going right into doing something. I got out in June of '14, and I started school here in August. In between that I was selling my house in

California and getting everything, so there wasn't a lot of stale time for me to think. I think that was the best thing, because I've noticed a lot of my brothers and sisters that I've served with, the more time they have to think, the harder it's been for them. I've always been kinda positive, that helps too, and I've got a good support channel around me. My wife has always been supportive. We're back in Texas, where her family is, so we've got a lot of support around here. I think a lot of veterans are having that disconnect, because they don't really know how to interact again with the community or even with civilians again. Even if you're in the military four years, a part of you has changed.

If I didn't have children and been married, and had been by myself, I think it could have been a whole lot worse. I didn't ever want my kids or wife to be like, "You haven't been the same since this." I mean, I know I'm not going to be the same, but you want to try to be positive, especially with young children, because they are going to feed off you. And wife or significant other, they're going to feed off your negative or positiveness as well. I think it could have been worse, but it was pretty rough, not going to lie. Still dealing with it at times. I still wish I was in. But at the same time, I try to look positive at it, because I wouldn't be in the shoes that I'm in without the military. I think it helped me become who I am.

"I still pray for her."

Joel Huffman

I realize that up to this point I've written mostly using first person plural pronouns: we, us, our, ours. I've made a conscious effort to do so, because this story is not mine alone; I have only one perspective of a much grander narrative that sweeps across continents and generations far beyond my scope.

But there was one event that abruptly shifted my focus from the deployment to my own life back home. One night in August when we had Internet access, I was checking my bank account—it was fun to see it climb with tax-free and combat pay benefits. I noticed that about $4,000 was missing, including a $2,000 charge for airplane tickets. Half alarmed, half confused, I investigated and discovered in my wife's email that the two tickets were to Costa Rica, for her and my best friend. (I prefer not to use their names out of respect.)

I tried to make sense of what little information I had. My wife was from Costa Rica, so I thought maybe she was visiting her relatives before her college classes started later that month. My friend was in the Air Force, and I knew he was preparing to come to Afghanistan for deployment the next month, but I thought that perhaps a terrible family emergency had happened, and he was being a great friend by accompanying her. I called her parents, my parents, and his parents, but no one knew anything about it.

I'll spare the details and emotional roller coaster of the next few weeks, but the condensed version is that a month earlier, in July, during his pre-deployment leave, he had gone back to our hometown, where she was living with my family while I was deployed. They got drunk together, he confessed his love to her, she told him she was planning to divorce me because I had gotten "too religious," and they slept together. Overcome with guilt, the next day he asked one of our friends for a gun so he could kill himself. Thankfully, God blocked that path. My wife and best friend couldn't undo what they had done, so instead they embraced it fully. They spent the rest of his leave together and soon after decided to leave to Costa Rica because they had a place to stay, and he wouldn't be in danger of being pursued by federal authorities for his desertion.

The next few weeks were tough. On one hand, I loved them both and told them I forgave them. I was trying desperately to resolve this situation without losing my best friend or my wife. I took seriously Jesus's prayer: "Forgive us our debts as we forgive our debtors." I've done some deplorable things in my life, and since God forgives me for those things, who am I to withhold forgiveness from others?

Plus, I was no better than they were. In fact, during my senior year of high school, things had not been going well at my house, so I had lived with my best friend's family. On graduation night, while he had stayed sober and was driving drunken friends safely to their houses, I was with his girlfriend, committing the same betrayal that he later committed with my wife. The difference between his act and mine was that I lacked the courage to admit what I did, even when he confronted me. It wasn't until years later that I actually told him; he had known the whole time and still remained friends with me.

With hurt and rage fueling my vengeful lust, I fantasized about things I can't put into writing. I wanted them both to feel the same pain I was experiencing. One person's offer for resolving the situation was "two Russians in Nicaragua" he knew who would kill them for a few thousand dollars. I thought about it for a minute, but couldn't bear the thought of the pain it would cause their families. It was a very dark time in my life, and I asked God's forgiveness constantly for wishing evil upon them.

In October we returned from Afghanistan. They returned to America in November, because life in Costa Rica was hard. He was arrested as he stepped off the plane in Houston, because he had turned himself in to the Air Force and told them his flight details. He spent a few months awaiting trial, and in January I served as a character witness on his behalf at his court martial. He's the nicest, most loyal, most generous person I've ever met. The colonel who presided over the case said my best friend had thirty-six character witnesses, far more than he had ever seen. This was a good guy who just made a bad mistake. He ended up spending time in jail, then got discharged from the military.

My wife moved back with me after returning from Costa Rica, but she seemed hardened and hollow. She didn't know how to accept forgiveness from the guilt and shame she felt. I told her I was sorry for the pain I had caused her. I had joined the military while we were dating without asking her, or anyone else, because I felt it needed to be my own decision, and she had always been torn between supporting me and hating war.

Over the next few years, she searched fruitlessly for lasting joy, instead finding only temporary happiness, followed by disappointment and frustration. She turned to academic success, art, drugs, dogs, political activism, and other things to find satisfaction and fulfillment, but beneath the surface she was angry, depressed, and anxious to find something to hope in. I tried to explain that everyone messes up—that's why we all need a Savior who offers us brand new life—but she wanted nothing to do with God, which distanced us further.

During my last deployment, she told me she needed time to figure things out on her own. I tried to win her back, but she said she just wanted to be alone, that getting married had been a mistake, and that if she had money she'd file for divorce. I said I'd never leave her because I took a vow—regardless of what she did—that I would love, honor, and cherish her until death. But later I realized that what was driving me was less nobility than pride. I didn't want to be seen as a failure in marriage, another divorce statistic, and by some Christians' standards disobedient to God's rules. After long, long hours of searching Scripture, praying, and asking others for wisdom, I filed for divorce, and sixty days later it was finalized. I still pray for her when I think about her and hope for the very best for her life.

"I didn't know what to do with myself."

Tami Tovar

I've lost touch with some that I wish were still around. Most are in touch. They're still on my Facebook but scattered to the four winds. I've been so many places after getting out, too. Some are still in the military. A couple have committed suicide, so that was hard. But I go over to the VFW and hang out with people. That helps but can have its own drama. Student Veterans Association has been a real help with connections. Especially in the hard times, having someone to relate to helps tremendously.

For me, everything about keeping in touch with my old job and co-workers is related to the contrast from being a soldier, to suddenly not being one. I suddenly went from everything is life or death twenty-four hours a day, 365 days a year on call, no matter what, to . . . what? This vacuum of nothing. At least I had my family. To be clear, in that job, you didn't just have one patient that you're taking care of that could accidentally die if you make a mistake. You're running tests on a machine, and if you do something wrong to the machine, you could put out thousands of inaccurate results that doctors base their treatment on, which could kill thousands of patients. It's very serious, and I went from that to being a stay-at-home mom with a navy blue carpet. Navy blue shows every speck of anything rather glaringly, if you're used to laboratory clean. I vacuumed eight times a day. I volunteered until I had no time left to think. I didn't know what to do with myself. I'd never had so much free time. The shock of the contrast: everything orderly, time to hang with buddies was limited to the rare breaks and slow times, but they were close by feeling it and dealing with all the same stuff as you, so it worked. Being out, it isn't the same.

I was then, and am still, really energetic. At some point, being faced with not really knowing what to do with myself, my family was like, "Yes, go back to school! Yes! Get out of our hair! You're driving us nuts!" I was always coming up with these bodacious projects. Like we had this one landlord lady whose husband had left who had been a builder, and he basically abandoned all his crap all over her yard. So I got in there and called Habitat for Humanity, and they got three semi truckloads out of that. I also got my kids and my husband involved in these projects out there, and we dug out the roots of the invasive weeds from her septic system. We put a fence around her yard to keep the foxes out. After that my family was like, "You need to go to school! You need a hobby that keeps you busy."

The job that I did as a soldier, even if you didn't have OCD, definitely kind of puts a layer of OCD on top of you, because everything has to be exact. Everything has to be perfect; there's no wiggle room. So of course that carried over. I still have a shoe display. It just looks nicer, you know? I believed more in my ability to be effective in my community. I've participated more in things by just driving down the road and noticing things like, "Hey, the road workers aren't even wearing orange jackets or carrying stop signs, but they're directing traffic into oncoming traffic down the street from an elementary school." I knew to call City Hall. Follow a hierarchy and protocol. I am possibly even more civic-minded now than before serving. There is a bigger picture. One that shows that everybody affects everybody, no matter how big or small.

I tried to reconnect to the people that were important to me before joining. The church my husband and I got married at, we'd been members at for years. Upon returning I found they had started this new program where you could have coffee, and it was a nice little fundraiser thing. All those years the church had been directed by one pastor, and we had just gotten a new guy before I left for the military. Up until then it didn't matter if you were rich or poor, a doctor or a janitor, everybody treated everybody the same, very equal. The stark realization that that was gone, really, really gone, was one day when I didn't have enough change at the bottom of my purse for a fancy coffee, so I was like, "Hey! What will sixty cents get me?" Which, by the way, you can do at Starbucks, and they won't worry about it. This lady lit into me like the Fourth of July. How dare I withhold funds from a charity? This was a fundraiser! I'm like, "Okay, yeah . . . " That was my stark realization that things had changed around here and my "anchor" of who I was, and where I came from, had stopped being the same and was not around anymore.

When I first got out I was really, really physically hurt; I faced a lot of challenges. While I was here at school, too. I had a slipped disc, a walker, the whole bit. It was awful. When I first got out my husband was still deployed, so it was just me and the young ones, and I told my neighbors that I couldn't push a lawnmower. Not one of them even offered to mow my lawn, not even for money. I was so agitated, and these were all people that went to different churches. Proudly boasting, "We go to such-and-such church!" "Really?" I wanted to scream, "Prove it!"

I was never deployed into theater, but my husband was, and when Obama came along saying he was going to bring everyone home, I was like, "Check yes!" After a while, though, I was like, "Yeah, he's not doing that. I don't even know why I voted for him." I voted for him in the primaries, but not in the election. Of course, he didn't bring my husband home. Instead my husband spent eighteen months straight in Iraq, so I was sad. That was just his first deployment; he ended up with back-to-back deployments. He went away, and the kids hadn't even learned to ride bicycles yet, but when he came back the girls were in training bras. He missed so much, and yeah, it was really hard; he didn't want to deal with them being big girls. He wanted them to be little tiny girls that crawled into his lap. "It's my homework, Daddy. You have to read me this oversized book." So he suffered a lot.

Do I feel differently about war? No. No, I think that technically it still serves its purpose. It sucks, and it is kind of a necessary evil to prevent bullies from taking over other people's peaceable liberties. Some people you can have a reasonable conversation with and come to an agreement with, and some people need a slap in the face, because that's the language they understand. I felt honored to be able to serve during a time when the military needed people. There were definitely times and circumstances that my leadership had my back, and it meant the world to me. And, because they had my back, I was willing to give more.

"I gotta maintain my filters."
Elyana Ramirez

Sometimes I still face challenges now, even in the workplace. You can't talk to someone and just be like, "This needs to get done." Sometimes you have to sugarcoat things for people. You have to play the politics game, as opposed to in the military you can just tell someone, "No, you're going to get this done. And if it's not done, then you can't go home. You can't go to sleep until it's done." It gave me more of an attitude of, "Oh there's a problem? Great. What's your solution? How are we going to fix this?"

My senior chief's famous words to me, with the division of twelve junior sailors, would be, "Ramirez, un-fuck this now." "Okay. Roger that, senior chief." And I kind of wish I could use that more now, because I manage design teams, so I need them to meet a certain schedule, but it's not crucial. Like, the ship is not going to sink if they don't turn in their thumbnails to me on time. But at the same time, how do I find that balance where I'm not too pushy? I just had my ninety-day review, and they were like, "You're doing good work, a lot of error-free stuff, we're going to give you a raise. You get the job done, you get the work done, you follow through. There have been instances where there have been heated discussions." And I'm like, "Are you kidding me? Really? Like, I haven't yelled at anybody." And they're like, "Although you maintained a professional manner, think of ways that you can talk it through." And I was like, "I don't understand. I thought feelings were secured at work. I thought you checked them at the door." Because it was kind of a joke in the Navy, like, "Feelings are secured!" And when shit got really bad? Happiness was secured. So those are some things I continue to struggle with even after being at TCU, you know?

I have a potty mouth. I gotta maintain my filters. My first orientation at TCU we were trying to shove everyone into an elevator and I was like, "All right, everybody, get in there! Butt to nut!" And they were just like, "You can't say that." And I was like, "Oh, I didn't know." The Navy had turned me from a lady into a sailor mouth. So it was things like that, especially as a woman, that were kind of different.

"That's who you really are at the core."

Jake Melton

There's nothing like time to point out how ignorant you used to be, that's for sure. But you know, you think you know yourself, but then combat just really reveals to you who you really are. It pulls back the layers and you can see yourself for your true self, and it's not always good and it's not always bad. I mean, it's truthful and it's realistic, and not everybody's ready for that. I wasn't ready for it. It takes a while to actually believe it. You know? You're like, "I'm not like that. I'm not that kind of person," or whatever. But slowly you start to realize that, yeah, you are, and that's who you really are at the core, at the base of everything. That's you. And it takes a while to come to terms with that, actually.

Q: *What did combat show you about yourself?*

Some of the good things were, it showed me that in a pinch, when everything is melting down, I can maintain and I can make clearheaded decisions, and I'm not gonna run. And if you're the guy standing next to me, then you've got somebody good standing next to you. And I take a lot of pride in that, the fact that the guy standing next to me can count on me to be there and not hiding behind a Humvee tire.

Some of the things that aren't so good, maybe that I'm the kind of person that can kill somebody simply because somebody else deemed that person to be a bad person. Following orders is necessary in combat, absolutely necessary, but when you look back and evaluate that, it's kind of absurd to just take somebody's word for it. "Hey, all those people over there? They need to die." "Oh. Yes, sir." I mean, that's pretty big for someone to just make that snap decision on a lot of people. Now, I'm sure just by sheer coincidence, we killed some bad guys that needed to be killed. I'm sure there are a few people that were collateral damage, didn't deserve it. Some people that were just defending their country against outsiders that come in and try to do them harm. I can actually respect that. I can. 'Cause I'd be that person if someone came to this country. I'd be that fool with a pistol and a shotgun and a whatever explosive device I could make to put on the side of the road. That'd be me. And here I am killing that person. A little counterintuitive. A little nonsensical, at times. Therapists have a name for that, when you start feeling empathy for the enemy. I don't know what it is, but I think I got a little bit of that.

But I'm capable of killing somebody and being okay with it. I would like to not be okay with that. I would like to just be broken up and feel terrible for that person. I feel empathy or sympathy for them, whichever the correct term there is. But I don't lose any sleep over it. I don't. I mean, because at the end of the day, they were shooting at me. So I shot back. I'm just a better shot. That's it. You're dead and I can respect you, but I don't feel bad for killing you. I do have respect for them, kinda the old Japanese Samurai type of deal. They had respect for the people they killed, but that person needed to be killed or whatever. Same basic principle. I would like to have more of a sense of responsibility for that person's life. I should feel bad about that. I really don't.

I don't necessarily look to the past to see how I was changed. I'm looking to the future to see how I'm gonna change, how I can change. 'Cause everybody changes. It's just the only constant through life. It's just a matter of how and when, under what circumstances, and I'm looking to be able to control that a little bit more than I've been able to in the past.

"My priorities are quite different."
Tommy Dunaway

After several more years, including another deployment and three years overseas, I left active duty and returned to the reserves. In 2014 I became a member of the TCU Executive Masters of Business Administration Class of 2015. Married now, with three kids and a business to run, life and my priorities are quite different than they were on 9/11. Even though it's part-time, I still wear the uniform, and the opportunity to lead Marines is always in the back of my mind. I graduated from TCU in December 2015, fourteen years after 9/11 and thirteen years after I tried and failed to fail my way out of college and into combat.

"I wouldn't go back in enlisted."
Paige McCloud

I grew up my whole life thinking that's what I was going to do and I was going to do it for twenty-plus years, and then I didn't. So I still feel like I didn't complete what I said I was going to do, but I wouldn't go back in enlisted. If I went back in, I would go back in as an officer. It's just such a better life on the ship. You know, you're in a berthing with forty or fifty other females when you're enlisted, and when you're an officer, there's two of you in the same room. So much better. They have better food, too.

My husband was a CS, a Culinary Specialist, on the ship, and he would bring me good food. We were not in the same division or even the same department, and we were the same rank until he got out, so we were doing nothing wrong. Just on the same ship, and it's huge. It's like six thousand people. That's bigger than my hometown. Oh, it's huge, three hangar bays to store the planes and like aircraft elevators where they can bring the planes from the hangar bay up to the flight deck, which is really cool. It gets really loud, though, because you have the arresting gear and the catapult. And I slept right under the arresting gear, which is towards the back of the ship and right under it; you could hear it. It gets loud but you get used to it, so now I sleep through anything.

I'm just really thankful for everything that I learned while I was there that helped me after the fact, helped me in college and especially getting into TCU, paid for and everything. I couldn't be more thankful for that.

"Women have had to handle every situation."

Barbara Wahl

When George came back from Vietnam, he was very quick to anger. He would say, "I have no emotions." His main emotion was anger. Everything would trigger him off. But I also have to say that he was coming out of Vietnam, where he was in very stressful military situations, where it's structured as much as it can be. He's still following what he's been taught, and it's the military structure in combat. He comes home and they send him to graduate school, which is totally different. He's having to deal with the family dynamics of a six-month-old baby and a two-and-a-half-year-old. Dealing with children is totally different than dealing with adults, even if you have adults who are childish. So it was very stressful, to say the least, because he's coming from very high impact to going to school, nothing but calmness and quiet. It's a horrible adjustment. I think the easier adjustment would have been to have gone back into a military unit where you're still in the structure, and then go from there, where it gives you a chance to calm down out of a very active situation into a less active situation, and then into a school situation. I think that was his biggest adjustment.

My biggest adjustment was having somebody around telling me what to do. You ask his mother. I know all men are like this, but military men in particular are always right, and their decision is the right decision. It's testosterone versus estrogen, that's exactly what it is. In the military, you'll find there are many divorces after there's a deployment. Women have had to handle every situation themselves. There's nobody there but you. You know how to do it. You pay the bills, you get the doctor's appointments, you do whatever. The men come back: "I'm king of the hill again." Well, excuse me. That was the biggest adjustment for me.

I'm kind of an adjuster. I'm the compromiser in every situation. I'm a caregiver. I'm an RN. You have to look at the good side because when you're moving around a lot, your husband's experiencing many, many different things. You just have to look at the good side. If you start looking at all the bad, it's just gonna bury you with frustration, that's it. I mean to tell you, depression can take over very easily in a lot of these situations. With him coming back after a year and wanting to rule the roost and in school, he's around almost twenty-four hours a day, so we're having our own adjustment battles and finding our own territory. It's very difficult, and I don't know anybody that says it isn't. They might say it, but they're not telling you the truth. He could go from being very happy to being very angry; horrible mood swings. Now, if I see him starting to go into it, I'll say, "George, take a deep breath. You're going to have to grab hold." I know it when it's coming. I can see all the signs. Now he's learned to turn it around, where before he'd be in a funk. We've been married almost fifty-two years, so you know we've survived. But he was definitely a changed man when he came back from the war.

One thing I want to make clear. When he came back from Vietnam, there was absolutely no counseling, absolutely nothing for the people coming back that had problems. I kept telling him to go take a pill, because sometimes I just couldn't stand it. I'd say, "Go talk to somebody. Go talk to the psychiatrist. Go to somebody. You have to overcome this, so you consider yourself to be what you need to be." He'd say, "They'll kick me out of the military if they see I have any psychology problems." He wanted this to be his career. We had to conquer and overcome this ourselves. Now, they all have to have psychiatric counseling, medication if they need the medication, and they are held as heroes because they are actually taking care of the situation and overcoming it, and they're allowed to continue in their military career.

"That lifelong gift of being responsible was never diminished."

William T. Howe Sr.

He was a perennial all-star in Little League baseball by age eleven. He excelled on defense in football at his school. By age fourteen he could harvest and field dress a South Texas white tail. With a single shot .410 shotgun he could hit a West Texas dove on the fly. Snow skiing by the time he was fifteen, he tamed all of the black runs in New Mexico, Utah, and Colorado. Active in his church youth group, volunteering time to help the less fortunate through various church ministries, and mature enough to make the decision to forego an important all-star game to attend his cousin's funeral. An above-average student in every subject, one of those who could simply read or listen to a lecture and ace a comprehensive test. Things came easy to this young man. I was privileged to see him grow up before my very eyes. He is my son, William T. Howe Jr.

My son always had an easy way about him. But that carefree attitude

William Howe Sr.
Courtesy of William Howe Jr.

was held in check by the ever-greater character trait of personal responsibility. Whether at college a thousand miles from home, or his first job just down the street, William excelled. It was easy to give him great responsibility, because he was greatly responsible.

After 9/11, William began to experience the ever-present pull of military service. Through boot camp, combat medic training, and his deployment to Iraq, my son continued to excel. But he changed. His carefree style was gone. The easy way about him diminished. Conversations with my son were, for the first time, hard pressed. He was detached, somber, overwhelmed by the success that simply doing his job brought him. A distance crept in. Not in geographic terms, but rather in terms of endearment. As a father I could pray, as often I did, and that was about all. My son was different. He was a man with the agony of human experience weighing heavy on his soul.

Then he came home. The worst was yet to come. I remember driving William home from Fort Hood to Fort Worth. On our trip there was a box on the side of the Interstate, that evidently had tumbled off a delivery truck or moving trailer. William asked me to get into the fast lane, as far from that box as possible. As we passed, my son had his face in his hands. Once with the bravery to jump fifty feet off a chair lift, land on his skis, and tackle the triple black ski run, now he was afraid of a box on the side of the road. More withdrawal, more somberness, more detachment. Words like carefree, fun-loving, passionate, and easy were the polar opposite of William's real emotional state.

But that one overriding trait, that lifelong gift of being responsible, was ever present and never diminished. It was not his responsibility toward his mom and dad, or his sisters, or his church, or the military—from which he was now medically retired—or even the responsibility to self that kept him moving forward. It was his responsibility to his only child, his little girl. In her eyes he had to be responsible, and he knew it and he dealt with it.

So, with the help of his VA benefits, the Texas Yellow Ribbon program, and TCU's commitment to help deserving veterans, William's life began to be rebuilt. Study was therapy. Tests were challenges. Writing assignments cleared his mind of the mental conflicts. William graduated with honors and continues his personal improvement today.

My son has come full circle. That which was easy became difficult; now the difficult is becoming easier. As a pastor I communicate often, to all who will listen, that each of us experiences two lives: one we learn with, one we live with. William has learned; now he is living.

"All I have is me."

Sau Le Hudecek

The US government decide to take in refugees from Vietnam. At the time, I'm only twenty-some-odd year old. I want to go so badly. My mom, she fifty-some-odd year old at the time, and she said, "Oh, I don't want to start my life all over."

So she's the one that stalled me there. She said that she's too old to start life all over again, so she want me to go by myself. But I don't want to go without her. So we delay for a couple year there, and then finally my brother and my sisters said, "Mom, you have to go. You have an opportunity to get out of here. Go." Eventually, she decide that, "Oh, yeah, maybe, if you all okay with it, then I go."

That's when we take an application. But doing the process of taking application doesn't guarantee that you can go, because they had to make sure that you truly had American children. They had to test your blood. They had to make sure that you had documentation, anything that's left from my father to my mother, or whatnot. Wedding pictures, or anything of that nature. Unfortunately, our family grow up in Hue, right in the heart of Viet Cong. So my mom, if she had any, she had to get rid of them at the time. So she don't have any picture, or not anything to prove that I'm American child except that I am half American, half Vietnamese. Therefore, I'm just stand out in the crowd. Taking the application, first you have to give up your Vietnamese citizenship. So it's a high risk to say, "Yes, this what I want to do."

I grew up in Communist Vietnam. Those people, they don't tolerate nothing. If you want to left the country, first you have to give up your citizenship. And then, what happen if you don't have a chance to go to America? You basically don't have a country to live in. But to me it's worth it, because grow up there, after the war and American children, it's really hard. So this opportunity cannot come soon enough for me. When I see that opportunity, I thought, whatever it takes, I will beg my mom if I have to, to get me out of there. I'm so grateful that I take that opportunity, and it work. Because a lot of kid, it doesn't work out as good as my situation. I think [my application acceptance] had a lot to do with the interview. Vietnam doesn't have different color makeup for different skin color. So I go into the interview, and I had makeup on made for white-skinned people, and here I am a color [half-Vietnamese, half-African American] woman and wearing white makeup.

So I never forget when I walk into the room with American man and translation with a Vietnamese woman. The American asked me, "Why did you wear that makeup?"

I said, "Well, this the only makeup that I have, in the market."

At the time I own a salon, and my job was to prep people for wedding and do all the beauty stuff. So I tell him that's the only makeup that they have in the market. He looked quite surprised. He looked at me and he look at the translation lady, Vietnamese lady, and she say, "Yeah, she right. That the only makeup that they have in the market."

He asked me a couple more question, then he look back to me and he said, "Where you go to, you not have to wear that makeup."

I remember that I can't took that in yet, because I'm still thinking he have to ask me more question, you know. But, few minute later, I realized that he said that I will go to America. At the time, I'm thinking, I don't know what he asked me next, but the point was that to make it through the interview, basically tell him the truth. The truth is that we don't have any evidence, any picture, anything at all. All I have is me.

"I felt like I was stepping into the past."

Nathaniel Peoples

I think the hardest part about it was connecting with people in America who have yet to travel outside of their city, their neighborhood, their state, or whatever. That was the most difficult part. Overseas you connected by your interests: what you like to do, how smart you are, how cool you are, if you're great at football, if you like chess, etcetera. Overseas it's no matter what your color was. You like each other. You're a big group. Over here, there was a big divide in race and religion and different social groups. Like the nerds with the nerds, the jocks with the jocks. But that's not bad, that's how you gain new friends, but it was a big social divide, and I felt like I was stepping into the past, coming to Fort Worth. I won't say America, because you've got places that are right there with Japan, like New York and California. It was very interesting coming from Japan to Fort Worth and actually having to adapt to the lifestyle here.

"I never want to go to combat again."

George Wahl

I finished up in 1991 and joined the civilian world in various human resource capacities. My bottom line was that I was not happy. Anyone who ever spent time in combat knows it is not pleasant. It's not the way to win friends and influence people, and I don't want to get into the political realm but, unfortunately, people who make the decision that this is what the United States is going to do, many times, not just in today's environment, but many times, those individuals never wore a uniform. I'm not saying they never were deployed in combat, that would be helpful, too, but they never wore a uniform. And the US military is expected to be the worldwide police force, making all safe for democracy so to speak. So that was probably to me, and subsequently, more troubling when Desert Storm came along, and Iraq and Afghanistan. It's not a win/win situation, it's a lose/lose situa-

Army veteran George Wahl.
Courtesy of George Wahl.

tion. It causes a lot of problems, not only for the individual transitioning, but for his or her family. It's difficult.

There is a personal side of it, and then there's a combat side of it. I was in all of the hot spot trouble areas, where the 173rd Airborne Brigade was fighting, to include Tuy Hoa and Dak To. Dak To is the bell ringer for me. That's where we lost many hundreds of Army paratroopers. It was a difficult time for me. That's the combat side of it. The personal side of it was all the stories you heard about what the hippies did to returning veterans. Thank God I don't see that today for returning Iraq and Afghanistan veterans. I came back on the tenth or eleventh of May 1968, had to go through LAX in order to get back to Cincinnati where Barbara and the family were, and to be taunted and spit upon by hippie-looking men and women was very personally degrading. I'll never forget that, as well as the combat experience. Going out to get the taxicab, I was spit upon. They were basically hippie, dirty, grungy clothes type. Four or five guys. And I don't think that's a good way to greet returning military servicemen. I guess I was more PO'ed than upset and, being a man of discretion, I said, "My mission is to get into the cab." I was by myself. I was on my way back to Cincinnati to return to my family, and that was my mission.

In Cincinnati my wife was at the airport and there were no demonstrations, and I think that's what I call the Midwest conservative syndrome, which now isn't universal in the Midwest, but in the mid-sixties it was, and it was just great to be home. And I said, "Thank God I'm home, I'm alive, and I never want to go to combat again, never."

I'm sure I'm going to espouse my own bias and my own bravado, but maybe Barbara is a better person to ask [about transitioning to civilian life]. I, at the time, personally, did not perceive that I had any problems. And I know now, in retrospect, that I had problems. I was quick to anger. I was quick to fly off the handle. I was quick to be extra hard on the kids. In fact, driving up here, Barbara reminded me of something that I did that I thought was perfectly harmless, and I guess it was me being self-centered. I like listening to classical music, and now I find out that our oldest son hated that Dad always had classical music on. But it soothes my savage breast, so to speak. Since I was not a direct combat infantryman, I probably did not have the experiences of PTSD that a lot of soldiers, sailors, and Marines have today, coming back from Iraq and Afghanistan. But I still have PTSD issues from Vietnam. Emotional issues that, for the most part, unless somebody asks me about them, I don't exhibit and are not normally something I talk about.

I think we are doing a better job with transitioning military members from the military to civilian life than we did when I came back from Vietnam. For example, when I came back from Vietnam, the Army didn't even have a transition program. Today not only does the Army have a transition program, but as of about two years ago, there is a mandated five-day transition assistance program to get people into the type of care they need, to give them the job-searching skills, how to write a resumé, how to look for a job. That was nonexistent in 1968. PTSD is an issue that I'm glad is being recognized, and I can see how it happens. All you gotta do is be in a combat zone and have certain experiences, and it'll affect you.

"Let's be better than we've been."
Jarrod McClendon

I worry that there are fires that are starting in the rest of the world, and because we're looked at as who we are, we might want to involve ourselves. I've always worried about this, actually. I think that there are other ways of handling things. Hopefully the powers that be are paying attention to the possibilities, rather than just going back into what we've done before. Because it's very obvious that that didn't work after almost fifteen years.

I'm not afraid of going into combat. I don't think that you should be afraid of things, but there's nothing wrong with having fear, because having a lack of fear is almost insanity. Like after I jumped out of a plane, I'd always get weak in the knees a little bit. It didn't mean that I was afraid, it just meant that there was fear to be had, and it's normal. But if there's a plane headed that way and my name's on the manifest, then so be it. But if I'm a part of whether or not we have to do this, then let's consider the options before we just jump into anything. We've wasted a lot of money and a lot of lives. I have a lot of friends that are not here anymore because of the things that we've done, and I would prefer that those would be the last that we would lose.

Just to be honest, there are certain parts of the world that are not as lucky as we are. We are very blessed in the things that we have, and I think that we could probably share that wealth with the rest of the world. And this isn't a communist viewpoint; I just believe that if I have the ability to build a running water system in Fort Worth, why can't I do that in sub-Saharan Africa? I just think that we can probably help more than we hurt, and we have a lot of assets to do so. We've spent over a trillion dollars on the war in Afghanistan and Iraq. I just think those assets could be used otherwise. I mean, let's be better than we've been before.

"There's a lot of work that still needs to be done."
Joddy Murray

I think as a vet, you always feel like you're a vet. The veteran identity carries with you. There's a strong community among vets that are connected, but vets are also diverse. You will meet people from all over the political spectrum, and they are vets. You'll meet LGBTQ identified people, or whatever other social or cultural advocates that are out there. You'll have strong opinions one way or the other, but not all uniform opinions. Even though we have a strong bond that's common to the military, we all are very diverse as well. I think that's an important thing. I don't like to be painted as a vet if that means I'm going to vote this way or I'm going to think that way. A lot of vets are selfless people who just want to contribute, and I think there might be a little too many people who are quick to call them heroes, when they feel like, "I was just doing my job."

On the other hand there are heroes, of course. But I guess what I mean is that there's an incredible amount of diversity, and there should be more diversity. We should have more women who want to work in combat. We should have more people of color in high leadership positions, women in high leadership positions. There's a lot of work that still needs to be done. But there are vets out there that are committed to doing a good thing.

"Let's pray we never forget."

Shawn Keane

At the VFW's Welcome Home Vietnam Vets event there was a dartboard with Jane Fonda's face on it, so veterans could throw darts at "Hanoi Jane." Fonda is known for being a famous actress who went to North Vietnam, and protested against both the war and the soldiers who were over there. She was one of the reasons why many of the soldiers who returned from Vietnam received a cold reception from civilians. Throwing darts at Jane Fonda's face made my husband feel good. He even encouraged the rest of the family to throw darts as well. He said, "Come on, Melissa, throw darts at her." So the rest of my children also threw darts at Jane Fonda.

I didn't participate, because I didn't care much about the dartboard. I just don't want to see the disrespect and hostility towards the Vietnam veterans ever happen again to any veteran.

Have we learned any lessons? I don't know. History will tell. Let's pray we never forget, though.

"I treat everybody equal."
Sau Le Hudecek

We have Hispanic, we have Vietnamese, we have white, we have black. I personally don't see people in color. I see people as a person. I believe that everybody, maybe because I grow up in Vietnam, go through such a bully and difficult time. I remember as a young child, I tell myself, I know what I don't want to do or don't want to repeat when I grow up. I remember vividly, I make a note of that in my mind that every time I hear something so, how you say it, so bad, so hard, I remember telling myself, make sure you don't be like that person. Make sure you don't be like that woman. Don't throw thing at kid, or yell at some child. In fact, I had couple customers who is color, and often they reference it that they in color. I tell them, "You don't have to feel that way. We in America. It the freedom that given to all of us. We have to look at that as we're all equal." I treat everybody equal and try my best to not do what they do to me.

"How do you get out of hell?"
Phil Ditto

Suicide is a dark and bitter reality known only to those who remain among the living. I have often thought deeply about what suicide means, why someone would turn to this "solution." I suppose there are many answers, as varied as those precious souls who agonized to come to this decision. After nearly eighteen years of service as a paramedic, many of which were spent as a medic in the Army, I have seen a great deal of death. I have also seen a great deal of life, both renewed and that which had just began. In this way, one can only be confronted with the duality of our existence.

Many know about the plaguing problem of suicide among veterans. It is estimated that twenty-two veterans a day kill themselves. Another staggering number is that we have lost more veterans from the war on terror to suicide than to enemy action. Why? I have my theories, but I think more than anything there are two main reasons. First, there is a tremendous loss of purpose when one leaves the military. The second is the loss of camaraderie and the loneliness that follows. You pair these factors with the stress of service, combat, unstable home environments, guilt, and a lack of strong support, and we might as well load the guns ourselves.

I had this one friend in the military. We served together on the East Coast, and he was revered. A stellar soldier, leader, and friend, "Joe" was loyal to the core. This loyalty had a way of inspiring loyalty in others, so much so that he was nicknamed the Don. You couldn't help but love this guy, and you certainly didn't want to disappoint him. One day, while driving around the local town, Joe was on edge. Sweating, eyes darting back and forth, speeding, his heart surely racing, something was wrong. I look down and see it. Joe has a loaded handgun under his thigh between the seat.

"Joe, why is that out?" He looked at me as if I was the stupidest person. My stomach sank.

"Phil, they are everywhere. You got to be ready."

"For what, Joe?"

He never did answer the question. I saw Joe a few days later, back to his normal self. I of course knew Joe was a great soldier, who had saved many lives with his unit in Iraq. A few months later he had departed for a new duty assignment, as was routine and is far too familiar of a cycle to those who have served. I never saw Joe again.

A couple years later, I learned that he had killed himself near the memorial to those killed in the war on terrorism of the fabled unit he had been a part of all those years ago. Stricken with what I am sure is an undeniable grief and guilt at the loss of the friends he could not save, etched into the marble wall in front of which he now lay dead. I often wonder what might have happened had I said something. We will never know.

I have lost more friends than should ever happen to suicide, mostly from the service. But many of us, far too many, have such similar stories. We are tragically and unbelievably connected by the exponential guilt that bonds those left behind. The travesty of suicide must end. To all those around the world who are in despair, who grieve and are tormented, lest you battle alone, we will walk together through the fires of hell. For, as the expression goes: How do you get out of hell? You keep on going.

"What have we done?"

George Wahl

When Saigon fell, in April 1975, we were in San Antonio. I remember watching it on TV and my heart sinking. "What have we done?" But it was just a matter of time. I knew it was going to happen. I just didn't know how or when. I just felt a loss. I thought of it in the same way I'm looking at Iraq today. God, the American lives we invested in Iraq, and the national decision-makers said, "We're pulling out a hundred percent, we're outta there." And, yeah, we're outta there, and now look at the troubles. I guess sometimes we don't learn from history. Or maybe we learn the wrong lessons. I don't know.

Leading the Way

The Story of Eldon Bielss

This first-person account by World War II veteran Eldon Bielss, who is believed to have passed away in 2017, was brought to the editors of this book by Adam Baggs, assistant vice chancellor for School and College Development at TCU and a member of TCU's Veterans Services Task Force. "Mr. Bielss originally reached out to me because he wished to donate copies of his self-published book to the Mary Couts Burnett Library at TCU," Adam told us. "From there, we struck up a correspondence via email. I shared my copy with many relatives and friends who are veterans. Mr. Bielss wrote the book to share his story while he still could. He was the last survivor of his crew."

T his is a story about the fantastic rescue of a large number of prisoners of war from a Romanian prison camp run by the Germans. This was the first prison rescue of World War II, and it received very little attention. To the people that were rescued, it was a tremendous event.

These POWs were all Air Force people that had been shot down during the course of the war over the oilfields and other targets in the area of Romania. The Germans had control of that whole area.

A lot of the prisoners were from the first raid from North Africa. There were groups of B-24s that were to bomb the oilfields at low level. The Germans were aware of the raid (through their spy network) and shot down about half of the bombers, approximately twenty-four crews, and these were the survivors that were able to bail out of the ships or survive the crashes. They had been in this prison for months and months.

Their clothing was all worn out, and they hadn't been able to shave or do other things. They were able to bathe once in a while. They were a pitiful bunch. The rest of the prisoners were survivors of the many raids we did after we went to Italy, but at high altitude.

The war was winding down, and the German Army were pulling back. They just pulled up and left the prison camp to take care of itself. The Romanian government had to take over. They were in short supply of food and other necessities for their own people, without the extra burden of having to take on over four hundred prisoners.

I think the hero of this story is, in part, a young Romanian officer. He volunteered to take their problem to the Allied Armed Forces in Italy. He flew a small plane across Yugoslavia and the Adriatic Sea into Italy. He landed on a United States Air Force field and told his story. He was flown to General Eaker's headquarters. General Eaker was the commander of the 15th Air Force in Italy. Of course, the general was more than interested to get his men back in Allied hands.

This is where I came into the picture. I had completed fifty-one combat missions and was waiting for orders to go home. The commander of our group asked me if I would fly over to Naples, Italy, to pick up some important people and bring them back to base. It was a chance to get out of the tent for a change. I was given a plane that had been stripped of armament and oxygen equipment plus the armor plates. Several hundred pounds of material had been taken out of the ship.

I was given instructions where to go. It was to a little airfield north of Naples in a vineyard field. It had been used as a fighter field but was abandoned as the war moved north.

It took about an hour to make the trip. I found the field, now to land this thing. Now you have to know how this ship handles with all the weight removed. There are ten less men, about a half tank of fuel (less 1400 gallons at six and a half pounds a gallon), no bomb load.

The airstrip is dirt but hard. I made a pass to land, and this darn thing just would not quit flying. It flew like a Cub. The time of day was dusk but plenty of light. I had to go around. This time I made a long approach and let down real low, just above the grapevines. I left the power on just enough to drag in. After I got over the last row of vines I chopped the throttle, opened the cooling flaps on the engines to increase drag. This time I made it real good. I taxied up to a little building about the middle of the field. The building was abandoned but had a telephone inside, and it was working. We waited and waited until about midnight, and made a call back to our base to find out what happened. They said, "The people are on the way, just wait."

About one or two o'clock, here come two large trucks loaded with supplies and five men. I never saw so much brass in one group: a Naval officer, an Air Force colonel, a Marine major, an Army captain, plus the Romanian.

I ask the colonel what this is all about. He tells me, "We will fly back to your base and join the group to go to Budapest and leave them there. The Romanian will tell us where to go."

I tell him that is impossible. We have no oxygen and only a limited amount of fuel. This airplane has been stripped of everything except engines.

He was very vocal about the problem, and went inside to call General Eaker. After a brief conversation, the colonel asked me to talk to the general. I explained the problem to him and said we could not make the trip. He cussed a little, then told me to fly back to the base and there would be a ship parked on the end of the runway. Transfer the equipment to it and they will go from there. I bet whoever took the call back at the base got a good chewing.

Sure enough, when we got back to the base about daylight, there was a ship waiting and a bunch of people to help load the equipment into the other ship.

About the mission. The loaded ship will go with the group that will bomb a target in the area where the Germans are still active. The loaded ship will leave the formation and go to Budapest, where it will land. The colonel will set up the radio equipment for the next day's landing for the evacuating ships. The other officers (I find out that they are doctors) will go to the prison camp to doctor the injured and get them ready to move about a mile to the airstrip to be picked up. The Romanians are helping to get things set up. There are guards around the field to keep any sympathizers or Germans away until the next day's evacuation.

The next day a group of twenty-eight B-17s were sent to Budapest from my group, from Foggia airfield. They started out with the 15th Air Force on a mission and broke away to proceed on to Budapest. With the help of the radio equipment set up the day earlier, the group were directed to the landing site. They all taxied and parked on the side of the runway.

The doctors had been busy all night evaluating the sick and wounded. They had to make preparations to move the bunch to the airfield.

The morning was started out with breakfast of hot cabbage soup and bread as usual. That's all they had had for a long time. There wasn't any food available for the prisoners by the Germans, and the Romanian government didn't want to get involved. All of the prisoners had lost a tremendous amount of weight.

All of the prisoners were excited beyond belief. They were going home. A lot of them didn't believe it yet.

Now is the time to move this bunch to the airfield. It's about a mile away. The biggest job is transporting the wounded and sick for that distance. Several of the people had been hurt getting out of damaged airplanes or hurt during the parachute landing. The doctors had done a fantastic job patching these people up. Makeshift drags and anything that would help move them to the airfield. Even the Romanian government helped by sending trucks to help move them. Now we have approximately five hundred people strung out over this mile.

They have made it to the airport and started loading the sick and wounded in first. There will be about sixteen or eighteen people loaded into each plane. They are finally loaded and ready for takeoff.

The group is loaded and taking off for home. Everything is going okay.

A fighter cover has been covering the rescue group while all this is taking place. They have a limited fuel supply and have to leave early. The 15th Air Force is to come by where the rescue group can join them and use their fighter cover for protection on the way home.

As they approach the home field, there are a bunch of ambulances lined at the end of the runway ready to take the sick and wounded off first. Also a large number of trucks lined up to take part of the prisoners to other nearby airfields. It would be impossible for one airfield to house the whole group of people.

This is happening around midday. Everybody is working feverishly to try to accommodate all of these people. Between the happy people on the ground and the prisoners, it was a beautiful sight. The prisoners had to be the most excited, because of all the suffering they went through. Some of them had been in this prison for months. Now it's over, and they're on their way home.

Contributors

Ed Adcock, United States Navy

Rodney Baker, United States Navy

Christa Banet, United States Marine Corps

Shirley Beck, United States Army

Eldon Bielss, United States Air Force

Michael Blackert, United States Army

Enrique Brown-Spence, Military Dependent, United States Marine Corps

Maria Brown-Spence, United States Army

April Brown, United States Marine Corps

Carl Castillo, United States Marine Corps

Alcee Chriss Sr., United States Marine Corps

Jeff Coffer, United States Army

Stesha Colby, United States Marine Corps

Bruce Cole, United States Marine Corps and United States Army Reserve

Charlotte Cole, Military Spouse, United States Marine Corps

Jordan Cole, Military Dependent

Tim Cole, United States Marine Corps

Jessica Dawson, United States Navy

Phil Ditto, United States Army

Bob Doran, United States Army

Tommy Dunaway, United States Marine Corps

William Dwiggins, United States Marine Corps

Eric Freedman, United States Marine Corps

Bill Galyean, United States Army

John Garcia, United States Marine Corps

Steven Gonzalez, United States Marine Corps

David Grantham, United States Air Force

Jim Hille, United States Navy

William Howe Jr., United States Army

William Howe Sr., Military Parent

Joel Huffman, United States Marine Corps

Jonathan Ide, United States Army

Michelle Johnson, United States Army

Shawn Keane, Military Spouse, United States Air Force

Chad Lackovic, United States Army

Andy Lahey, United States Marine Corps

Charles Lamb, United States Army

Felicia Lawson, United States Navy

Sau Le Hudecek, Vietnam Refugee

Jim Lee, United States Navy

Harold Leeman Jr., United States Army

Marty Leewright, United States Army

Jon Lippens, Belgian Army combat soldier

Robert MacIvor, United States Army

Virginia MacIvor Meyn, Daughter of Robert MacIvor, United States Army

Jarrod McClendon, United States Army

Paige McCloud, United States Navy

Jake Melton, United States Army

Jason Mendoza, United States Army

Gabe Merigian, United States Marine Corps

Megan Morris, United States Air Force

Cristina Mungilla, United States Army

Leo Munson, United States Air Force

Brad Murphey, United States Air Force

Joddy Murray, United States Air Force

Mary Newcomer McKinney, Daughter of James Newcomer, United States Army

James Newcomer, United States Army

Nathaniel Peoples, Military Dependent, United States Navy

Richard Puett, United States Marine Corps

Elyana Ramirez, United States Navy

Stephen Rivera, United States Navy

Thaddeus Rix, United States Marine Corps

Martin Ruch, United States Navy

Israel Sanchez, United States Marine Corps

Benjamin Schmidt, United States Marine Corps

David Schmidt, Military Parent, United States Marine Corps

Teresa Schmidt, Military Parent, United States Marine Corps

Nick Sellman, United States Marine Corps

Alexandria Smith, United States Army

Rey Soto, United States Marine Corps

Dan Southard, United States Marine Corps

Richard Spence, United States Marine Corps

John Thompson, United States Army

Aaron Tombleson, United States Marine Corps

Tami Tovar, United States Army

Joe Vera, United States Army

Barbara Wahl, Military Spouse, United States Army

George Wahl, United States Army

Jeffrey Waite, United States Air Force

Michael Washington Sr., United States Army

Mark Wassenich, United States Air Force

Steve Weis, United States Navy

David Ziomek, United States Air Force

Rachel Ziomek, Military Dependent, United States Air Force

It Takes Teamwork

Acknowledgments

The plural first word of this book's title is crucial to its purposes and intentions. *Voices of America* is just that, and the project of seeking out and amplifying a wide and representative range of American voices for inclusion between one pair of covers has necessarily involved cultivating and welcoming a wide range of partners and allies. And that is as it should be, because the varieties of human experience are what make our military, and our country, what they are.

The two of us began interviewing student veterans at Texas Christian University in January 2015. At first we had no concrete plan for how or even whether to publish the stories; we only knew that it was important for us to hear them, and perhaps for the veterans themselves to tell them. At that early period in the journey that led to the publication of this book (and, we hope, beyond), multiple conversations were taking place around the TCU campus on how best to support what became known informally as "the Veterans Project." Participants in those earliest conversations included James English, Harry Parker, Sarah Robbins, and Dan Williams. Sarah, in her capacity at the time as interim dean of TCU's Honors College, was extremely supportive both morally—which we deeply appreciate—and materially, in her ready agreement to Dan's proposal to teach a series of four colloquium classes in which Honors students would interview TCU students, faculty, and staff who are military veterans or family members, as a class requirement. Those interviews provide most of the narrative material included in this book, and all of the Honors students who took part are credited as assistant editors.

Among Dr. Williams's students, the one who has truly stood out is Kit Snyder, whose involvement in the project began when she approached us at an informal Honors College breakfast, deepened when she enrolled not once but twice in the colloquium, then continued in her role as a student worker at TCU Press. Over time Kit grew into an invaluable and integral member of the team that brought this book to fruition; her acumen, sheer editorial and administrative competence, and rock-solid reliability proved crucial to bringing it across the finish line.

Dan Williams himself is another person who merits singling out for special mention. His early and steadfast enthusiasm not only led to the series of four Honors colloquia but also provided a home for the book. Dan steered the project into port in his role as director of TCU Press.

Harry Parker's early interest led to Michael Skinner of TCU's Department of Theatre writing a script using some of the veterans' and family members' stories in the book, which was then performed twice on campus: a reading at the fall 2017 TCU Veterans Celebration Luncheon, and a full production during the Spring 2018 semester at the Hays Theatre. The production was directed by Jennifer Engler. One of the performers in the theatre project was Professor Till Meyn, who went on to enlist his mother, Virginia Meyn, to write the account of her father's World War II service that appears in this book. We also wish to thank Professor Mary Newcomer McKinney and Adam Baggs, for bringing to us the other two "Leading the Way" accounts of World War II service.

Professor Ed McNertney and John Singleton and James English of TCU's Office of International Student Services led the ambitious effort to internationalize TCU via the Discovering Global Citizenship initiative between 2013 and 2019. DGC generously shared its resources, most importantly by bringing Ethan Casey to TCU many times and allowing much of his campus time to be devoted to the Veterans Project. The position of Discovering Global Citizenship's administrators, expressed explicitly and often over the course of the project, was that the experience of American veterans serving overseas is legitimately international experience—at least as much so as any traditional undergrad studying abroad or grad student doing field research—and thus deserved DGC's support.

Professor Jan Ballard helped lead a contest for graphic design students to propose designs for the cover, and Kara Vuic, TCU's LCpl. Benjamin W. Schmidt Professor of War, Conflict, and Society in Twentieth-Century America and an adviser to the Student Veterans Alliance, provided important information and advice.

Along the way, we as the book's editors, along with many of the student veterans and family members featured in the book, took part in quite a few panel discussions, "meet and greets," ceremonies, and other campus events, where the dialogue has continued and become enriched, and where we have met and cultivated many more partners and supporters. We have also spoken about the project at national, regional, and local conferences, including the 2016 National Collegiate Honors Council Annual Conference, the 2018 NASPA Symposium on Military-Connected Students, and the 2019 National Conference on Race and Ethnicity.

Voices of America, the book, is thus the product and expression of many relationships and cross-pollinations among students, faculty, staff, and institutions and individuals in the wider community, and it illustrates and models some of the many ways that those who wish to support and celebrate veterans can raise awareness, find each other, and effectively work together. The book itself does some of the needed work by being a vehicle for allowing often silent or unheard voices to be heard. It models some of what we all can do, as a nation and as families, institutions, and other communities, to support veterans and military family members. One direction for further effort that we hope our work will inspire is expressed in the preface and perhaps merits reiteration:

> The governing criterion for inclusion—affiliation with TCU as defined by us, the editors—turned out to be this book's "special sauce," because its arbitrariness renders the range of stories otherwise remarkably representative, first of all locally for TCU and Fort Worth and more widely for Texas, but also nationally. There are lessons and truths in that, for all of us as Americans. One of those is that any American university could—and perhaps should—compile and publish a similar book.

We want to mention a number of people whose often quiet but significant support for this ambitious and complicated project might otherwise have gone unremarked. Our families have supported the two of us, and Kit, personally as well as through the sustained interest they have taken in the book's content and development. TCU's administration, led by Chancellor Victor Boschini, has also been supportive throughout, as have the members of the TCU Veterans Services Task Force, the TCU Student Veterans Alliance, and TCU's Student Affairs office, especially the staff in charge of Inclusiveness and Intercultural Services, Veterans Services, and International Student Services. Darron Turner, both in his present role as TCU's Chief Inclusion Officer and previously as associate vice chancellor for Student Affairs, has been a strong and staunch supporter.

In the wider community, we especially thank Colonel William Dwiggins (USMC, ret.) of the Texas Veterans Commission for being such a warm and vocal advocate for veterans and for honoring this book by contributing its introduction as well as a personal account of his own service. Col. Dwiggins's frequent and enthusiastic visits to TCU to show support for student veterans have been wonderful for everyone's morale, including ours; he models what military leadership should always be. We also wish to thank Allies in Service, American Legion Post 569, the Arlington (Texas) Veterans Center, The Art Station, Behavioral Health-Veteran Programs (MVPN), DNAWorks: Dialogue and Healing through the Arts, the Fort Worth Veterans Center, Healing Waters Fly Fishing, Marriage Management, Inc., the Soul Repair Center at Brite Divinity School, the Tarrant County Veterans Coalition, United States Marine Corps MAG 41 Fiscal/Family Readiness, the Veterans Administration North Texas Health Care System, and the Veterans Freedom Retreat.

Thanks to Elaina Brown-Spence for designing the book's cover, and to the staff of TCU Press: Rebecca Allen, Melinda Esco, Molly Spain, and Kathy Walton.

Finally, and above all, our heartfelt gratitude to the veterans and military family members whose stories are featured in this book, for their extraordinary generosity and honesty in sharing their experiences with the civilian members of the American public we hope will read this book. By doing that, they have served their country all over again, in a deeply important way.

April Brown and Ethan Casey
June 2020

Personal Notes from the Editors

April Brown

I would like to thank my father, Norman Brown, a retired Air Force veteran, who led the way and set an example for my service and the service of my brother, Paris Brown. I remain grateful to my late mother, Anna Marie Brown, as a military spouse, for showing me that military family members make a sacrifice and should be supported and acknowledged in their role in supporting those who serve. I would like to thank my husband, Richard Spence, for standing by my side, and my children, Maria Brown-Spence, Elaina Brown-Spence, and Enrique Brown-Spence, for recognizing that, although they did not choose military life, they could make the best of their journey by adapting and having a positive attitude wherever we were ordered to go.

Ethan Casey

Compiling and editing this book has been an enormously complicated collective labor of love: love for members of the TCU community who love their country enough to have given years or decades of their lives, and in many cases their very lives, to serve it honorably in the military; love for TCU; love for the work itself; love of learning through hearing and sharing each other's stories. For me, as an adopted member of the TCU family, it has been deeply gratifying. It has brought me lasting friendships with April and Kit, as well as with Dan Williams, director of TCU Press. As mentioned in the acknowledgments, Ed McNertney, John Singleton, and James English were crucial by generously sharing my campus time with this project, and I want to acknowledge here that all three have also become important personal friends to me.

I also am humbled that this book has given me friendship with a substantial subset of the veterans in it. I choose not to name these for fear of inadvertently leaving unmentioned anyone who should be mentioned, but I hope they know who they are and that they have both my friendship and my respect.

My wife, Jennifer Haywood, has been staunchly supportive of this book from the start, including (but not limited to) by tolerating my frequent absences from our home in Seattle. My parents (Dayle and Judy, both TCU grads) and my brother Aaron also will be pleased finally to see it in print. (My father and April's father actually met each other at a campus event related to this project.) My in-laws, Art and Elaine Haywood, likewise will enjoy and appreciate it; Art's long Air Force career included a year in Vietnam (1966–67) that included flying spotter planes in harm's way. I also want to thank my cousin and cousin-in-law Kelly and Carolyn Rominger, and their grandchildren Kendall and Karly, for their warm hospitality on weekends at their East Texas farm, and for following this book's progress with enthusiastic interest. Here it is!

Kit Snyder

I would like to thank my grandfather, Navy veteran Robert E. Snyder, and my family for their support of this project. Grandpa, thank you for your support, for answering my many questions, and for inspiring me to work on this project!